MICROSOFT OFFICE 365
FOR BEGINNERS 2022

8 BOOKS IN 1

THE MOST UPDATED ALL-IN-ONE GUIDE FROM BEGINNER TO ADVANCED, INCLUDING MICROSOFT EXCEL, WORD, POWERPOINT, ONENOTE, ONEDRIVE, OUTLOOK, TEAMS, AND ACCESS

JAMES HOLLER

TABLE OF CONTENTS

BOOK 3: MICROSOFT POWERPOINT 2022

BOOK 4: MICROSOFT ONE NOTE 2022

BOOK 5: MICROSOFT ONE DRIVE

BOOK 6: MICROSOFT OUTLOOK 2022

BOOK 7: MICROSOFT TEAMS

BOOK 8: MICROSOFT ACCESS 2022

BOOK 1:
MICROSOFT EXCEL 2022

The Most Updated Crash Course from Beginner to Advanced
Learn All the Functions, Macros, and Formulas
to Become a Pro in 7 Days or Less

CHAPTER 1:
Introduction

Microsoft Excel is an essential yet challenging application to learn and master. This is why it's sometimes preferable to refer to an easy-to-understand guide in learning how to use MS Excel effectively. Whether you are a student looking to learn how to use an excel spreadsheet for a school project, a professional looking to learn Microsoft Excel, or a person looking to increase your knowledge and gain new abilities, this book is for you. You will be guided with examples, hints, and tricks to understand the software better. You will also learn all Excel fundamentals, allowing you to operate with Excel more confidently daily.

Getting Started with Microsoft Office Excel in 2022

Excel is one of the most exemplary spreadsheet programs for crunching figures, creating dashboard reports, and storing and organizing data. This software initially emerged on the market in 1987 and has since evolved to become one of the most prominent ones of home or business software.

A table made up of columns and rows is what an Excel spreadsheet is. Columns are typically assigned alphabetical letters, whereas rows are typically assigned numbers. A cell is the intersection of two columns or rows. The letter representing a column and the number representing a row make up a cell's address.

Why Should I Learn Microsoft Excel?

We all deal with numbers to some degree. We all have everyday expenses we pay for using the money we earn every month. To spend appropriately, one must first understand their income vs. expenditure. When we need to record, analyze, and save numeric data, we can use Microsoft Excel.

How Can I Obtain Microsoft Excel?

Microsoft Excel can be obtained in a variety of ways. You can get it from a computer hardware store that also offers software. Microsoft Excel is an application that is included in the Microsoft Office suite. You may also get it through Microsoft's website, but you'll have to pay for the license key.

Features and Uses of MS Excel

Excel is a spreadsheet application that enables you to manage, store and analyze information. While you may believe that only specific people use Excel to process complex data, anyone can study how and when to use the program's sophisticated features. In addition, Excel makes it simple to work with various data types, whether you're tracking a budget, compiling a training log, or preparing an invoice.

This program has a variety of practical applications that are just waiting to be explored. As a result, Microsoft Excel is a beneficial application to master, whether you are a novice or have some experience.

In this chapter, we are going to discuss some significant features and uses of MS Excel:

Features of MS Excel
- ***Add Header and Footer***
In MS Excel, we can maintain the header and footer of our spreadsheet file.
- ***Replace and Find Command***
MS Excel allows us to discover the required data (text and numbers) in the worksheet and replace it with new data.
- ***Password Protection***
Using a password enables users to safeguard their workbooks from unwanted access.
- ***Filtering of Data***
Filtering is a quick and simple method for locating and working with a subset of data in a range. A filtered range shows only the rows that fulfill the column criteria you provide. For filtering ranges, Microsoft Excel supports two commands:
AutoFilter offers filtering by selection for simple measures.
For more sophisticated criteria, you can also use the Advanced Filter.
- ***Sorting Data***
The process of arranging data in a logical order is known as data sorting. Data can be sorted in either ascending or descending order in MS Excel
- ***Pre-Programmed Formulas***
MS Excel offers a plethora of built-in formulas for sum, average, minimum, and so on. We can apply those formulas as needed.
- ***Design Various Charts (Pivot Table Report)***
MS Excel allows us to generate charts such as bars, pies, lines, etc. This allows us to evaluate and compare data simply.
- ***Automatically Edits the Result***
If any modifications are made in any of the cells, MS Excel immediately modifies the result.
- ***Auditing of Formulas***
We may graphically depict or trace the relationships between cells and formulas using formula auditing with blue arrows. For example, we can follow the precedents (cells that offer information to a certain cell) or the dependents (the cells that depend on the value in a specific cell).

MS Excel Uses in 2022

- ### *Using Excel to Store and Analyze Data*
With MS Excel, one may easily examine a large amount of data to check for new trends. Charts and graphs assist you in better summarizing and retaining data.

- ### *Ease Your Workload*
MS Excel provides excellent capabilities that assist us in saving time by making our work easier.
There are amazing tools available for filtering, sorting, and searching. Combining these fantastic tools with pivot tables and table etch can help you finish your project faster.

- ### *Data Recovery and Spreadsheets*
One of the best applications of Excel is that if your data is lost for whatever reason, you can easily recover it. This also makes work more accessible and consistent.

- ### *Mathematical Formulas Make Calculation Easy*
Another excellent feature of Excel is the availability of various formulas for performing multiple operations, such as calculating averages, sums, and so on, allowing you to perform complex calculations efficiently.

- ### *Security*
Security is essential since it protects your personal information. MS Excel protects all of your files by password-protecting them using basic visual programming.

- ### *Make Data Presentations More Sophisticated*
The next benefit of using MS Excel is that it allows you to add more sophistication to your data presentations. For example, you can improve the data bars, highlight any specific areas you want to highlight, and make your data much more attractive.

- ### *Online Access*
The finest usage of Excel is that you can readily utilize it online from anywhere and at any time, regardless of where you are or if you have your smartphone with you. You can access Excel online by going through this link – https://office.live.com/start/excel.aspx

- ### *Manage Expenses*
Microsoft Excel can help you manage your expenses. For example, you may quickly create a table of your spending and compute the total amount using the mathematical procedures given by MS Excel.

- ### *Assist in the Development of Future Strategies*
It enables you to create charts and graphs so that you may establish goals for yourself with the help of graphs, and pie charts allow you to track your progress.

- ### *Stores Data in a Single Place*
It is also one of the efficient applications of Excel. You may put your data in a single spot, making it easier to find your files. In addition, it saves you time because you don't have to examine the files in multiple folders.

CHAPTER 2:
Excel Layout

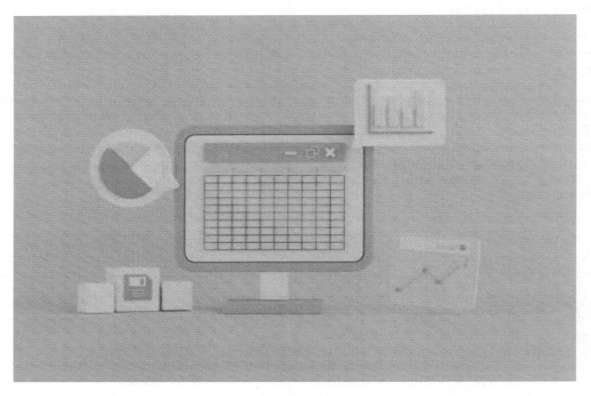

The Excel Start Screen will appear the first time you open Excel. You can create a new workbook, select a template, and see your recently changed workbooks from this page.
To access the Excel interface, go to the Excel Start Screen and find and select Blank workbook.

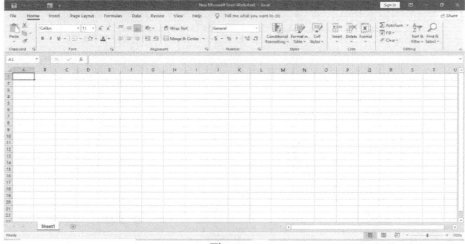

Figure 1

A workbook is a Microsoft Excel file with one or more worksheets (sometimes called spreadsheets). Depending on the number of new workbooks opened, Excel will assign a file name to the workbook, such as Sheet1, Sheet2, Sheet3, and so on. After starting Excel, the figure above shows a blank workbook. Take some time to get acquainted with this display. Your screen may look slightly different depending on whatever version you're using.

Layout Overview
Parts of the Excel Window

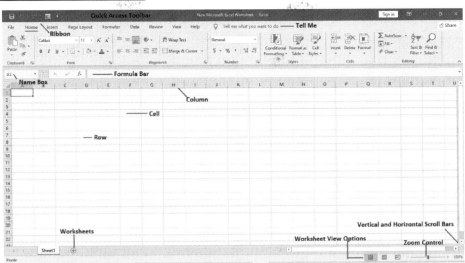

Figure 2

All Microsoft products share some components of the Excel window (such as the Ribbon and the scroll bars). However, other spreadsheet features, such as the formula bar, name box, and worksheet tabs, are more specialized for spreadsheets.

- **The Ribbon**

The Ribbon provides all the commands you'll need to do common Excel tasks. In addition, it features various tabs, each with a different set of commands.

- **Quick Access Toolbar**

Regardless of the tab chosen, the Quick Access Toolbar allows you to access popular commands. In addition, you can personalize the commands to suit your needs.

- **Name Box**

A selected cell's location, or name, is displayed in the Name box.

- **Tell Me**

The Tell me box functions similarly to a search bar, allowing you to locate tools or commands quickly.

- **Formula Bar**

You can enter or change data, a formula, or a function that will show in a specific cell in the formula bar.

- **Column**

A column is a set of cells that runs from top to bottom on a page. Columns in Excel are denoted by letters.

- **Cell**

A cell is a rectangular area in a workbook. A cell is a point where a row and a column meet. To choose a cell, simply click it.

- **Row**

A row is a set of cells that spans from left to right across the page. Numbers are used to identify rows in Excel. Workbooks are Excel files that contain worksheets. There are one or more worksheets in each workbook. To switch between tabs, click them, or right-click for more choices.

- **Worksheet View Options**

A worksheet can be seen in three different ways. To select the desired view, simply click a command.

- **Zoom Control**

To utilize the zoom control, click and move the slider. The zoom percentage is represented by the number to the right of the slider.

- **Scroll Bars (Vertical and Horizontal)**

The scroll bars can go up and down or side to side. To do so, click and drag the vertical or horizontal scroll bar.

Workbooks, Worksheets, Cells, and Formula Bar

- **Workbooks and Worksheets**

A worksheet appears on the screen by default when you open Microsoft Excel XP. There are three worksheets in each workbook. A worksheet is a cell grid that has 65,536 rows and 256 columns. Text, numbers, and mathematical formulas are inserted into different cells of a spreadsheet.

The gray boxes across the Excel screen, beginning with column A and finishing with column IV, contain alphabetic characters that refer to column titles.

Numbers appear on the left and flow down the Excel screen to relate to rows. For example, the first row is referred to as row 1, and the last row is referred to as row 65536.

- **The Cell**

Columns and rows make up an Excel spreadsheet. The intersection of these columns and rows results in the formation of cells, which are little boxes. A dark border surrounds the active cell or the cell that can be acted upon. The rest of the cells have a light gray border. Each cell is given a name. It has two elements to its name: the column letter and the row number.

- **The Formula Bar**

The formula bar shows data that has been entered into the current or active cell or that is being entered as you type. You can also use the formula bar to alter a cell's contents.

- **Horizontal and Vertical Scroll Bars**

PageUp and PageDown on the keyboard move the pointer up and down one screen at a time. Ctrl+Home, which sends the cursor to the top-left corner of the spreadsheet, or cell A1, and Home, which brings the cursor to the first column on the current row, are two other keys that shift the active cell.

To move around the worksheet:

You have numerous options for moving about the spreadsheet. To move the cell pointer, do the following:

- To activate a cell, use the mouse to point to it and click.
- Use the keyboard arrow keys to move the pointer one cell to the left, right, up, or down.
- To move around the worksheet, use the following commands:
- To go up or down the spreadsheet, utilize the vertical scroll bar on the right border of the screen. To scroll left or right across the spreadsheet, use the horizontal scroll bar at the bottom of the screen.

To move between worksheets:

Each workbook comes with three worksheets by default. Sheet1, Sheet2, and Sheet3 are the tabs displayed at the bottom of the Excel window to represent these workbooks.

To move from one worksheet to another, follow these steps:

Select the sheet tab you wish to see—Sheet1, Sheet2, or Sheet 3—and click it.

Understanding the Ribbon

Figure 3

The Microsoft Excel ribbon is a row of tabs and icons at the top of the Excel window that allows you to easily locate, comprehend, and use commands for accomplishing a task. It appears to be quite a complicated toolbar, which it is.

Excel 2007 introduced the ribbon, which replaced the previous version's traditional toolbars and pull-down menus. In addition, Microsoft added the option to customize the ribbon with Excel 2010.

The four primary components of Excel's ribbon are tabs, groups, dialog launchers, and command buttons.

Ribbon tab: Multiple commands are appropriately subdivided into groups on the Ribbon tab.

Ribbon group: A ribbon group is a collection of connected commands usually executed as part of a bigger task.

Dialog launcher: A dialog launcher is a little arrow in the group's lower-right corner that displays more related commands. Dialog launchers occur in groups with more commands than there is room for.

Command button: A command button is a button you press to perform a specific action.

Ribbon Tabs

The following tabs are found on the standard Excel ribbon, from left to right:
- **File** – opens the backstage view, which provides all the necessary file-related commands and Excel settings. This tab was added to Excel 2010 to replace the Office button in Excel 2007 and the File menu in previous versions.
- **Home** – includes the most commonly used commands, including copying and pasting, sorting and filtering, formatting, and so on.
- **Insert** — This command can add photos, charts, PivotTables, hyperlinks, special symbols, equations, headers, and footers to a worksheet.
- **Draw** - You can draw with a digital pen, a mouse, or a finger based on your device. This tab is present in Excel 2013 and beyond; however, it is not shown by default, just like the Developer tab.
- **Page Layout** - gives options for controlling the appearance of worksheets on screen and in print. These tools control theme settings, gridlines, page margins, object alignment, and print area.
- **Formulas** — this section offers tools for inserting functions, naming variables, and regulating computation choices.
- **Data** – this section contains commands for handling worksheet data and connecting to external data.
- **Review** — allows you to double-check the spelling, keep track of changes, make comments and notes, and password-protect worksheets and workbooks.
- **View** – allows you to switch between worksheet views, freeze panes, and view and arrange multiple windows.
- **Help** – appears only in Excel 2019 and Office 365. This tab provides quick access to the Help Task Pane and allows you to contact Microsoft support, send feedback, suggest a feature, and view training videos.
- **Developer** – gives you access to advanced features like VBA macros, ActiveX and Form controls, and XML commands. This tab is disabled by default and must be enabled first.
- **Add-ins** – This option appears only when you open an older workbook or load an add-in that modifies the toolbars or menu.

Contextual Ribbon Tabs

The Excel ribbon has context-sensitive tabs, also known as Tool Tabs, that appear only when you choose a specific item, such as a table, chart, shape, or picture, in addition to the constant tabs described above. For example, the Design and Format tabs will appear under Chart Tools if you select a chart.

Show/Hide Ribbon in Excel

Show Ribbon in Excel

Don't be alarmed if the ribbon has vanished from your Excel UI. You can quickly recover it by employing one of the methods listed below.
- **Display the Collapsed Ribbon in Full View**

If the Excel ribbon has been minimized so that only the tab names are visible, do one of the following to restore it to its full display:
- **Ctrl + F1 is the Ribbon Shortcut**

To re-show the entire ribbon, double-click on any ribbon tab.

Right-click any ribbon tab and deselect Collapse the Ribbon in Excel 2019 - 2013 or Minimize the Ribbon in Excel 2010 and 2007.

The ribbon should be pinned. To do so, temporarily display the ribbon by clicking on any tab. In Excel 2016 and 2019, a small pin icon (the arrow in Excel 2013) will appear in the lower right corner, and you can click on it to always show the ribbon.

Hide Ribbon in Excel

You can collapse the ribbon to reveal only the tab names or conceal it entirely if it takes up too much room at the top of your worksheet, mainly if you use a laptop with a small screen.

Reduce the Ribbon's Size

Use any of the following techniques to see only the tab names and no commands, as shown in the screenshot below:

Excel ribbon shortcuts are hidden in the Ribbon. Ctrl + F1 is the quickest way to hide the Excel ribbon.

Select a tab by double-clicking it. By double-clicking an active tab, you can also collapse the ribbon.

The arrow button Another quick way to hide the ribbon in Excel is to click the up arrow in the ribbon's lower-right corner.

How to Get Excel Ribbon Back?

If the ribbon vanishes from your Excel, it's most likely due to one of the following reasons.

The tabs appear, but the commands have vanished.

Perhaps you inadvertently obscured the ribbon with a misplaced keystroke or mouse click. To re-display the commands, press Ctrl + F1 or double-click any ribbon tab.

- **The Whole Ribbon Missing**

Your Excel most likely went into "full screen" mode. To restore the ribbon, click the Ribbon Display Options button in the top-right corner and select ShowTabs and Commands. This will keep the ribbon where it should be at the top of the Excel window. Please see How to Unhide the Ribbon in Excel for more information.

- **Disappearing of the Contextual tabs**

If a specific object's Tool Tabs (such as a chart, image, or PivotTable) are missing, that object has lost focus. Simply select the object to bring up the contextual tabs again.

- **Add-in's Tab Missing**

You've been using an Excel add-in (for example, our Ultimate Suite) for a while, and the add-ribbon has vanished. Excel most likely disabled the add-in.

To resolve this, navigate to File > Excel Options > Add-ins > Disabled Items > Go. Choose the add-in from the list and click the Enable button.

Customize the Ribbon in Excel

You can also easily personalize the ribbon to your needs to know exactly where everything is.

The Customize Ribbon window under Excel Options is your starting point for most customizations. And the quickest way to get there is to right-click on the ribbon and choose to Customize the Ribbon from the context menu:

You can create tabs with commands, rearrange tabs and groups, show, hide, and rename tabs, and much more.

Show the Developer Tab in Excel

The Developer tab is a handy addition to the Excel ribbon that gives you access to various advanced features such as VBA macros, ActiveX and Form controls, XML commands, and more. The issue is that the Developer tab is, by default, hidden. Fortunately, it's very simple to enable. To do so, right-click the ribbon, select Customize the Ribbon, Developer under Main Tabs, and OK.

Similarly, you can activate other tabs in Excel that are not visible on the ribbon, such as the Draw tab.

Keyboard Circuits to Navigate the Ribbon

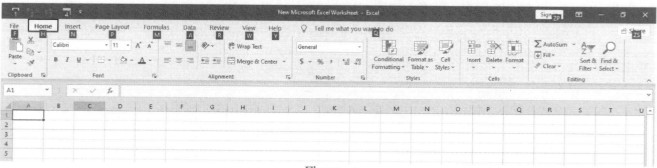

Figure 4

The ribbon organizes related choices into tabs. On the Home tab, for example, the Number group offers the Number Format choice. As demonstrated in the image below, pressing the Alt key displays the ribbon shortcuts, known as Key Tips, as letters in miniature images next to the tabs and options.

You may create shortcuts for the ribbon choices by combining the Key Tips letters with the Alt key. For example, Alt+H will open the Home tab, and Alt+Q will take you to the Tell me or Search area. Press Alt again to show KeyTips for the selected tab's settings.

Many of the old Alt key menu shortcuts still work in Office 2013 and Office 2010. However, you must be aware of the entire shortcut. For example, press Alt, then one of the classic menu keys such as E (Edit), V (View), I (Insert), and so on. A message appears informing you that you are using an access key from an earlier version of Microsoft

Office. Go ahead and utilize it if you know the whole key sequence. Suppose you are unaware of the sequence, press Esc and instead use Key Tips.

For ribbon tabs, use the Access keys.

To navigate directly to a ribbon tab, use one of the access keys listed below. Depending on your worksheet selection, additional tabs may display.

1. **Shortcut key: Alt+Q, then enter the search term.**

Enter a search phrase for assistance or Help content in the Tell me or Search section on the Ribbon.

2. **Shortcut key: Alt+F**

A backstage view is available when you open the File page.

3. **Shortcut key: Alt+H**

Open the Home tab and use the Find tool to format text and numbers.

4. **Shortcut key: Alt+N**

Insert PivotTables, charts, add-ins, Sparklines, photos, shapes, headers, or text boxes using the Insert tab.

5. **Shortcut key: Alt+P**

Navigate to the Page Layout tab and experiment with themes, page setup, scale, and alignment.

6. **Shortcut key: Alt+M**

Insert, trace, and customize functions and calculations using the Formulas tab.

7. **Shortcut key: Alt+A**

Connect to, sort, filter, analyze, and deal with data using the Data tab.

8. **Shortcut key: Alt+R**

Check to spell, add notes and threaded comments, and protect sheets and workbooks by opening the Review tab.

9. **Shortcut key: Alt+W**

Go to the View tab to examine page breaks and layouts, display and conceal gridlines and headings, adjust zoom magnification, manage windows and panes, and view macros.

CHAPTER 3:
Customizing Excel

If you customize Excel to your preferences, working with it can be a smooth experience. You can control how Excel looks and what information is displayed on different screens. Use the instructions in this chapter to learn how to customize Excel to make it the ideal spreadsheet program for your requirements.

Customizing Toolbars and Menus

When generating and updating spreadsheets, taking the time to customize the Excel toolbars (particularly the Standard and Formatting toolbars that Excel shows automatically when you begin the software) and pull-down menus saves you time.

Excel's multiple toolbars and pull-down menus can be customized regarding position, behavior, and content. This customization involves separating the Standard and Formatting toolbars, always displaying full pull-down menus, and modifying the buttons and command options found on both built-in and custom bars and menus.

Quick Access Toolbar in Excel

The Toolbar is a section of Excel where you may add various commands and tools. It is visible in the upper right corner of the Excel window by default, above the ribbon with several tools. However, they've been made adjustable to make toolbars more user-friendly based on how frequently particular tools are used. In addition, excel allows us to select and design a Quick Access Toolbar instead of a group of tools. This will enable you to access the tools you need quickly. As a result, the toolbar is known as the Quick Access Toolbar.

Looking at the very top of the excel screen, you will see the quick access toolbar. The default will look similar to this:

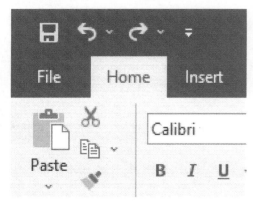

The floppy disk icon is for quick saving, then you have Undo and Redo options, followed by a drop-down for more options. By adding your items to the fast access toolbar, you can quickly customize it. In the next part, you'll learn what a data form is. On the other hand, data forms have been hidden away and are no longer visible on the Excel ribbon. The data forms icon will be added to the quick access toolbar.

To find Data Forms, go to the top left corner of Excel and click the file button. Then, at the bottom of the File menu, select More options:

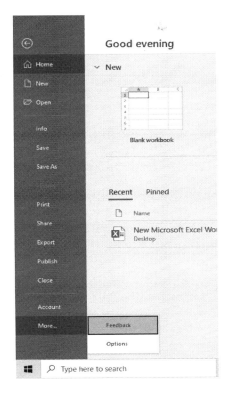

When you click the Options button, you'll see this dialogue box popping up:

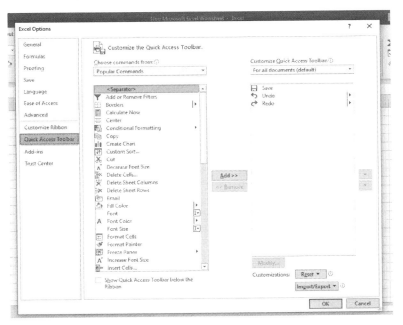

On the left, click the Quick Access toolbar button. You may put whatever you want on the Quick Access toolbar at the top of your Excel worksheet. You select one from the list and then click the middle Add button.

Click the Choose Commands From drop-down list to add the Data Form option to the Quick Access toolbar. You should look into this (we have cut a few options in the picture).

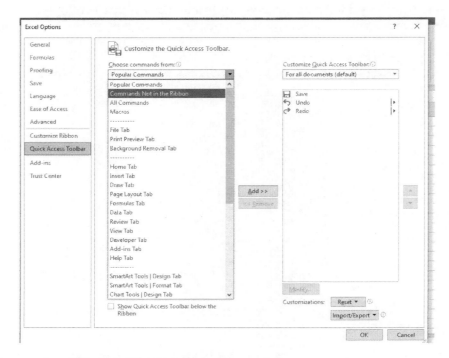

Select 'Commands Not in the Ribbon and the list box changes:

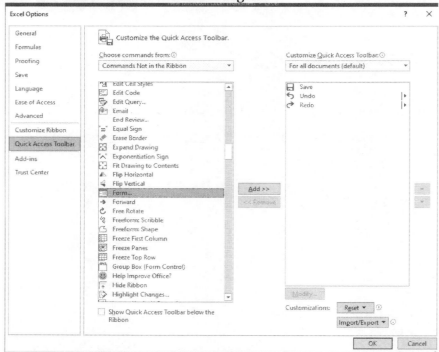

Select 'Form' from the list of Commands Not in the Ribbon. Then, in the middle, click the Add button. The right-hand list box will then appear like this:

Find out what else you can put on the Quick Access toolbar. There's a good chance you'll discover your favorite there!

After selecting OK in the choice dialogue box, you'll be taken back to the excel spreadsheet. In the Quick Access toolbar, your new item should be displayed:

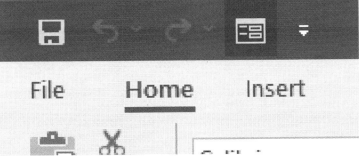

The Data Form item is highlighted in the image above.

Creating, Editing, and Running Macros

You can record a macro to automate actions in Microsoft Excel that you perform frequently. A macro is a single action or a series of activities you can repeat as often as you like. You record your mouse clicks and keystrokes when you construct a macro. You can alter a macro after its creation to make minor adjustments to its functions. Assume you produce a report for your accounting manager once a month. Customers with past-due accounts should have their names formatted in red and bold. You can use a macro to apply these formatting changes to the cells you select swiftly.

Create a Macro

- Click the Office button and then click Options.
- In the left pane, click popular and select the Show Developer tab in the Ribbon.
- Click the Developer tab and click the macros button.

- Type a name for the macro.
- Click the Macros in the list arrow and click All open Workbooks.
- Click create.
- The Microsoft Visual Basic window opens.
- Click the Module window, and then type new Visual Basic Commands.
- To run the macro, press F5.

Assign a Macro to a Toolbar

- Click the Quick Access toolbar list arrow, and then click More Commands.
- Click the Choose command, and then click Macros.
- From the left column, select Macro and then click Add.
- To rearrange the order, use the Move Up and Down arrow buttons.
- Click Modify.
- Type a name for the button. Then, click an icon in the symbol list.

Run a Macro

- Click the Office button, and then click Options.
- In the left pane, click Popular and Select the Show Developer tab in the Ribbon.
- Click the Developer or View tab.
- Click the macros button.
- Click the macro you want to run. Click Run.

Delete a Macro

- Click the Office button, and then click Options.
- In the left pane, click Popular and Select the Show Developer tab in the Ribbon.
- Click the Developer or View tab.
- Click the macros button.
- Click the macro you want to delete. Click Delete.
- Press Ctrl + Break to stop a macro.

Debug a Macro Using Step Mode

- Click the Office button and then click Options.
- In the left pane, click Popular and Select the Show Developer tab in the Ribbon.
- Click the Developer or View tab.
- Click the macros button.
- Click the macro you want to debug. Click Step Into.
- The Microsoft Visual Basic window opens.
- Click the Debug menu and Step Into to proceed through each action.

Edit a Macro

- Click the Office button and then click Options.
- Click Popular in the left pane, then select the Show Developer option in the Ribbon.
- Toggle between the Developer and View tabs.
- Select the macros option from the drop-down menu.
- Then click edit on the macro you wish to change.
- Click the Visual Basic code in the Module window.
- Edit the commands that are already there.

Record a Macro

- Click the Office button, and then click Options.
- In the left pane, click Popular and Select the Show Developer tab in the Ribbon.
- Click the Developer or View tab.
- Use the Use Relative References Button to record a macro with actions relative to the initially selected cell.

- To record a macro, press the Record Macro button.
- For the macro, type a name. To run the macro, assign a shortcut key. To utilize macros whenever you use Excel, click Store macros in the list arrow and pick Personal Macro Workbook.
- To utilize the macro in new workbooks, create a new workbook.
- This worksheet is the only one that uses macros.
- Type a description and click OK>
- Execute the commands.
- Click the Stop Recording button.

Save a Workbook with Macros

- Select Office from the drop-down menu, then click Save As.
- Give your workbook a name.
- After that, select the Save as type list arrow.
- Workbook with macros in Excel. VBA code is contained in a workbook (.xlsm).
- Excel Macro-Enabled Templates are another option. A spreadsheet template (.xltm) with pre-approved macros.
- Select Save.

Open a Workbook with Macros

- Select Office from the drop-down menu, then select Open.
- Select the macro-enabled worksheet you wish to open, then click Open.
- In the Security Warning, select Options.
- Select OK.

Sign a Macro Project

- Click the Office button and click Options.
- Click Popular in the left pane. In the Ribbon, click the Show Developer tab.
- Go to the Developer tab. To open the Visual Basic Window, click the Visual Basic button.
- Then select Digital Signature from the Tools menu.
- Select the one you want.
- Choose a certificate from the drop-down menu.
- To view a certificate, first select View Certificate, then OK.

Create a Self-Signing Certificate for a Macro Project

- Go to Office Tools and select Digital Certificate for VBA Projects.
- Type in a name, then click OK.
- Office apps will only trust a self-signed certificate if it was created on the same computer.

Change Macro Security Settings

- Click the Office button, and then click Options.
- In the left pane, click Trust Center. Then, click Trust Center Settings.
- In the left pane, click Macro Settings and select the option for macros:
  - Disable all macros except digitally signed macros.
  - Disable all macros with notification.
  - Enable all macros.
  - Disable all macros without notification.

If you're a developer, choose the Trust access to the VBA project object model check box.

Excel Add-Ins and Tools

Excel is a business application that has withstood the test of time regarding workplace efficiency. Rapid technological advancements are making their way into this world. Excel is also constantly improving with new add-ins and tools to work with each passing day. Here are a few add-ins that make working with data more fun and interesting:

ASAP Utilities

ASAP Utilities has one of the most extensive customer bases. It's used in a variety of worldwide companies as well as student groups. The add-in gives users various options, from choosing cells to sorting multiple items.
Among the responsibilities are selecting specific cells, applying formulas, and selecting and deselecting cells. This add-in also can import and export worksheets. The ability to sort tabs by name or color makes the add-in much more enticing. It's also available in ten additional languages.

Power Pivot

Thanks to Power Pivot, sharing data analysis findings has never been easier. The ability to import enormous amounts of data from various platforms distinguishes this add-on. These platforms import data from text files, spreadsheets, and cloud-based online services.
A component on mastering Power Pivot is now included in specialized Excel certification training. Working with large databases is part of the training. Power Pivot guarantees that data is processed quickly and accurately, resulting in high-quality reports.

Kutools

More than 200 functions and tools are included in this add-in. Working with Excel becomes much easier, and jobs can be completed in less time. In addition, it has a lot of features that make working with data enjoyable. While undergoing Excel certification training, learning Kutools can be advantageous.
The View utility is one of the most essential features. The Navigation Pane, Work Area, Reading, Column, Worksheet, and Show/Hide views are all included. Select, Insert, Delete, Text, Format, and Link Tools are all included in the Editing tool. Workbook and Sheets are also available.

Quandl

Quandl extends Excel's capability to allow users to work with massive datasets. This add-in lets you download large amounts of data that may be used to create reports. When this add-in is used, the possibilities for data investigation in various forms are endless.
Professionals in the financial sector can gain access to databases through this add-in to give insights; data analysts develop reports. These findings include venture capital, stock research, and hedge fund management.

Analysis Toolpak

This add-in provides tools for working with complex datasets in the statistical and engineering sectors. Analyst reports in the financial industry can also benefit from this add-on. For formulas and macros, a distinct set of skills is required.
Covariance, descriptive statistics, and Fourier Analysis are examples of analysis tools. Many analysts employ tools like the histogram and random number generation.

Data Burst

Data burst for Excel is an add-in that lets you make sunburst data visualizations in Excel. Many reporting analysts find the data appealing because it makes for appealing viewing. In addition, the visual value of data representation in this format is added.
Support for formulas, hidden columns, slicers, and filters are a few features. It works on the web, on mobile devices, and on tablets. It also has a feature for weather and geographic data.

Audible Charts

This add-in is unique because it allows you to present data in an audio format. For example, in the visualization reports, analysts can hear their data in ascending sequence of the pitch. Because reports are visual and audio, this is a unique feature of making them.
These are a handful of the most popular add-ins for Excel that improve its functionality and make it a more productive tool. Several tools you can easily access on the web enhance Excel's present functionality. It is essential to utilize some time to explore and learn about these tools and add-ins.

CHAPTER 4:
Basics of Organizing and Analyzing Data

Microsoft Office Excel has many features that enable data organizing and analysis in a snap. Organize and structure data in a worksheet according to the instructions to reap the most of these features.

Construction and Application of Customized Formulas

Although Microsoft Office Excel has many built-in worksheet functions, it is unlikely that it has a function for every calculation you conduct. This is because Excel's creators couldn't possibly anticipate every user's calculation needs. So, instead, an Excel spreadsheet provides you with the ability to create custom functions, which are explained below:

Creating a Simples Custom Function

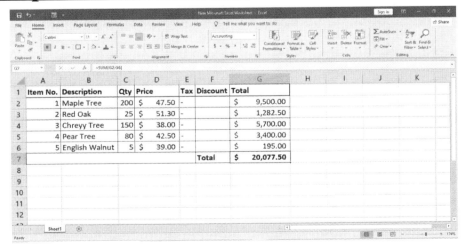

The Visual Basic for Applications (VBA) programming language is used to create custom functions, such as macros. They are distinct from macros in two ways. First, instead of sub-procedures, they utilize function procedures. Instead of starting with a Sub statement, they begin with a Function statement and end with an End Function rather than an End sub. Second, instead of taking action, they perform computations. You'll learn how to construct and use custom functions in this chapter:

Assume that your company offers a 20% quantity discount on the sale of a product if the order totals more than 100 units. You will create a function to calculate this discount in the following paragraphs.

The worksheet in the figure below shows an order form that lists each item, the quantity, the price, the discount (if any), and the resulting extended price.

We are now going to calculate the discount for each item ordered in column F. Follow these steps to make a custom DISCOUNT function in this workbook:

> Press Alt + F11 to open the Visual Basic Editor, then click Insert, Module. A new module appears.
> Type the code in the new module as below.

```
Function Discount (quantity, price)
If quantity > = 100 Then
        Discount = quantity * price * 0.1
Else
        Discount = 0
End If
        Discount = Application.Round (Discount, 2)
End Function
```

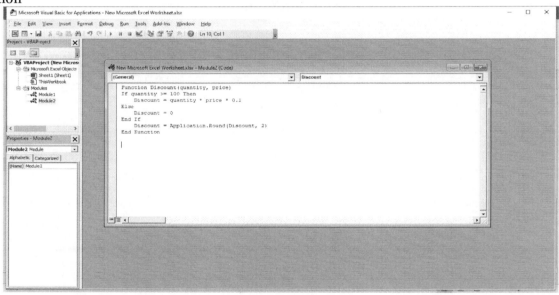

<u>Using Custom Functions</u>

Now, you are ready to use the new DISCOUNT function. Press Alt + F11 to switch to the worksheet shown above. Select cell F2, and type the following:

=DISCOUNT(C2, D2)

Excel calculates a 10% discount on 200 units at $47.50 each, totaling $950.00.

The DISCOUNT function requires two arguments, price and quantity, as stated in the first line of your VBA code, Function Discount. Those two arguments must be included when executing the function in a worksheet cell. In the formula =DISCOUNT(C2, D2), C2 is the quantity argument, and D2 is the price argument. Then, you can copy the DISCOUNT formula to F3:F6 to get the worksheet shown in the figure below.

This worksheet displays the DISCOUNT custom function's output.

The If statement in the next block of code checks the quantity argument to see if the number of products sold is higher than or equal to 100:

```
If quantity >= 100 Then
        Discount = quantity * price * 0.1
Else
        Discount=0
End If
```

If the number of products sold is higher than or equal to 100, VBA performs the following expression, which divides the quantity by the price, then divides the result by 0.1:

The result is saved as the Discount variable. A VBA statement that holds a value in a variable is called an assignment statement. It examines the expression on the right side of the equal sign and assigns the result to the variable name on the left. The value contained in the variable Discount is returned to the worksheet formula called the DISCOUNT function since the variable Discount has the same name as the function procedure.

VBA executes the following statements if the quantity is less than 100.

```
Discount = 0
```

Finally, the value allocated to the Discount variable is rounded to two decimal places using the following statement:

```
Discount = Application.Round(Discount, 2)
```

The ROUND function is not available in VBA, although it is available in Excel. To use ROUND in this sentence, you tell VBA to look in the Application object for the Round method (function) (Excel). By putting the term Application before the word Round, you can achieve this. Use this syntax when you need to call an Excel function from a VBA module.

Understanding Custom Function Rules

A function must begin with a Function statement and end with an End Function statement to be considered custom. The Function statement typically specifies one or more arguments besides the function name. However, you can design a function that takes no arguments. RAND and NOW, for example, are two built-in Excel functions that don't require arguments.

The function procedure, which comes after the Function statement, contains one or more VBA statements that make judgments and execute calculations based on the arguments supplied to the function. Finally, you must insert a statement in the function method that assigns a value to a variable with the same name as the function. This value is returned to the function-calling formula.

Using VBA Keywords in Custom Functions

The amount of VBA keywords that can be used in custom functions is less than that of macros. Custom functions cannot do anything other than return a value to a worksheet formula or an expression utilized in another VBA macro or function. Custom functions, for example, cannot resize windows, update a cell's formula, or change the font, color, or pattern options for text in a cell. If you use this type of "action" code in a function procedure, the function will return the #VALUE! Error.

Aside from conducting computations, the only thing a function procedure can do is display a dialog box. Input from the user executing the function can be obtained using an InputBox statement in a custom function. Likewise, a MsgBox statement can communicate information to the user. Custom dialog boxes, also known as UserForms, are another option outside this tutorial's scope.

Application of Advanced Filters

The steps involved in the advanced filter implementation are as follows:
- Select the headers
- Copy them
- Paste the headers, having 2-3 rows free.
- Write the criteria under the header according to your decision to extract certain data, for example, '>= 80' under the 'Marks in Maths' header and '>=400' under the 'Total Marks' header.
- Now, click anywhere inside your data.
- Then click on the 'Data' tab, and under the group' sort & filter,' select 'advanced.'
- A new pop-up window with the title 'Advanced Filter' appears, and the listed range is automatically selected in the worksheet and entered in the text box next to the 'list range' in the pop-up window.
- In the textbox next to the 'criteria range,' you can also enter the range manually.
- Finally, click OK and observe that your data has been filtered according to your specified conditions.

Performing Data Analysis Using Automated Tools

Add/Install Data Analysis Add-in
- Click the Office button and then click the option.
- Click the Add-in and click the Data Analysis in the list.
- Click GO
- Select Data Analysis add-in in the list. Click OK.
- Click OK to install Data Analysis, and the Data Analysis button is added to the Data tab.

Use Data Analysis Tools
- Select the Data tab. Select the Data Analysis option. Load the add-in if it isn't already installed.
- To use the analysis tool, simply click it.
- Click Help to acquire more information about each tool.
- Click the OK button.
- Choose an input range. The Collapse Dialog button can be used to pick a range, and the Expand Dialog button can be used to return.
- Click OK after specifying any other tool-specific parameters.

When developing complicated statistical or engineering analyses, Microsoft Excel provides a suite of data analysis tools, and Analysis Toolpak, that you could employ to save time. You enter data and settings for each analysis, and the program applies suitable statistical or engineering macro functions before displaying the results in an output table. In addition to generating tables, some utilities generate charts.

Tools in Analysis ToolPak

Other statistical, financial, and engineering spreadsheet capabilities are also available in Excel. Some statistical functions are pre-installed, while others are added once you install the Analysis Toolpak.
The following tools are included in the Analysis ToolPak:

Anova

Different forms of variance analysis are available with the Anova analysis tools. The tool you should use is determined by the number of factors you want to test and the number of samples you have from the populations you want to analyze.
- **ANOVA: Single Factor**

This program analyzes variance in data from two or more samples. The study compares the hypothesis that each sample is chosen from the same underlying probability distribution against the alternative hypothesis that the underlying probability distributions for all samples are not the same. You can utilize the worksheet function T.TEST if you just have two samples. However, there is no practical generalization of T.TEST when there are more than two samples; hence the Single Factor Anova model is used instead.

- **Anova: Two-Factor with Replication**

This analysis tool comes in handy when data may be categorized along two separate dimensions. For example, in an experiment to assess plant height, the plants could be given different fertilizer brands (A, B, C) and kept at varying temperatures (low, high). We have an equal number of observations of plant height for each of the six potential couples of fertilizer and temperature. We can use the Anova tool to test:

Whether the various fertilizer brands' plant heights are derived from the same underlying population, temperatures aren't considered in this study.

The plant heights for the various temperature levels come from the same underlying population. Fertilizer brands are not taken into account for the objectives of this study.

Regardless of whether the effects of differences in fertilizer brands found in the first bulleted point and changes in temperatures found in the second bulleted point have been accounted for, the six samples representing all pairs of fertilizer and the temperature values are drawn from the same population. As a result, the alternative theory is that, in addition to changes based merely on fertilizer or temperature, there are effects owing to specific fertilizer and temperature pairings. This analysis tool comes in handy when data is categorized on two dimensions, as in the Two-Factor example with replication. However, for this tool, it is assumed that each pair (for example, each fertilizer and temperature pair in the last example) has only one observation.

Correlation

When data on each variable are observed for each N participant, the CORREL and PEARSON worksheet calculate the correlation coefficient between the two variables. (Any subject with no observations is omitted in the analysis.) The correlation analysis tool is especially effective when there are more than two measurement variables for each N subject. It generates a correlation matrix, which displays the CORREL (or PEARSON) value for each conceivable pair of measurement variables.

Like the covariance, the correlation coefficient measures how much two measurement variables "vary together." Unlike covariance, the correlation coefficient is scaled so that its value is unaffected by the units in which two measurement variables are expressed. (If weight and height are the two measurement variables, the correlation coefficient remains the same when the weight is converted from pounds to kilograms.) Any correlation coefficient must be between -1 and +1 inclusive.

You can make use of the correlation analysis tool to examine each pair of measurement variables to see if they seem to move in the same direction — that is, whether greater values of one variable are associated with greater values of another (positive correlation), small values of one variable are associated with greater values of another (negative correlation), and so on.

Covariance

When you have N separate measurement variables observed on a group of individuals, you can utilize both the Correlation and Covariance tools at the same time. Each Correlation and Covariance tool produces an output table, a matrix, that displays the correlation coefficient or covariance between each pair of measurement variables, respectively. The only difference is those correlation coefficients are scaled from -1 to +1 inclusive. The covariances of the corresponding covariances are not scaled. The correlation coefficient and covariance measure how much two variables "variate together."

For each pair of measurement variables, the covariance tool computes the value of the worksheet function COVARIANCE.P. (When there are just two measurement variables, such as N=2, using COVARIANCE.P instead of the Covariance tool is a suitable alternative.) The entry on the diagonal of the Covariance tool's output table in row I column I represents the covariance of the i-th measurement variable with itself. The population variance for that variable, as computed by the VAR.P worksheet function, is just this. The Covariance tool can examine each pair of measurement variables to see if they tend to move together. That is, whether large values of one variable are associated with large values of the other (positive covariance) or whether small values of one variable are associated with small values of the other (negative covariance) (negative covariance).

Descriptive Statistics

The Descriptive Statistics analysis tool produces a report of univariate statistics for data in the supplied range, revealing information about your data's central tendency and variability.

Exponential Smoothing

The Exponential Smoothing analytical tool forecasts a value based on the prior period's forecast, corrected for the prior forecast's mistake. The constant smoothing controls how strongly the forecasts respond to flaws in the prior forecast, and its value defines how powerful the tool is.

F-Test Two-Sample for Variances

The F-Test Two-Sample for Variances analysis tool compares two population variances using a two-sample F-test.

For example, you can use the F-Test tool to compare two teams' times in a swim meet. The tool displays the outcome of a null hypothesis test that these two samples come from distributions with equal variances, as opposed to the alternative that the variances in the underlying distributions are not equal.

Fourier Analysis

Using the Fast Fourier Transform (FFT) approach to transform data, the Fourier Analysis tool addresses problems in linear systems and analyzes periodic data. Inverse transformations, in which the inverse of changed data returns the original data, are also supported by this tool.

Histogram

Individual and cumulative frequencies for a cell range of data and bins are calculated using the Histogram analysis tool. In addition, this tool calculates the number of times a value appears in a data set.

You can, for example, determine the distribution of scores in letter-grade categories in a class of 20 pupils. The letter-grade limits and the number of scores between the lowest and current bound are displayed in a histogram table. The data's mode is the single most common score.

Moving Average

The Moving Average analysis tool predicts values for the forecast period based on the variable's average value across a set of previous periods. A moving average reveals trends that would be hidden by a simple average of all past data. This tool can predict sales, inventories, and other patterns. The following formula is used to calculate each forecasted value.

The formula for calculating moving averages is as follows:

$$F_{(j+1)} = \frac{1}{N} \sum_{j=1}^{N} A_{(-j+1)}$$

Where:
- N represents the number of prior periods to include in the moving average
- F j is the forecasted value at time j
- A j is the actual value at time j

Random Number Generation

The Random Number Generation analysis tool generates independent random numbers from one of several distributions and fills a range with them. A probability distribution can be used to characterize the participants in a population. For example, a normal distribution can describe the population of people's heights. In contrast, a Bernoulli distribution of two possible outcomes can describe the population of coin-flip results.

Rank and Percentile

The Rank and Percentile analysis tool generates a table that lists each item in a data set's ordinal and percentage rank. Thus, you can look at how values in a data collection compare to each other. The spreadsheet functions RANK.EQ and PERCENTRANK.INC is used in this tool. Use the RANK.EQ function to treat tied values as having the same rank, or the RANK.AVG method returns the average rank for the tied values if you want to account for them.

Regression

This tool operates linear regression analysis by fitting a line through a set of observations using the "least squares" method. You can look at how the values of one or more independent variables affect the values of a single dependent variable. For example, you can look at how age, height, and weight affect an athlete's performance. Based on a set of performance data, you can assign shares in the performance measure to each of these three components and then use the results to estimate the performance of a new, untested athlete.

The LINEST worksheet function is used by the Regression tool.

Sampling

By treating the input range as a population, the Sampling analysis tool creates a sample from a population. A representative sample might be used when the population is too vast to analyze or chart. If you believe the input data is periodic, you may also build a sample that only contains values from a specific cycle region.

T-Test

The Two-Sample t-Test analysis tools examine the population means that underpin each sample for equality. The three tools use distinct assumptions: that the population variances are equal and not equal and that the two samples represent before-and after-treatment observations on the same people.

A t-Statistic value, t, is computed and displayed as "t Stat." This value, t, might be negative or nonnegative, depending on the data. If t 0, "P(T <= t) one-tail" offers the probability of observing a t-Statistic value that is more negative than t under the assumption of equal underlying population means. If t >=0, "P(T< = t) one-tail" indicates the likelihood of observing a t-Statistic value that is more positive than t. The cutoff value is "t Critical one-tail," hence Alpha's chance of seeing a t-Statistic value greater than or equal to "t Critical one-tail."

The probability that a value of the t-Statistic is bigger in absolute value than t will be seen is given by "P(T \< = t) two-tail." The cutoff value is "P Critical two-tail," and the probability of an observed t-Statistic greater in absolute value than "P Critical two-tail" is Alpha.

Z-Test

z-Test performs a two-sample z-Test for means with known variances using the z-Test: Two-Sample for Means analytical tool. This tool is used to test the null hypothesis that no difference exists between two population means against alternative hypotheses that are either one-sided or two-sided. If the variances are unknown, use the spreadsheet function Z.TEST instead.

When using the z-Test tool, make sure to read the result carefully.

When there is no difference between population means, "P(Z = z) one-tail" is truly P(Z >= ABS(z)), which is the probability of a z-value further from 0 in the same direction as the observed z value. When there is no difference between population means, "P(Z = z) two-tail" is truly P(Z >= ABS(z) or Z= -ABS(z): probability of z-value further from 0 in either direction than observed z-value. The one-tailed result is simply multiplied by two to get the two-tailed result. The z-Test tool can also be used in cases where the null hypothesis is that the difference between two population means has a specific nonzero value. This test can be used to compare the performance of two car models, for example.

Creating Pivot Table and Pivot Chart Reports

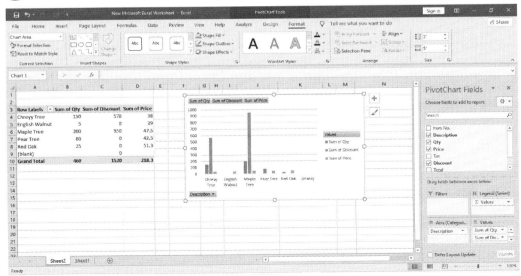

Follow the steps below to create a PivotTable or PivotChart Report:
- Click anywhere within the table rang
- Click on the Insert tab and click the PivotTable button. After that, click PivotTable or PivotChart.
- Click the Select a table or range option or the Use an external data source option. Next, click Choose Connection, and then select a connection.
- Click the New or Existing worksheet option, and specify a cell range.
- Click OK.
- Choose the checkboxes next to the fields you want to use to add them to empty PivotTable.
- Create a PivotChart Report from a PivotTable Report.
- Click the Options tab under PivotTable tools and click the PivotChart button.
- Click the chart type and click OK.

Application of Build-In Functions and Formulas

One of Excel's most important features is the option to create formulas that calculate the value of the data you enter into its columns and rows. Excel can perform time, percentages, averages, and other arithmetic and statistical calculations. This popular software's built-in functions make creating the formulas you need simple.

Simple Math Formulas

- Launch Microsoft Excel by double-clicking the Desktop shortcut or selecting it from the Windows Start menu. You will be given an Excel Workbook by default. The Workbook has three blank worksheets labeled Sheet1, Sheet2, and Sheet3.
- Remember that each column has a title that Excel can use in calculations and that each row has a number, a column letter, and a row number. A1 is the first cell at the top of the worksheet. B1 is the cell to the right.
- In Sheet 1, begin typing the figures you want to compute. You can enter the numbers in a single column or over multiple rows. You can also enter information in more than one column or row.
- Place the cursor on the first empty cell beneath the data in your column or at the end of your first row. Excel shows the cursor location and cell name beneath the toolbars at the top of the screen.
- Begin each formula with the equal sign. Excel immediately shows it in the Formula Bar, which is located above the first row of the worksheet.
- Select the first cell in your formula by clicking it. Excel automatically inserts the cell name into your formula. Enter a mathematical function here. Use the + sign on your keyboard to add numbers. The negative symbol is used for subtraction. To split, press the slash key while holding down the question mark key. Excel utilizes an asterisk above the number 8 on the keyboard to multiply.
- Click each cell in the formula you wish to use, then input the required arithmetic function. When your formula is finished, click the green check mark at the top of the formula bar.

AutoSum

- For a speedier addition of one column or row of integers, use Excel's AutoSum button. It will be far more convenient than clicking on each cell and inputting the plus sign.
- Put your cursor in the first empty cell following your numbers. Select the AutoSum option. It looks like a fancy capital letter E and is located on the editing toolbar in Excel. Excel will highlight every cell in the column above until it reaches an empty cell. Excel chooses data to the left of the cursor for data in rows.
- To finish the formula, click the green checkmark in the formula bar.

Using Excel Functions in Formulas

- Create a formula using the built-in mathematical functions in Excel by first placing your cursor on an empty cell. Then, to begin the formula, type the equal sign. In Excel 2007, select Formulas, then Insert Function. Click to open the Insert menu in Excel 2003, then select Function from the drop-down list.
- Choose the desired function. Financial, date, time, statistical, engineering, trigonometric, logical, and many other categories are available. Select All from the category drop-down box to see all of the features.
- Highlight the function that you require in the function list. Insert it into your formula by clicking on it. Excel inserts it into the formula bar. To test this, use the functions COUNT or AVERAGE.
- Complete your formula by clicking on each cell you wish to include. When you're done adding cells, click the green check mark. The results of your function's calculation are displayed in Excel.

Use of Tool Menu Commands: Goal Seek and Formula Auditing

When unsure of the initial value, Goal Seek is utilized to get a particular result. For instance, what is the second number if the result is 56 and the first number is 8? Is it 8 times 7 or 8 times 6? You can find out by using Goal Seek. We'll start with that example and move on to a more practical one.
Make the worksheet below in Excel.

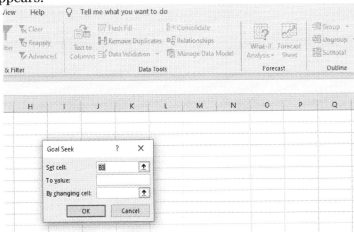

We know that we want to multiply the number in B1 by the number in B2 in the spreadsheet above. We're not sure about the number in cell B2. Cell B3 will hold the solution. Our current answer is incorrect because we have a Goal of 56. Try the following to find the solution using Goal Seek:
Click Data in the Excel menu to access the Data Tools panel and the What-if Analysis item.
Select Goal Seek from the What-If Analysis option.
The following dialog box appears:

The first thing Excel looks for is "Set cell." This isn't a very good name. It implies, "Which cell contains the Formula that you want Excel to use?" This corresponds to cell B3 for us. B3 has the following formula:
= B1 * B2
So, if it isn't already there, type B3 into the "Set cell" box.
The "To value" option says, "What result are you seeking?" This is 56 for us. Simply enter 56 into the "To value" box.
The section you're not sure about is "By Changing Cell." This section of Excel will be altered. It was cell B2 for us. We couldn't determine which number when multiplied by 8, which yielded the answer 56. So, enter B2 in the box. Your Goal Seek dialogue box should look something like this:

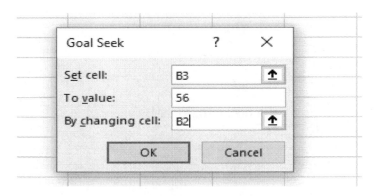

If you click OK, Excel will notify you whether it has found a solution:

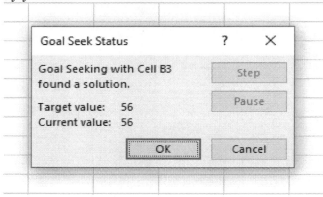

Because Excel has discovered the solution, click OK once again. Your new spreadsheet will look something like this:

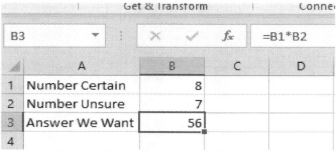

Spreadsheet displaying the result of a Goal Seek

As you can see, Excel has altered cell B2 and replaced the 6 with a 7 - the correct answer.

Formula Auditing

Excel provides useful formula auditing tools for tracing the link between the formulas in your worksheet's cells and locating the cell causing your problems.

Tracing the relationships allows you to test formulae to identify which cells, known as direct precedents in spreadsheet language, directly feed the formulas and which cells, known as dependents, rely on the formula results. Excel even allows you to graphically track the various sources of an incorrect value in a cell's formulas. The formula-auditing tools can be found in the Formula Auditing group on the Formulas tab of the Ribbon via the command buttons. Among these command buttons are the following:

- **Trace Precedents**

When you click the Trace Precedents button, Excel draws arrows to the cells (the so-called direct precedents) that are referenced in the formula inside the selected cell; when you click this option again, Excel inserts 'tracer' arrows that show the cells (the so-called indirect precedents) that are referred to in the direct precedents' formulas.

- **Trace Dependents**

If you click this button, Excel generates arrows from the selected cell to the cells (referred to as direct dependents) that use or rely on the formula results in the selected cell. When you click this option again, Excel adds tracer arrows to the cells that refer to formulae in the direct dependents (the so-called indirect dependents).

- **Remove Arrows**

Selecting this button (or the Remove Arrows option in its drop-down menu) removes all arrows drawn, regardless of whatever button or command you used to draw them. Remove Precedent Arrows from the drop-down menu to remove the arrows drawn when you selected Trace Precedents, and Remove Dependent Arrows to remove the arrows drawn when you clicked Trace Dependents.

- **Show Formulas**

Displays all formulas in their worksheet cells rather than their computed values (similar to pressing Ctrl+).

- **Error Checking**

When you choose this button or the Issue Checking option from its drop-down menu, Excel shows the Error Checking dialog box, which details the nature of the error in the current cell, provides assistance, and allows you to trace its antecedents. Click the Trace Error option in the drop-down menu of this button to find the cell containing the original formula that has an error. Click the Circular References option in this button's drop-down menu to display a menu with a list of all the cell addresses in the active worksheet that include circular references.

- **Evaluate Formula**

When you click this button, Excel displays the Evaluate Formula dialog box, where you may have Excel evaluate each portion of the formula in the current cell. The Evaluate Formula functionality may be handy in formulae containing several functions.

- **Watch Window**

When you click this button, the Watch Window pane appears, displaying the workbook, sheet, cell location, range name, current value, and formula in any cells you add to the watch list. To add a cell to the watch list, select it in the worksheet, click the Add Watch button in the Watch Window pane, and finally click Add in the Add Watch dialog box that opens.

Defining, Modifying, and Using Named Ranges

To add up a column of integers, instead of =SUM(A2:A5), you may replace the A2:A5 component of the function with a more descriptive term. This is referred to as a Named range. Take a look at the spreadsheet below:

Cell B5 in the Results Row is the sum of cells B2 and B4. The formula used is =SUM (B2:B4)

Examine the same spreadsheet, but this time using a Named Range:

This time, cell B5 lacks the formula =SUM (B2:B4). It has =SUM(Monthly Totals), as you can see. This time, cell B5 lacks the formula = Sum (B2:B4). It has =SUM(Monthly Totals), as you can see. This is the B1 label. We've made a Named Range. Cell B5's formula is now more detailed. We can know what we're adding up at a look. Excel has replaced the B2:B4 section with the name we assigned to it. But, behind the scenes, we continue accumulating numbers in cells B2 through B4. Excel has just concealed cell references under our name.

You will now learn how to make your own Named Ranges.

- **Creating a Named Range**

Begin a new spreadsheet with the same data as seen in the image below:

Check that the formula in cell B5 =Sum is the same (B2:B4). Next, we'll make a Named Range and then paste it into cell B5. Then, to create a Named Range, perform the following steps:

From B2 through B4, highlight the B column (Do not include the formula when highlighting).

Right-click and select Define Name from the drop-down menu. As shown below, a submenu appears:

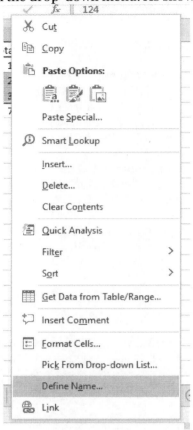

Setting up a Named Range is a two-step process. The first step is to choose a name. Your formula is then given the name.

So, from the submenu, choose Define name.

The Define Name dialog box appears. This is the one:

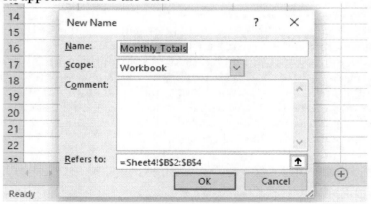

When you highlight the B column, Excel will utilize your label at the top as the name (Monthly Totals for us). However, you have the option to alter it if you choose to.

Take note of the small text box at the bottom that says "Refers to." This displays the highlighted cells.

Click OK on the dialogue box.

You are taken back to your spreadsheet. Nothing is going to happen. This is because we haven't completed step two of the two-step procedure to apply the name.

To add your new name to a formula, follow these steps:

Click within the cell containing your formula, B5, in our example.

From the menu bar, select Insert.

Choose Name from the drop-down option.

Click Apply from the submenu that displays.

A dialogue window will open, displaying a list of all the Names you have configured

You'll just have one Name set up, so there's not much else to do than hit the OK button.

When you click OK, Excel should make the necessary changes to your formula in cell B5. If you've done everything correctly, your spreadsheet should look like this:

| B5 | ▼ | ⋮ | × | ✓ | f_x | =SUM(Monthly_Totals) |

	A	B	C	D	E
1		Monthly Totals	Monthly Tax		
2		124	12		
3		234	23		
4		344	34		
5	Results	702	69		
6					
7					

As you can see, cell B5 now contains the formula =SUM(Monthly Totals).

Ensure you highlight the cells in your formula before clicking Insert > Name > Define. Make certain that there is a formula in cell B5 that states = SUM (B2:B4).

We may add another Named Range for our Monthly Tax column and column C. Here's a breakdown of the Two-Step method for creating a Named Range.

- Step 1 - Define the cell range
  Enter your Formula here. (Enter = SUM(C2:C4) in cell C5.)
  Highlight the cells that will be used in your formula.
  Click Insert > Name > Define from the navigation bar. Accept the name given to you by Excel in the Specify Name dialogue box, or write your name for the range of cells you're about to define. Click the OK button.

- Step 2 - Use the Name
  Click within the cell containing the formula (cell C5 for us)
  Click Insert > Name > Apply from the navigation bar.
  Select the Name you want to use in the Apply Name dialogue box
  Click the OK button.
  If possible, Excel will insert the name and conceal your cell references behind the name.
  Insert a Named Range for cell C5 now.
  Cell C5 no longer has the formula = Sum (C2:C4). Instead, in cell C5, we have a Named Range.

CHAPTER 5:
Formatting Data and Contents

Creating and Modifying Customized Data Formats

Small formatting changes may make or break a Microsoft Excel file. With a splash of color and a font change, your worksheet transforms from a sea of rows and columns into an ordered, attractive data table. Microsoft Excel has many options that allow users to customize how their data is displayed. And there's a solid reason for it: formatting cells can help attract attention to essential data or show it more correctly.

Following data preparation, or all of the data cleansing, enrichment, organizing, and standardizing that is necessary to prepare data for analysis, Excel formatting is an optional step.

In Excel, a style is a collection of formatting options named and kept as part of your current spreadsheet file. The new style may then be instantly applied to data and cells in the spreadsheet.

Custom Formatting Style in Excel

- Choose a single spreadsheet cell.
- Apply all necessary formatting choices to this cell.
- On the ribbon, click the Home tab.
- Click the Cell Styles option on the ribbon to enter the Cell Styles gallery.
- To access the Style dialog box, click on the New cell styles option at the bottom of the gallery.
- In the Style name box, give a new style a name.
- The formatting choices already applied to the chosen cell will be presented in the dialog box.

Add New Formatting Options or Change Existing Ones

- To launch the Format Cells dialog box, click the Format button in the Style dialog box.
- In the dialog box, select the relevant tab.
- Make the necessary adjustments.
- To exit the Format Cells dialog box, click OK.
- To exit the Style dialog box, click OK.
- The new look has been added to the gallery's top.

Apply the New Style to Cells in Your Spreadsheet

- Choose the desired cells.
- On the ribbon, select the Home tab.
- Click the Cell Styles option on the ribbon to enter the Cell Styles gallery.
- At the top of the gallery, click on the new style name.
- The formatting of the style is instantly applied to the selected cells.

Using Conditional Formatting

Conditional formatting can assist you in visually exploring and analyzing data, detecting key issues, and identifying patterns and trends.

Conditional formatting allows you to highlight noteworthy cells or ranges of cells easily, highlight uncommon values, and show data by utilizing data bars, color scales, and icon sets that correlate to specific variations in data. A conditional format alters the look of cells based on the circumstances you define. If the criteria are true, the cell range is formatted; otherwise, the cell range is not formed. There are numerous pre-existing ailments, and you may add your own (including by using a formula that evaluates to True or False).

Highlight Cells Rules

Execute the following steps to highlight cells that are greater than a value.

1. Choose the range A1:A10.

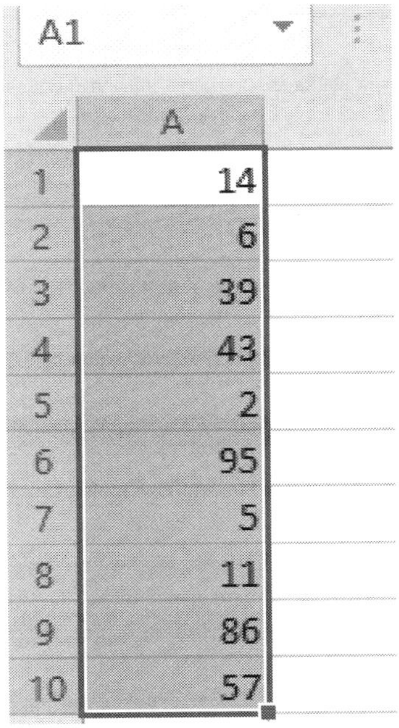

2. Select Conditional Formatting from the Styles category on the Home tab

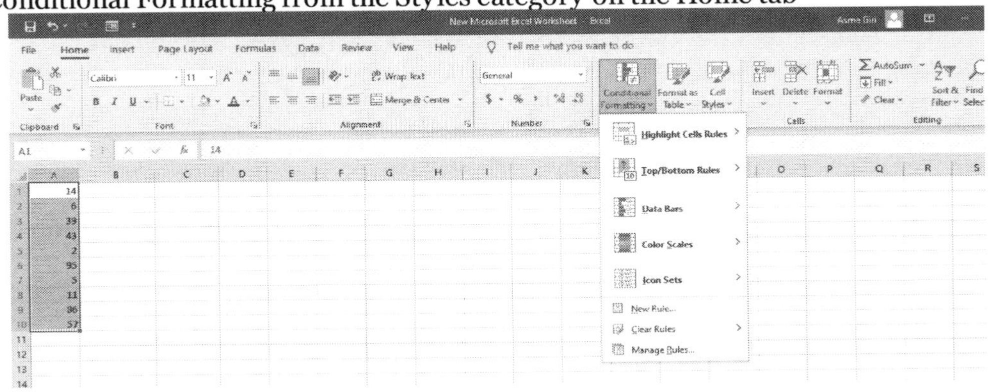

43

3. Select Highlight Cells Rules, Greater Than, from the drop-down menu.

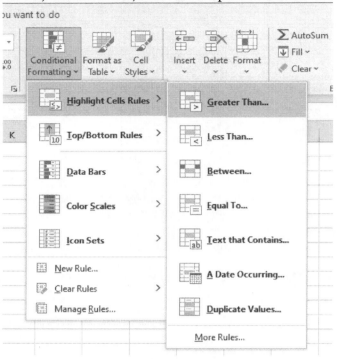

4. Enter the number 80 and choose a formatting style.

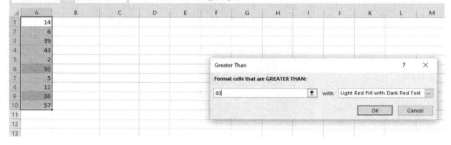

5. Press the OK button.
Excel emphasizes cells with a value greater than 80.

	A
1	14
2	6
3	39
4	43
5	2
6	95
7	5
8	11
9	86
10	57
11	

6. Change cell A1's value to 81.
As a result, Excel automatically adjusts the format of cell A1.

	A
1	81
2	6
3	39
4	43
5	2
6	95
7	5
8	11
9	86
10	57
11	

Clear Rules

Execute the following procedures to clear a conditional formatting rule.
- Choose the range A1:A10.
- Select Conditional Formatting from the Styles category on the Home tab.
- Pick the Clear Rules from Selected Cells from the menu.

Top/Bottom Principles

Execute the following procedures to highlight cells that are above average.
- Choose the range A1:A10.
- Select Conditional Formatting from the Styles category on the Home tab.
- Select Top/Bottom Rules, Above Average from the drop-down menu.
- Decide on a formatting style.
- Click OK.

Conditional Formatting with Formulas

- Use a formula to select which cells to format to take your Excel abilities to the next level. Conditional formatting formulas must evaluate to TRUE or FALSE.
- Choose the range A1:E5.
- Select Conditional Formatting from the Styles category on the Home tab.
- Select New Rule.
- Check the box next to 'Use a formula to select which cells to format.'
- Type in the formula =ISODD (A1)
- Click OK after selecting a formatting style.
- Choose the A2:D7 range.
- Repeat steps 2 to 4 above.
- Type =$C2="USA" into the formula box.
- Choose a formatting style and then click OK.

CHAPTER 6:
Sharing and Security

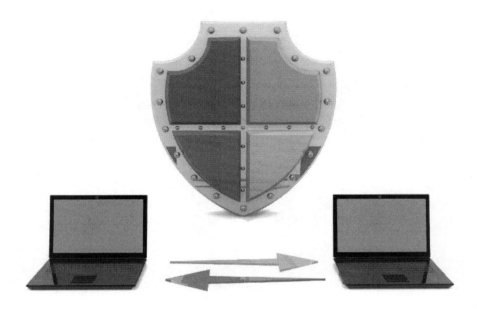

Protecting Cells, Worksheets, and Workbooks

When you distribute a worksheet to other people, to prevent data from being altered, you may want to safeguard data in certain worksheet elements. You may also require users to provide passwords to change certain protected worksheets and workbook elements. You may also restrict users from altering the structure of the worksheet.

Protecting Worksheet Elements

When you secure a worksheet, all of the cells on the worksheet are locked by default, and users cannot make changes to a protected cell. For example, they cannot edit, alter, remove, or format data in a locked cell. When you secure the worksheet, you can specify which components users will be able to modify.

Locking, hiding, and protecting workbook and worksheet components is not designed to assist in safeguarding any private information you store in the workbook. It only helps to conceal data that could confuse other users and prohibits them from accessing or changing such data.

Excel does not encrypt data that is hidden or locked in a spreadsheet. To help keep sensitive data confidential, you may want to limit access to workbooks containing such information by storing them in a place accessible only to authorized users.

Before safeguarding the worksheet, you may unlock the ranges in which users want to edit or enter data. You can unlock cells for all users or select users.

When you lock a worksheet or workbook elements to secure it, providing a password to modify the unlocked elements is optional. The password, in this case, is solely meant to provide access to certain users while aiding in preventing modifications by other users. This degree of password protection may not ensure the security of all sensitive data in your worksheet. To help protect a workbook from unwanted access, you should secure it using a password.

When you use a password to secure worksheet or workbook items, you must remember the password. You cannot unprotect the workbook or worksheet without it.

You may lock a workbook's structure, which prohibits users from adding or removing worksheets or revealing hidden worksheets. You may also stop users from changing the size or position of the worksheet windows. The structure of the workbook and window protection applies to the whole workbook.

Simply enter the following to secure the entire worksheet:

- Click Protect Sheet on the Review tab, under the Changes group.
- Select the elements you want users to be allowed to alter in the Allow all users of this worksheet to list.
- Type a password for the sheet in the Password to unprotect sheet box, click OK, and then retype the password to confirm it.

Only specific elements of a worksheet can be protected in the following ways:

- Choose the worksheet that you wish to safeguard.
- Choose each cell or range you wish to open to allow other users to alter any cells or ranges you have unlocked. Next, click Format, then Format Cells, on the Home tab, in the Cells group. Clear the Locked check box on the Protection tab, then click OK.
- To allow users to alter any graphic elements (such as images, clip art, shapes, or Smart Art graphics), perform the following: Hold CTRL and click on each visual item you wish to unlock. This brings up the Picture Tools or Drawing Tools and the Format tab. Next, click the Dialog Box Launcher (small box with an arrow pointing diagonally left) next to Size on the Format tab. Next, check the Locked check box on the Properties tab and, if present, the Lock text check box.
- Select the Review tab now, and in the Changes group, click Protect Sheet to lock the rest of the spreadsheet.
- Then, in the Allow all users of this worksheet to list, check the boxes next to the items that you want users to be able to modify. Next, type a password for the sheet in the Password to unprotect sheet box, click OK, and then retype the password to confirm it.
- It should be noted that the password is optional. If you do not provide a password, any user will be able to unprotect the document and modify the protected parts. Therefore, make sure you select a password that is simple to remember since if you forget it, you will be unable to access the worksheet's protected parts.

Excel does not encrypt data in a worksheet that is hidden or protected. To assist in keeping sensitive data confidential, you may limit access to workbooks containing such information by storing them in a place accessible only to authorized users.

Always remember to keep your info secure!

Enable Workbook Sharing

Using OneDrive, Excel makes it simple to share and collaborate on workbooks. Previously, you could send a file as an email attachment to someone if you wished to share it with them. While this approach is convenient, it also generates several copies of the same file, which can be challenging to organize.

When you share an Excel worksheet, you essentially provide people access to the same file. This allows you and the individuals you share the workbook to modify the same document without keeping track of several versions.

A worksheet must be saved to your OneDrive before it can be shared.

To share a worksheet, open the Backstage view by clicking the File tab, then click Share.

Return to Normal view by clicking Share Excel, which opens the Share panel on the right side of the window. You may invite others to share your document from here, see a list of who has access to it, and specify whether they can edit or simply read it.

Merging Workbooks

When other users update a shared workbook and want to compare the changes they made before updating the workbook, you may use the Compare and Merge Workbooks command. However, it is not available with other shared workbook commands on the Review tab of the Changes group, but it may be added to the Quick Access Toolbar.

A shared workbook may only be merged with copies of that worksheet created from the same shared workbook. Therefore, the Compare and Merge Workbooks command cannot be used to merge workbooks that are not shared.

To utilize the Compare and Merge Workbooks function, all shared workbook users must save a copy of the shared workbook, including their modifications, with a file name that differs from the original workbook. All copies of a shared worksheet should be kept in the same folder as the original.

Follow the steps below to Compare and Merge Workbooks command:
- Select the picture of the Microsoft Office Button, and then click Excel Options.
- Click All Commands in the Customize category.
- Choose commands from the list.
- Click Compare and Merge Workbooks in the list, then Add and OK.
- Open the shared worksheet copy into which you wish to combine the modifications.
- Select Compare and Merge Workbooks from the Quick Access Toolbar.
- Quick Access Toolbar includes a button to Compare and Merge Workbooks
- Save the worksheet if asked.
- Click a copy of the workbook that includes the changes you wish to combine in the Select Files to Merge into the Current Workbook dialog box, and then click OK.

Tracking, Accepting, and Rejecting Changes to Workbooks

When editing Excel files in collaboration with others, it's critical to keep track of the changes and accept or reject modifications. Excel has a "Track Changes" feature, often known as the "tracking mode," for this purpose. This feature allows you to graphically highlight changes, log them tabularly, and undo them later if required. The approval of workbooks is inextricably connected to the tracking of modifications in Excel. Both functionalities are frequently utilized in tandem. The feature to approve workbooks is no longer available in later Office versions that are cloud-optimized since they are intended from the start for collaborative working.
In Excel, you have two choices for tracking changes. We'll take a look at both of them here.

Keeping Track of Changes

Open the "Review" menu item from the main menu bar. Next, choose "Track Changes" from the dropdown menu, followed by "Highlight Changes...".
Excel: Tracking menu choices in Excel
You may configure your tracking settings in the dialog box.
Selecting "Track changes while editing" is a simple option. This also distributes your workbook." as well as "Highlight changes on screen." The modifications are now logged in Excel and marked by a remark next to the cell. The workbook is published automatically. All other options stay unaltered with this default configuration.

Accepting or Declining Changes

The "Accept/Reject Changes" button may accept or reject monitored modifications in an Excel sheet. This option is accessible via the "Track Changes" menu item, which is situated in the "Changes" section of the "Review" tab. Initially, a notice telling you that you must save the worksheet will display; acknowledge the message by clicking "OK." You may specify which modifications to examine in the following dialog box. Similar to the options in Excel for recording changes, you may filter by time, user, and range here. All modifications that have not yet been checked are checked by default.
In Excel, pick the "Accept/Reject Changes" menu option.
You will be guided through the individual modifications via a dialog window. You can accept or reject modifications individually or all at once. If you reject a modification, the associated cell is restored to its previous state. You can inspect each modification and approve or reject it if a cell has been updated many times.
You can evaluate changes individually or all at once in the "Accept or Reject Changes" dialog box.
Even whether you approved or refused the modification, the modified cells are marked after review. When you disable track changes in Excel, the highlighter disappears.

Turning Off Track Changes

- Take these steps if you no longer want Excel to track changes:
- From the main menu, select the "Review" tab.
- From the "Changes" section, select "Track Changes."
- Select "Highlight Changes."
- Deactivate the "Track changes while editing..." checkbox.

- When you deactivate track changes, the changes history is erased. You can, however, store the history separately ahead of time. To do this, follow the steps in "Log changes in a new worksheet" and duplicate the "Change History" worksheet to another Excel workbook.
- Joint editing of the worksheet is no longer available after disabling track changes. A warning message will appear. When another user saves their worksheet version after disabling track changes, previously saved versions are overwritten.

CHAPTER 7:
Managing Data and Workbooks

Importing/Exporting Data to/from Excel

Aside from the standard .xlsx format, Excel can import and export various other file formats. If your data is shared between programs, such as a database, you may need to store data in a new file format or import files in a different file type.

Export Data

When you need to transfer data from one system to another, export it from Excel in a format that other applications can understand, such as a text or CSV file.
- Navigate to the File tab.
- Click Export on the left.
- Click the Change File Type button.
- Choose a file type from Other File Types.
  - Text (Tab delimited): A tab will be used to separate the cell data.
  - CSV (Comma delimited): A comma will be used to separate the cell data.
  - Formatted Text (space-delimited): A space will be used to separate the cell data.
  - Save as a Different File Type: When the Save As dialog box displays, choose a new file type.
The kind of file you choose will be determined by the application that will consume the exported data.
- Save As is the default option.
- Choose where you wish to save the file.
- Save your work by clicking the Save button.
A dialog box informs you that some of the workbook's capabilities could be lost.

Import Data

Excel can import data from a variety of external data sources, such as other files, databases, or websites.
- On the Ribbon, select the Data tab.
- Select the Get Data option.

Some data sources may need specific security access, and the connecting method is frequently complicated. Enlist the aid of your organization's technical support personnel.
- Choose From File.
- Choose from Text/CSV.
- Select one of the Get External Data category choices if you have data to import from Access, the web, or another source.
- Choose the file you wish to import.
- Select Import.
- If a security warning displays while importing external data, stating that connecting to an external source may not be safe, click OK.
- Check that the preview is correct.

Because we asked that commas split the data, the delimiter is already established. You may do so if you want to alter it from this menu.
- Choose 'Load.'

Creating And Editing Templates

Microsoft Excel templates are a valuable component of the Excel experience and a fantastic way to save time. Once you've built a template, it will only make small changes to meet your present needs and can thus be applied to new circumstances and utilized repeatedly. Excel templates may also assist you in creating consistent and appealing papers that will amaze your coworkers or superiors and make you appear your best.

Excel calendars, budget planners, invoices, inventory, and dashboards are a few examples of commonly used document types that benefit from templates. What could be better than getting a ready-to-use spreadsheet that already has the appearance and feels you desire and can be quickly customized to meet your specific needs?

A Microsoft Excel template is precisely that - a template. A pre-designed workbook or worksheet in which the majority of the work has already been done for you, sparing you from having to reinvent the wheel

Making a Workbook from an Existing Excel Template

Rather than beginning from scratch, you may rapidly build a new workbook based on an Excel template. The correct template may truly ease your life since it uses complex formulae, advanced styles, and other Microsoft Excel capabilities that you may not even be aware of.

There are many free Excel templates accessible and ready to be used. Follow the instructions below to create a new workbook based on an existing Excel template.

In Excel 2013, go to the File tab and select New to view a variety of templates offered by Microsoft.

In Excel 2010, you have two options:

Choose from the Sample templates, which are simple Excel templates already on your computer.

Look in the com Templates area, click on a category to see the template thumbnails, and then download the desired template.

Simply click on a template to see a preview of it. A preview of the chosen template will be displayed, along with the publisher's name and other information on how to utilize the template.

If you like the template preview, click the Create button to download it.

That's all - the selected template is downloaded, and a new workbook is immediately generated based on it.

Where Can I Get Additional Templates?

Enter a matching term in the search field to obtain a larger variety of Excel templates:

If you're looking for anything specific, you may sort the Microsoft Excel templates accessible by category.

Searching for a template in Microsoft Excel displays all relevant templates from the Office Store. Some templates are developed by third-party providers or individual users, while Microsoft Corporation creates others. This is why you may get the message below, asking if you trust the template's publisher. If this is the case, click the Trust this app option.

How to Make a Custom Excel Template?

It is simple to create your own Excel templates. You begin by creating a workbook traditionally, and the most challenging aspect is getting it to appear precisely the way you want. It is worthwhile to put some time and effort into both the design and the content because all formatting, styles, text, and pictures used in the workbook will appear in all future workbooks based on this template.

You may store the following parameters in an Excel template:
- The quantity and kind of sheets
- Formats and styles for cells
- Page layout and print areas for each sheet
- Hidden regions make specific sheets, rows, columns, or cells invisible.
- Areas that have been shielded to avoid alterations in certain cells
- Text that you wish to show in all workbooks based on a specific template, such as column labels or page headers.
- Formulas, hyperlinks, charts, pictures, and other graphics are all examples of graphics.
- Options for Excel data validation include drop-down menus, validation messages or warnings, and so on.
- Calculation and window view settings, such as freezing the header row
- Custom forms using macros and ActiveX controls

After you've generated the worksheet, save it as a .xlt or .xltx file (depending on whatever Excel version you're using) rather than the usual .xls or .xlsx. Here are the detailed steps if you need them:
- Click File > Save As in Excel 2010 and 2013. Click the Office button in Excel 2007, then Save as.
- In the Save As dialog, in the File name box, provide a name for the template.
- If you're using Excel 2013, 2010, or 2007, choose Excel Template (*.xltx) as the Save as type.
- Select Excel 97-2003 Template (*.xlt) in older Excel versions.
- Choose Excel Macro-Enabled Template (*.xltm) if your workbook contains a macro.
- When you choose one of the template types listed above, the file extension in the File Name field changes to the relevant extension.
- Please keep in mind that when you save your workbook as an Excel Template (*.xltx), Microsoft Excel switches the destination location to the default templates folder, which is generally C:\Users\<User Name>\AppData\Roaming\Microsoft\Templates
- If you wish to store the template somewhere else, modify the destination after selecting Excel Template (*.xltx) as the document type. Regardless of the destination folder you select, a duplicate of your template will be saved to the default templates folder.
- To save your newly generated Excel template, click the Save option.
- You may now create new workbooks and share them with other users using this template. Excel templates, like regular Excel files, can be shared in various ways, such as storing them in a shared folder or on your local network, saving them to OneDrive (Excel Online), or emailing them as attachments.

Create a Template for Excel

If you have a favorite Microsoft Excel template, you may set it as the default template and have it open immediately when Excel starts.

Microsoft Excel allows you to create two unique templates – Book .xltx and Sheet .xltx - the foundation for all new workbooks and worksheets. So, the main point is to choose the sort of template you want:

Workbook template in Excel. This sort of template consists of many sheets. Create a workbook with the desired sheets, insert placeholders and default text (e.g., page headers, column and row names, and so on), add formulae or macros, and apply styles and other formatting that you want to see in all future workbooks produced using the template.

Worksheet template in Excel This template type requires only one sheet. So, remove two of the workbook's default three pages and edit the remaining sheet to your taste. Apply the necessary styles and formatting, then add the information you wish to show on all new worksheets created using this template.

Once you've chosen your default template type, continue with the instructions below.
- Click File > Save As in the worksheet you wish to use as your default Excel template.
- Select Excel Template (*.xltx) from the Save as type box drop-down list.
- Select the target folder for the default template in the Save in box. This should always be the XLStart folder; nothing else will suffice.
- In Vista, Windows 7, and Windows 8, the XLStart folder is often seen C:\Users\<User name>\AppData\Local\Microsoft\Excel\XLStart

- In Windows XP, it is usually located in:
  C:\Documents and Settings\<User name>\Application Data\Microsoft\Excel\XLStart
- Finally, give your Excel default template the appropriate name:
- When creating a workbook template, type Book in the File name. • When generating a worksheet template, type Sheet in the File name.
- The screenshot below shows the development of the default workbook template:
- Creating the Excel default workbook template • • Click the Save button to complete the procedure and dismiss the window.

You may now restart Excel and check if it produces a new workbook based on the default template you've just set.

Where to Download Excel Templates

Office.com, as you are undoubtedly aware, is the greatest site to seek Excel templates. Here you can discover many free Excel templates organized into several categories, such as calendar, budget, invoice, timeline, inventory, project management, and more.

These are the same templates you see in Excel when you go to File > New. However, searching on the web may be more effective, especially if you seek anything specific. It's a little weird that you can only filter the templates by application or category, not both, but you should have no trouble locating the template you want:

Simply click on an Excel template to download it. This will summarize the template and the Open in Excel Online option. As you might imagine, selecting this button generates a workbook in Excel Online based on the specified template.

Click File > Save As > Download a Copy to save the template to your desktop Excel. This will launch the classic Windows Save As dialog box, where you can choose a destination folder and click the Save button.

Aside from Office.com, several more websites provide free Excel templates. Naturally, the quality of third-party templates varies, and some may perform better than others.

CHAPTER 8:
Tips and Tricks for Improving Your MS Excel Skills In 2022

Microsoft Excel skills have quickly become one of the most valuable assets in our life. Microsoft introduced it in 1985 and it was first used primarily for commercial purposes. However, as time has passed, it has become so common that we utilize MS Excel in nearly every area of our lives, whether for educational, government, professional, or even personal reasons.

Many computer applications have been developed since Excel. But, it hasn't lost its allure; its popularity is growing by the day! So, as you can see, having Excel abilities is critical for advancing in any professional sector. Here are some Excel tips and tricks. These techniques can help users increase productivity while making this application simpler and smoother.

- **Work from Left to Right At All Times**

Implementing Microsoft Excel tips and techniques is simply because data naturally flows from left to right. By default, Excel will compute data at the upper left corner, go to the right, and continue to the bottom. As a result, independent values must be kept in the left corner of the spreadsheet, while dependent values must be stored on the right side.

While this may not significantly impact tiny spreadsheets with minimal data, working in this manner will be beneficial when there is a large amount of data and computations involved.

- **Try to Keep All of Your Data in a Single Worksheet**

Excel takes significantly longer to calculate the relevant data values when data is dispersed across several spreadsheets.

Arranging data once distributed across several sheets may be time-consuming; keep this in mind when adding new data and variables.

- **Delete Unnecessary Data on the Workbook**

It is critical to delete any data that you are no longer using. In this manner, you can avoid unnecessary misunderstandings later on and reduce the document's usage range.

By pressing control and end, users may quickly determine the utilized range of the Excel documents. Following that, this user can store the worksheet for future use.

- **Tips On Excel Shortcut Keys are a Lifesaver**

Shortcut keys are a godsend for individuals who use the software daily since they allow users to do activities more quickly, increasing productivity.

Autofill (where data is automatically put into columns and rows), choosing a whole row quickly (press shift and spacebar), and calculating the sum of an entire column by using alt and = are just a few of the shortcut keys that users may utilize to make their job easier.

- **Filters can be Helpful for Individuals who Deal with a Large Amount of Data**

If you use a spreadsheet with many data sets, you may learn to filter them so that you only see the information you need. Filters are helpful in this situation because they allow users to filter data based on specific criteria.

Users may add a filter by selecting the data tab and the filter option. For example, if you have a worksheet of all Harry Potter students, you may apply a Gryffindor filter to view just students from that house.

- **Customized Lists Might Help You Save a Lot of Time**

Many individuals deal with redundant data, meaning we enter it repeatedly.

This is why it can be a good idea to develop a bespoke list based on your unique needs.

The user may build a custom list by selecting choices from the Tools menu and then the Custom Lists tab.

Enter every item in the list in the list entries control, one entry on each line, precisely in the order you desire.

After creating the list, click Add, and it'll be copied to the custom lists control.

After that, click OK to exit the choices dialog. After that, anytime you add a name from the list to the cell, the list will be immediately added to your data.

- **For Constants and Ranges, Use Specified Names**

If you have a lot of data in percentages or other similar variables, user-defined names make your work easier and faster. For example, simply choose a cell and select a name from the Insert option.

After that, click define, give it a descriptive name, say discount, and then click okay. This is a specified term; you can use the name discount instead of excel to get your result.

This function has two advantages: on the one hand, it makes updating straightforward and avoids data entering mistakes. Excel hints and techniques

- **Insert Several Rows or Columns at the Same Time**

While many people are familiar with adding columns and rows to a spreadsheet, you can simply add numerous columns and rows to a spreadsheet. Excel hints and techniques

This might speed up your job because manually adding columns and rows can be tiresome and time-consuming. So, if you want to add four new rows to an existing table, choose four rows from below or above and then right-click to insert the rows.

This will create a dialog box where users may specify the precise action to be performed on the rows and columns.

- **Use Autocorrect to Correct Spelling Errors in Your Spreadsheet**

Small and insignificant spelling errors can significantly impact your overall presentation. That is why Excel includes an auto-correct option that can assist you in avoiding such a situation. Users may utilize auto-correct by going to file settings, proofing, and autocorrect options.

Users will see a dialog box that allows them to change text with the right spellings. When this term is misspelled again, Excel will not only rectify your present errors but will also automatically correct them.

- **Data can be Extracted from a Web Page and Entered into an Excel Spreadsheet**

Users may quickly take data from a website and evaluate it in a spreadsheet. This is a simple method that saves a lot of time that would otherwise be spent entering content/data from a website into an excel spreadsheet

Knowing this can go a long way toward assisting users in better managing their time and efforts.

- **Sparkline Micro Charts in Excel can Aid in Comparisons**

Sparkling micro charts are tiny graphs that may be placed next to data in a cell. They are a wonderful tool for increasing numbers' visibility by displaying the data's value in a graph.

To use this function, users must first choose the data from which they want to make sparkling and then go to line from inset. After you've chosen the target location for your dazzling chart, the graph will be put in the appropriate column immediately.

- **Hide Everything but the Working Area to Avoid Distractions While Working**

It is possible to conceal columns or rows, either to safeguard data and excel or to work solely on the columns/rows that are necessary.

Users can conceal unneeded rows by selecting the row under the final row and pressing the control, shift, and down arrow to choose the rows that need to be hidden.

This will prevent essential data from being destroyed while allowing you to work in a distraction-free environment.

- **If You Must Print Your Worksheet, Provide the File Name in the Header/Footer Region**

An employee's schedule includes the printing of an Excel spreadsheet regularly. It is a good idea to enter the project name in either the header or footer region so that the file may be easily identified.

You can input the worksheet's name by selecting the Header/Footer tab in the File menu in Excel 2007.

- **You may Simply Limit the Numeric Data Value in the Spreadsheet, Simplifying Your Job**

Users may demand just a certain set of values in the spreadsheet sometimes, especially when it may cause difficulties with the final result. Data validation in Excel allows you to restrict the data.

The range of numeric data that may be used in the system is limited by data validation. For example, if you enter data validation between 500 and 1000, you will get all data between these values.

- **The Watch Pane Enables You to Keep Track of Data Methodically**

Excel is similar to a large spreadsheet, and the more data there is, the more likely there will be errors. Modifying one area might occasionally impact the totals and calculations in another, particularly in quantitative form.

Furthermore, if your spreadsheet is distributed throughout a broad region, certain modifications may go overlooked by you, resulting in a huge number of mistakes in the long term.

Furthermore, because it is not feasible to keep going forward in your data area, it is a good idea to activate Watch Windows, which displays the values of cells that have changed due to your current contributions.

To open a Watch Window, click the left mouse button on the cell you wish to monitor. Then, on the Ribbon toolbar, select Excel and Window watch. When the watch window dialog box displays, click Add to finish setting up the same.

- **Enhance Productivity by Customizing the Toolbar Area**

The primary goal of the toolbar area should be to allow you to work more efficiently and straightforwardly. You can put tools you regularly use in this section so that you don't have to go back to the tabs to access them.

BOOK 2:

MICROSOFT WORD 2022

The Most Updated Crash Course from Beginner to Advanced
Learn All the Functions and Features to
Become a Pro in 7 Days or Less

INTRODUCTION

Welcome to Microsoft Word 2022, an up-to-date tutorial that teaches you everything you need to know about Microsoft Word to stay current, confident, and productive. This book will teach you how to use MS Word's most helpful and remarkable features without stress. You'll learn how to create, edit, and format a document from the ground up like an expert, operate confidently and efficiently using MS Word's best shortcut commands, and quickly insert and format photos, shapes, tables, charts, and much more.

Microsoft Word, popularly called **MS-Word** or **Word,** is a word processing application developed by Microsoft Corporation. Word is part of Microsoft Office Suite and was launched in **1983**. It competed with WordPerfect (the most popular word processor then) to become the world-leading word processor in the **1990s** till date. The latest office suite is **Office 2021 and Office 365**. It can run on Windows, macOS, iOS, and Android operating systems.

Most essential Microsoft Word features have been around for a long time, and the fundamentals remain consistent across all editions. Keep reading if you have an older version of Word, Word 2021, or Word 365; this book will benefit you.

MS Word allows you to create, edit, format, save, and print a wide range of professional-looking personal and business documents, including books, graphics, bills, resumes, reports, letters, photographs, emails, invites, catalogs, notes, certifications, newsletters, and more. It features a simple user interface and is very easy to use.

Getting Started

To start using MS word, you must install it on your computer or use it online. Some computers come with Microsoft Office preinstalled, but if you do not have it, you can get it following the steps below:

Buy MS Word

1. Open your web browser, e.g., Google Chrome.
2. Go to the official website: www.office.com.
3. Click on **Get Office** if you want an office or MS Word on your desktop and buy from the available options:
    - **Office 365 Family** vs. **Office 365 Personal**: Office 365 Family can be shared with up to six individuals, while one person can only use Office 365 Personal. They serve the same purpose, and both demand ongoing subscriptions. For anyone who wants access to the most up-to-date office software and cloud services, Office 365 is the ideal alternative. It is compatible with Windows 11, 10, 8, 7, and Mac OS X.
    - **Office Home & Student 2021**: This is the latest version of office available for a one-time payment and contains only the essential apps (Word, Excel, PowerPoint, Access, Outlook, OneNote, Team, and Publisher). You can only use it on Windows 11, 10, and macOS.
4. Install Microsoft Office, and MS word is available on your desktop.

Use MS Word Freely

You can download it for free from the Microsoft website if you don't want to buy Microsoft Office. The online version of Word is brand new and does not have all of the functionality found in the desktop version. Because the website version cannot work when there is no internet connection, the offline/ desktop version is a more viable option.

To use MS word freely online:
- Visit their website, www.office.com.
- Sign in if you have an existing account or,
- Create a new one if you do not have one, and MS word will be available for your use.

Opening and Pinning MS Word

To open an MS word:

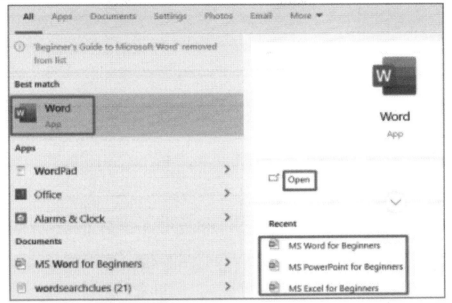

1. Type **Word** in your computer search bar.
2. Left click on the word icon or **Open** to open a new MS word file.
3. You can also click any recent lists to open an already existing file.

If you often use Word, it will be better to pin it to the start or taskbar.

To pin an MS Word to start or taskbar:

1. Right-click on the Word icon. A menu appears.
2. Select **Pin to Start** or **Pin to taskbar** as desired from the menu.

MS Word Start Screen

The start screen Home page appears when you first open MS Word, as illustrated below. A blue vertical bar on the left side of the page contains tabs for the right-side contents. The Home page has links to the shortcuts for the remaining tabs.

You have a **Blank** document on the **Home** screen that you can use to start from scratch. Also available are several learning tutorials and **templates** that can quickly get you started with MS Word. Click on more templates or the New tab at the left-hand bar if you want more templates.

Below the templates is the list of the **Recent** Word document. The **Open** tab at the left-sidebar or the **More documents** link opens more available documents at the right bottom corner of the list. Frequently open documents can be pinned and accessed in the **Pinned** beside the **Recent** list.

CHAPTER 1:
Introduction to Microsoft Word

Practically everyone uses Microsoft Word. This is due to the prevalence of word processing tasks in our daily life. A word processor may assist you in creating letters, memos, reports, and even emails, which are commonplace in everyday life. Word processors can swiftly and easily edit, alter, and rearrange text. As a result, you'll discover the fundamentals of Microsoft Word 2022 in this chapter and how to use the most crucial features and capabilities to help you compose documents quickly.

Note: Microsoft Word can be found in the Microsoft Office Suite, and there are other applications in the Microsoft Suite Office, such as Microsoft Excel, Microsoft PowerPoint, Microsoft OneNote, Microsoft Outlook, Microsoft Access, and Microsoft Publisher. However, we're only going to focus on just Microsoft Word.

The Concept of Microsoft Word 2022

Microsoft Word is a word processing program developed by Microsoft in 1983 to assist individuals in writing. It works on a computer, desktop, laptop, or mobile device. It is a component of the Microsoft Office suite, which is utilized by a variety of people, including teachers, students, professionals, business owners, and people of various ages and backgrounds. It creates professional-looking documents, such as letters, reports, and resumes. Another benefit of a word processor is that it makes it simple to make modifications such as spelling corrections, additions, deletions, formatting, and text movement. Once the document is complete, it may be swiftly and correctly printed and stored for future modifications.

Features of Microsoft Word 2022

Microsoft Word has different versions from its inception. But what makes the Microsoft word 2022 version unique include;
- **Simplified Word Processing** - Make, manage, and even edit documents without ever having to work hard. Users worldwide use Microsoft Word to make and share all their documents; this current version makes it easier to achieve this.
- **Rapid Document Editing** – Make changes to documents with unmatched ease and speed. Correct a document's spelling, test its readability, and change its grammar with tools meant to improve the document.
- It lets you save any original file in a lot of different formats, like .doc, .pdf, .txt, .rts, .dot, .wps, and many more formats can be used to make documents.
- You may easily create visually appealing and well-designed papers because of its fantastic user interface! Microsoft Word offers a user-friendly interface that allows even the most inexperienced computer users to create excellent documents.

Getting Microsoft Word 2022

It is possible to get Microsoft Word 2022 applications in various ways:
- The first option, which is common with students, is to buy a license and then download and install Word on your computer. Students often select this option because Microsoft gives a big discount to students.
- The second option is to pay for a year's worth of service (Office 365).
- Another alternative is to utilize Microsoft Word online. You can use the online version of Word for free, but you must access it through your browser. You will, however, require a Microsoft Word 365 account, and the online version will only allow you to access documents saved on your OneDrive.

Components of Microsoft Word 2022

Now, let's talk about the components or parts of MS Word. These features allow you to do many different things with your documents, like save, delete, style, modify, or look at the content of your documents.
1. **The File**: It has options like New, which is used to make a new document; Open, which is used to open an existing document; Save, which is used to save documents; Save As, which is used to rename a document and save it, Info; Options, etc.
2. **The Home Tab**: The "Home" tab in MS Word is the first tab you see when you open the software. The most common groupings are Clipboard, Font, Style, and Editing. It allows you to customize your text's color, font, emphasis, bullets, and location. Aside from that, it can cut, copy, and paste. You will have additional alternatives to work with after hitting the home tab.
3. **Insert:** This part can be used to input anything into your document. You can insert tables, words, shapes, hyperlinks, charts, signature lines, time, shapes, headers, footers, text boxes, links, boxes, equations, etc.
4. **Draw:** Freehand drawing can be done with this tool in MS Word. Different types of pens for drawing are shown on this tab
5. **Design**: Here, you can choose from documents with centered titles, off-centered headings, left-justified text, and more. You can also select from different page borders, watermarks, and colors in the design tab.
6. **Layout**: You can use it to make your Microsoft Word documents look how you want them to look. It has options to set margins, show line numbers, set paragraph indentation, apply themes, control page orientation and size, line breaks, and more.
7. **The References Tab:** This option allows you to add references to a document and then create a bibliography at the end of the text for easy reference. The references are frequently maintained in a master

list that may be used to add references to other documents. It has a table of contents, footnotes, citations, bibliography, captions, an index, a table of authorities, and a smart look.

8. **Review:** The Review Tab has commenting, language, translation, spell check, word count, and other tools for you to use. A good thing about it is that you can quickly find and change comments. These options will display when you click on the review tab.

9. **Mailing:** One of the best things about Microsoft Word is that you can write a letter, report, etc., and send it to a lot of people at the same time, with each person's name and address in the letter.

10. **View**: In the View tab, you can switch between single and double pages. You can also change how the layout tools work. You can use it to make a print layout, outline, website, task pane, toolbar, and rulers, as well as to make a full-screen view, zoom in and out, and so on.

Getting into the Microsoft Word Environment

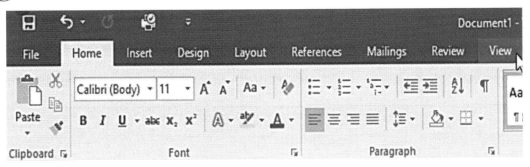

Quick Access Toolbar

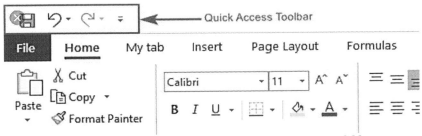

The Quick Access Toolbar has icons for the tools you use the most. You can add buttons to this bar that you use a lot, and you can make them bigger.

Ribbon

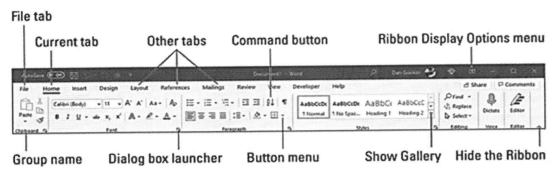

The Word Ribbon is an essential component of the Word interface. It can take the shape of an improper button, input box, or menu.

The Ribbon is separated into tabs, each with a group of commanding buttons. The ribbon can be used in a variety of ways. You can find what you need by clicking on a tab and then looking through the group names. Finally, press the button to activate the command.

Status Bar

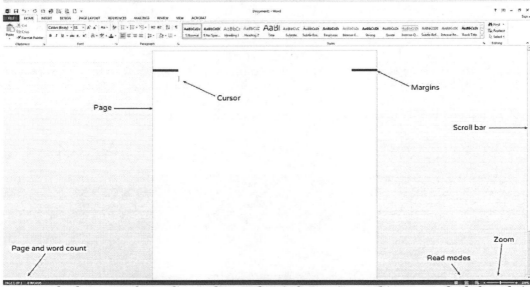

This bar shows up at the bottom of Word's window. It has information and icons on the left and right sides. The information on the left shows how many pages and words are in the text. You can work with grammar and spelling tools by clicking the grammar icon.

Across the right side of the status bar, some icons can be used to change how the document is shown to you. Most of the time, there are three views: Print view, which is used for editing and seeing how the pages would look if they were printed; read mode, which is like a magazine layout; and HTML view, which is how the text looks when it is viewed with a browser. Another tool you can use while viewing a document on the right side is a zoom slider. This lets you change the document size as you look at it.

Starting the Word Program

First, you must find and open Microsoft Word (MS) on your computer.

From the computer's home screen:
- Double-click on the MS Word icon if it's on your computer's home screen.

But if it's not on your home screen, then do the following:
- Find the Start menu.
- Then click on Programs.
- Then click on Word, 2022.

Note: Keep in mind that Microsoft Word may be in the Microsoft Office folder. If this is the case, you first need to click on Microsoft Office before clicking on "Word." Then you'll see a blank document where you may write your content and do various things.

Working on the Word Start Screen

Start screen: You can use it to open an already-opened document, start a new document from a template, or begin from scratch with a blank document. Choose to start a new document once and open it. Then, start writing.

Opening a New Document

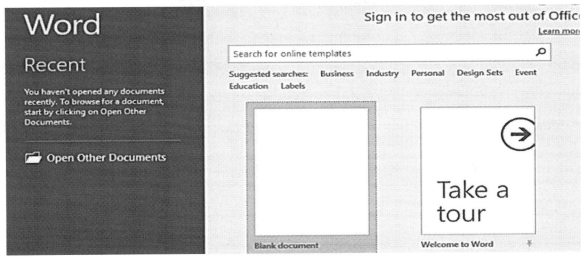

- To open a document:
- Choose **the File tab** on the ribbon and click on the **Open option**.
- Then the screen opens where you can click the blank document to start a new document
- The document is opened and shown on the screen. It's ready for anything.

Note: You can save the document, and when you save a document for the first time, you give it a name.

Changing the Size of Text

Employee Name	Customer Achieved (2018)	Sales (INR)
Vihan Aryan	200	100,000
Taijul Sharma	30	30,000
Advait Nagrwal	95	
Mohsin Pinjari	188	376,000

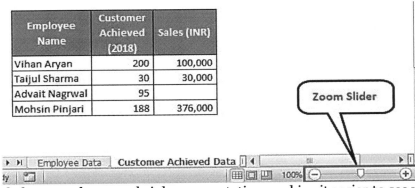

A zoom command can help you enlarge or shrink a presentation, making it easier to see what you're looking at. You don't have to change the font size to make the information in Word bigger. To zoom in or out, go to the Zoom command as shown.

Quitting Word

When you're finished with a word processor and don't expect to use it again soon, it's best to close it. Select the "X" icon in the upper right corner of the screen to do so.
Remember that you must shut all open word document windows before declaring that you are finished with the document. It's also a good practice to save your work before closing the word processor.

Setting the Word Aside

You can minimize your word document to work on other things on your computer. The minimize button is on the upper right corner of the screen.

In the image shown, the first is the minimize icon, and the second is the maximize icon.

To shrink the word window to a button on the taskbar, click the **Minimize** button, and it will be possible for you to do other things with your computer. You can click the maximize button to bring the word document back to the screen. How the Minimize and maximize icon looks is shown in the figure.

CHAPTER 2:
Typing Documents

If no other gadgets work with the computer, it will be useless. These various gadgets can interface with the computer and do multiple tasks. This chapter will cover the two primary typing input devices and everything about typing in Microsoft Word.

Input Devices Set Up

You can enter information into a computer with a device called an input device. The two most important input device is the Keyboard and the Mouse. These two input devices are very important for communicating with your computer.

1. The PC Keyboard

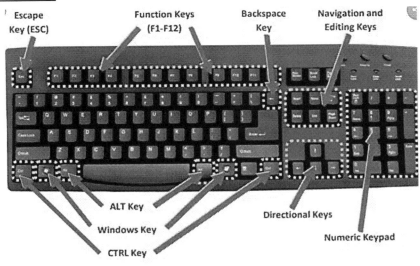

A computer keyboard is a piece of hardware that lets you type in data (text, numbers, punctuations, etc.) and commands to a computer. In most cases, your keyboard is the best way to get information into your computer. You can type a letter, number, symbols, punctuation marks, etc., by pressing the keys on your keyboard.

The keys on your keyboard can be broken down into different groups based on how they work:

- **Using (alphanumeric) keys to type:** These keys have the same letter, number, punctuation, and symbol keys that you find on a typewriter.
- **The function keys:** The function keys are used to do certain things. They're called F1, F2, F3, and so on, until F12. These keys can do different things in different programs.
- **The navigation keys**: These keys move around and alter the text in documents and web pages. There is an arrow next to each of these buttons. The Home and End keys are also present.
- **The numeric keypad**: It makes it easy and fast to enter numbers. All the keys are in a block like an old calculator or adding machine.

Some primary keys on the keyboard are the Shift key, Caps lock, Tab, Enter key, Spacebar, Backspace, Alt key, and Arrow Keys.

Note:

- There is a Desktop Keyboard and the Laptop Keyboard.
- Most laptop keyboards don't have a numeric keypad.
- The cursor keys are close together around the typewriter keys in weird and creative ways.
- The function keys may be accessed by pressing certain keys together.
- Each key has two symbols, showing that it has two different functionalities.

Putting Words on a Document

A vertical line blinks when you need to input something in software, email, or text box. The cursor or insertion point is this line. It indicates where the text you'll write will begin. You can move the cursor by using the mouse to click where you want it to go or by using the keys. The four arrow keys that go up, down, left, and right can be used to move your cursor in Microsoft Word.

Using the Onscreen Keyboard

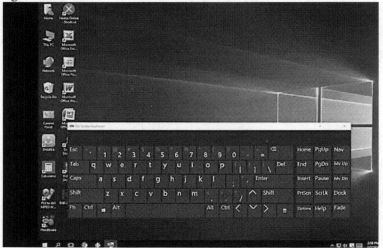

When you want to use the On-Screen Keyboard:

- Go to **Start** on your computer
- Then select **Settings**
- Click on **Ease of Access**
- Click on the Keyboard and turn on the toggle next to Use the On-Screen Keyboard to use the keyboard on the screen
  Immediately, you will see a keyboard that you can use to move around the screen and type text. The keyboard will stay on the screen until you shut it down.
- Open a document in any program where you can write text. Then, with your mouse, click the keys on the onscreen keyboard to type in the text you want.
- To close it, choose "Close" and then click "OK" on the screen keyboard to remove it from your screen.

Note: Here are some things to note about using an on-screen keyboard:

- The onscreen keyboard is nearly identical to a physical keyboard. You can type with your fingers, but you won't be able to do so as rapidly as you would on a real keyboard.
- Some special keys (function, cursor, and so on) are hard to get to. Some of the time, you can get them by switching to a different touchscreen keyboard layout, but most of the time, they're not there at all.
- Using the Ctrl key on the onscreen keyboard requires two steps: first, tap the Ctrl key, and then tap another key.
- Some of the Ctrl-key combinations in Word can't be made by using the on-screen keyboard.

2. The Mouse

The mouse is yet another input device that can be used to type or enter commands into Microsoft Word. You can move the cursor or pointer on a computer screen with a mouse by dragging it across a flat surface, such as your desk or table. The name "mouse" came to be known as "mouse" because it resembles a little, corded, oval-shaped instrument. Some mice contain built-in functions, such as extra buttons that may be programmed and utilized for various purposes.

Early mouse devices were connected to computers by a cable or cord and had a roller ball as a movement sensor on the bottom of the device. While modern mouse devices are now optical technology, this signifies that a visible or invisible light beam is used to move the cursor. Many models have wireless connectivity through radio frequency (RF) and Bluetooth, among other technologies.

The three main types of mouse are:
- **Mechanical:** The mouse has a trackball under it and mechanical sensors that make it easy to move in all directions.
- **Optomechanical**: The same as mechanical, but optical sensors instead of mechanical ones are used to detect the movement of the trackball.
- **Optical:** The most expensive. It has no moving parts, uses a laser to detect movement, and reacts faster than previous varieties.

Understanding How the Mouse Pointer Works

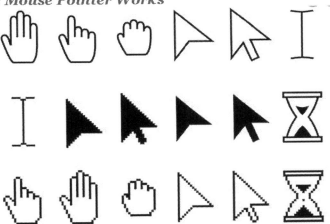

A mouse pointer or cursor is a visible item on a computer screen. Computer users can move the mouse pointer around the screen by moving the mouse, which moves the mouse pointer. You can move around the document and select text with it too.

The mouse pointer on a computer is typically in the shape of an arrow or a hand. The arrow usually points to the top of the screen and tilts slightly to the left. Arrows represent where the mouse is on the screen, and a line-like pointer shows where text can be inserted in graphical user interfaces. Instead of arrows or hands, text-based interfaces can utilize a rectangle to show where items are.

Cursors often change how they look on a screen because they are used and manipulated.
- If you want to edit any text, the mouse pointer turns into an I-beam.
- In some documents, users might see hand cursors.
- A mouse pointer at 11 o'clock is used to choose items.
- When you want to select lines of text, you use the mouse pointer at 1 o'clock to do it.
- In some document types, users might be able to press a mouse button and see that the pointer responds by "grabbing" the document page or an object in it.

- When the user works with graphical editing software, the cursor might change to match the function they are using.

Note: The mouse pointer changes when the click-and-type capability is enabled. Below the I-beam mouse pointer, tiny lines appear to the left and right of the mouse cursor. When you point your mouse at a word tool, you'll see a pop-up information bubble appear. The bubble text may provide insight on how to utilize the command.

Also, as a person moves the mouse, the mouse pointer will move around the screen similarly. When the mouse pointer is over where text can be typed, the pointer can blink as it thinks about typing. If a user wants to stop the cursor from blinking, he might be able to change the pointer's settings, such as how visible it is and how quickly it blinks. This will depend on the interface.

Keyboard "Do's and Don'ts."

Knowing how to type on a keyboard is essential since it will allow you to learn a few aspects of typing specific to word processing. Although learning to type is not required, it is recommended that you do so to avoid unnecessary stress.

- **Following the Insertion Pointer**

The text you write in Word shows up where the insertion pointer is. As soon as you move the pointer, it looks like a moving vertical bar: When you move the insertion pointer, a character comes up in front of it one by one. It moves to the right after adding a character, making room for more text.

Note: The Insertion Point can be moved to a new place, and the key moves the insertion point to wherever you want it to be.

- **Pressing the Space Bar**

The space bar is used to type blank lines in your text. The space bar is a key on a keyboard that looks like a long horizontal bar. It's in the bottom row and significantly bigger than the rest of the keyboard's keys. You can use it to enter a space between words while typing swiftly.

When typing, the most important thing to remember about the space bar is that you only need to press it once. There is only one space in between words and after punctuation. That's everything!

Note: Any time you think you need two or more spaces in a document, use a tab instead. Tabs are the best way to indent text and line up text in columns, so they are suitable for both.

- **Backspace and Delete Key**

When you make a mistake while typing, you push the backspace key on your keyboard. It deletes a character by moving the insertion pointer back to one character. The Delete key also deletes text, but only to the right of the insertion pointer, so it doesn't completely erase it.

- **Pressing the Enter Key**

The Return key is another name for it. The keyboard key tells the computer to enter the line of data or instructions just typed into the computer. You only use the Enter key in word processing when you've reached the end of a sentence.

Note: If your text reaches too near the right margin in Word, it will automatically transfer your last words to the following line. You don't have to press Enter at the end of a line because of this word-wrap feature.

As you type your text quickly, with your fingers pounding the keys on the keyboard, you might see a few things on the screen. You may see spots, lines, and boxes that may appear. We are going to look at some major stuff that happens when you type

- **Text Prediction**

Microsoft Word helps you write faster as you type. As you type, the app anticipates your next words and presents them for you to accept, allowing you to go through your manuscript faster than ever. Continue typing after accepting the suggested text with the Tab or Right-arrow key on your keyboard. Simply continue typing or press Esc to dismiss the recommendation.

- **Keep an Eye on the Status Bar**

A status bar is a type of graphical control element that shows a section of information at the bottom of a window. As you type, it shows you how your document is doing. The status bar shows a collection of data that starts at the left and moves right.

The information that shows up on the status bar can be changed. It talks about how to control what shows up on the status bar and how to hide things.

It can be broken up into sections so that you can group information. Its main job is to show information about the current state of its window, but some status bars have extra features. For example, many web browsers have sections that can be clicked on to show security or privacy information.

Some good things about status bars: They let you see messages and the whole screen at the same time, they let you write while you look at your status data, and status data is shown in a way that lets you see other menu options at the same time, and they show how things are going at all times.

- **Notice the Page Breaks**

A page break in your text indicates where the current page ends and the following one begins. After that, you can click anywhere to open a new page. Click the Insert tab at the top of the screen to add a page break. The Page Break button is on the right of the screen in the Pages group; click it to make the page break visible.

Inserting Page Breaks Manually

It's best to put your insertion point where you want the page break to be. To change your page layout, click on the Page Layout ribbon. Then click on Breaks and then choose Page. Page break becomes visible.

Note: The Pages group has a button called "Blank Page." If you want to add a blank page at the break, click that button.

Remove the Page Break

You should first show the formatting marks to find and remove page breaks quickly.

- Click the **Home button.**
- The **Show/Hide button i**s on the right.
- This shows punctuation characters like spaces, paragraph markers, and the most important for this lesson, page, and section breaks.

- Double-click the **page brea**k to pick it up.
- Press the **delete key.**
- The page break is gone.

A page break you put in now can be taken out at any time if you change your mind.

- **Collapsible Headers**

While typing, you may notice a little triangle to the left of some of your document's headings. With these triangles, you can modify the size of all the text in the header section. To hide the text, click once; to reveal it, click twice. The page does not appear to be empty because of the collapsed sections. They do an excellent job at reducing the size of the page to make it easier to read.

- **Getting Rid of Spots and Clutter in the Text**

Seeing dots or spots in your writing does not necessarily indicate something is wrong. Characters that can't be read are what you're seeing. Spaces, tabs, the Enter key, and other symbols are used in Word to represent usually hidden items. These dots and titles appear when the Show/Hide feature is enabled. If you need to remove them again, click the Show/Hide button.

- **Understanding the Colors of the Underlines**

Word underlines your text without your permission and alerts you to something wrong with how things are going. These underlines are not text styles. At times, you might see these:

- o **Red zigzag**: This indicate there is a mistake in the word
- o **Blue zigzag**: It indicates errors in grammar and word choice
- o **Blue single line**: When you write a document, Word adds blue underlined text to show where web page addresses are. You can press Ctrl+click the blue text to go to the web page.
- o **Red lines:** You might see red lines in the margin, below the text, or even through the text. It means that you're using Track Changes in Word.

CHAPTER 3:
Editing on Microsoft Word 2022

Making text is what typing is all about. Going through and revising your words is also a part of the process. Word contains many commands that can cut, slice, stitch, and so on to assist you with text editing. The instructions are a crucial aspect of word processing, and they perform best when dealing with large amounts of text. Writing initially and then editing is a smart strategy.

Therefore, this chapter will cover how to edit text, how to delete lines and sentences, split and join paragraphs, how to use the Redo command to undo what you did, etc. will all be discussed in this chapter.

Deleting a Single Character

You can use the keyboard to add and remove text when you write in Word. Many keys make text, but Backspace and Delete are the only keys that can delete text. These keys become more powerful when used with other keys, or even the mouse, that help them delete large amounts of text.

- **The Delete Key** removes characters to the **right** of the insertion pointer
- **The Backspace Key** deletes characters to the **left** of the insertion pointer.

Deleting a Word

The Ctrl and Backspace or Delete keys can be used to delete an entire planet. These keyboard shortcuts can be used in two ways. They operate best when the insertion pointer is at the beginning or end of a word. Delete commands are utilized when the pointer is in the middle of a word. These commands only delete from that middle point to the start or end of the word. The shortcut to delete is illustrated as follows:

- The word to the leftward of the insertion pointer is deleted when you press **Ctrl+Backspace.**
- The word to the rightward of the insertion pointer is deleted when you press **Ctrl + Delete.**

Note: When you use Ctrl+Backspace to delete a word to the left. The pointer is at the end of what comes before it. When you use Ctrl+Delete to remove a word, the cursor moves to the start of the next word. This is done to make removing several words in a row easier.

Deleting More than a Word

The keyboard and mouse must work together to remove chunks of text bigger than a single letter or word. The first step is to choose a chunk of text and then delete that chunk of text.

Remove a Line of Text

A line of text starts on one side of the page and goes to the other. If you want to remove the line, you can:
- Make sure the mouse pointer is next to a line of text by moving it to the left.
- Then click on the mouse.
- The text line is chosen and shown in a different color on the screen.
- Press the delete key to eliminate that line.

Delete a Sentence

A sentence is a group of text that begins with a capital letter and ends with a period, question mark, or exclamation point, depending on what you're trying to communicate. To do this:
- Place the mouse pointer where the sentence you want to delete lies.
- Press then hold down the Ctrl key simultaneously as you click the mouse.
- Using Ctrl and a mouse click together, you can choose a sentence of text that you want to delete.
- The Ctrl key can be let go, and then you can hit delete.

Deleting a Paragraph

A Paragraph is a group of sentences formed when you press the Enter key. If you want to delete a whole paragraph quickly, here's how to do it:
- Click the mouse **three times.** In this case, the triple-click selects the whole paragraph of the text.
- Press the **Delete button.**

Another way to select a paragraph is to click the mouse two times in the left margin, next to the paragraph, to make it select and then click on delete.

Deleting a Page

Page of text is everything on a page from top to bottom. This part of the document isn't one that Word directly addresses with keyboard commands. You'll need some sleight of hand to get rid of a whole page of text. Take these steps:
- Press the keys **Ctrl+G.**
- The Find and Replace dialogue box comes up, with the Go To tab at the top of the list of tabs.
- On the Go to What list, choose Page and then type the number of the page you want to remove.
- Click the Go To button, then the Close button. And the page shows up.
- Press the **Delete** button.
- All the text on the page is taken off.

Split and Join Paragraphs

A paragraph, as earlier defined, is a group of sentences that all say the same thing about a thought, idea, or theme. In Word, a paragraph is a chunk of text that ends when you press the Enter key. You can change a paragraph in a document by splitting or joining text.

To split a single paragraph in two:

When you need to start a new paragraph, move the cursor to the desired location. That point belongs at the start of a sentence. To begin, press the Enter key. Word splits the text in half during this process. The paragraph above the insertion pointer becomes the current paragraph, while the paragraph below becomes the next paragraph.

Making a Single Paragraph Out of Two Separate Ones

To combine two paragraphs and make them one, do this; When you place the insertion pointer at the start of the second paragraph, use the keyboard or click the mouse to move the insertion pointer where you want it to be, press the Backspace button.
This implies that you have removed the entered character from the paragraph before this one, thus making two paragraphs into one.

Soft and Hard Return

The **Return or Enter key** is pressed at the end of each line when typing on a keyboard. This indicates that you've finished one paragraph and are ready to go on to the next. However, when you set your page margins, Word knows that your text should wrap to the next line automatically when you get to the right margin.
There may be times when you wish to stop writing a line before it reaches the right margin. In these situations, you have two options for terminating a line. The first way is to type in the line's endpoint and press Enter. As a result, the document has a hard return on it. This action (pressing Enter) indicates that you've reached the end of a paragraph and want to start a new one.
Another approach to end a line is to hit **Shift+Enter,** which will insert a soft return, also known as a line break or newline character, into the document. The end of a paragraph is indicated by hard returns, whereas soft returns indicate the end of a line.
A hard return displays on your screen as a paragraph mark (a backward P), while a soft return appears as a down-and-left pointing arrow.

The Undo Command

The Undo command can undo anything you do in Word, like changing text, moving blocks, typing, and deleting text. It does this for everything you do in the program. If you want to use the Undo command, you have two ways to do it:

- The shortcut method is to Press **Ctrl+Z.**
- Alternatively, you can click the Undo command button on the Quick Access toolbar to get back to where your previous work is.

Note: In some cases, you can't use the Undo command because there's nothing to undo. For example, you can't go back and undo a file save.

The Redo Command

If you make a mistake and accidentally undo something, use the Redo command to restore things to their previous state. Assume you type some text and then use Undo to erase it. And, you can use the Redo command to go back and type again. It's your choice. You can choose

- The shortcut method is to press **Ctrl+Y.**
- Alternatively, look at the **Quick Access toolbar** and click the **Redo button.**

Note: The Undo command does the opposite of the Redo command. So, if you write text, Undo removes the text, and Redo puts the text back.

The Repeat Command

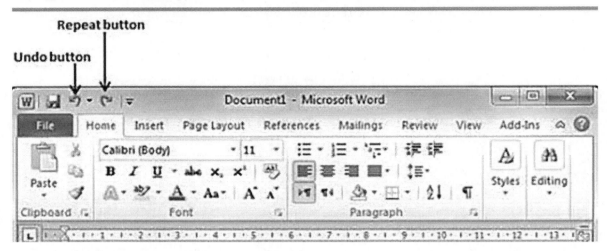

To repeat what you did in Word last time, use the Repeat command to do the same thing again. This could be typing new text, formatting it, or doing many other things.

Using the Repeat command, you can keep the same picture. The Redo command turns into the Repeat command whenever there is no more to redo.

To do this:

- The shortcut method is to Press **Ctrl+Y**, which is the same keyboard shortcut as to redo something.

Finally, now that you know how to utilize Word's fundamental tools to create a document, this chapter has covered several additional editing tools and easy formatting effects to improve the appearance of a document. Other chapters will go through other editing tools.

CHAPTER 4:
Document Formatting

Formatting with Styles and Themes

Styles and **Themes** are powerful Word features that you can quickly and easily use to create a professional-looking document. A **style** is a Word predefined combination of all font, and paragraph formatting elements (e.g., font size, font type, color, indent, etc.) applied to a selected text or paragraph. At the same time, a **theme** is a group of formatting choices with a unique set of colors, font, and effects to change the appearance of the entire document.

You can choose from a variety of styles and themes in Word. The steps for applying, modifying, and creating styles and themes are outlined here.

Applying, Modifying, and Creating Styles

To apply a style:

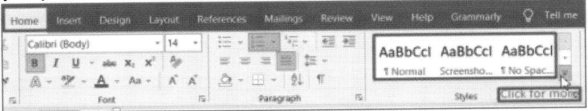

1. Select the text or paragraph you want to apply a style.
2. Go to the **Home** ribbon.
3. Select the style you want in the **Style** group. You can hover over each style to see the live effect in your document before applying. To see the additional style, click the **More** dropdown arrow.

To modify a style:
1. Select the style you want to modify.
2. Right-click and select Modify in the dropdown list. A **Modify Style** dialog box appears.
3. Set as desired all the formatting groups. You can as well change the style name.
4. Click on the **Format** button for more formatting options and control.
5. Check the **Automatically update** box to update the style changes anywhere you have applied them in your document.
6. Press **OK** when you are done.

To create a style:
1. Go to the **Home** ribbon.
2. In the **Style** group, click the **More** dropdown arrow.
3. Select **Create a Style**. A dialog box appears.

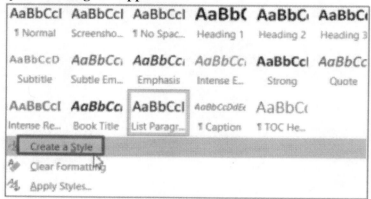

4. Input your desired name.
5. Click the **Modify** button, modify as explained above, and a new style will appear in the style gallery.

To remove a style from the list, right-click on the style and select **Remove from Style Gallery.**

Creating Your Document with Word Headings

To create your document with Word Headings:
- Go to the **Home** ribbon, under the **Style** group.
- Select all your chapters or section headings and click **Heading 1** in the **Style** group.
- Select all the sub-topics or sub-sections and click **Heading 2** in the **Style** group.
- Select all your sub-sub-topics and click **Heading 3** in the **Style** group. Continue to your last headings.

You can customize your headings following the steps in **Section 7.1.1**

Changing, Customizing, and Saving a Theme

A theme is a collection of colors, fonts, and effects that alter the overall appearance of your page. The default Office theme is used whenever you create a document in Word.

To change the theme of your document:
1. Click the **Design** tab.
2. Click the **Themes** command in the **Document Formatting** group. A drop-down list appears.
3. Hover your cursor over a theme to preview it in your document.
4. Click your desired theme to apply it.

Customizing a theme: You can change any theme element (i.e., color, font, and effect) to create a unique look for your document.

To change themes colors:
1. Go to the **Design** tap.
2. Select **Colors** command. A drop-down color palette appears.

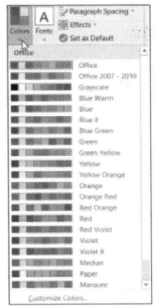

3. Select the desired color palate or click customize the color to combine your colors.

To change a theme font:
1. Go to the **Design** tab.
2. Click the **Font** command. A drop-down menu of fonts appears.
3. Select your desired theme fonts or Select **Customize Font** to customize your font.
4. Set your desired font in the dialog box that appears and presses **Ok**.

To change a theme effect:
1. Go to the **Design** tab.
2. Click the **Effect** command. A drop-down list of all the available effects appears.

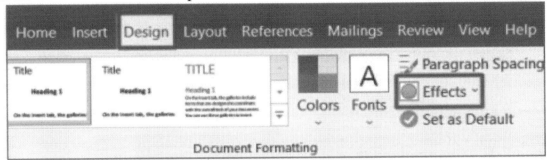

3. Select the desired effect. You can see the live preview of any effect you hover on.
You can save your current or customized theme for later use.

To save a theme:
1. Click the **Design** tab.
2. Click the **Themes** command in the **Document Formatting** group. A drop-down list appears.
3. Select **Save Current Theme**.
4. Input a file name for your theme and press **Save** in the dialog box that appears.

Setting Paper Size, Margins, and Orientation

Margins

Margins are the spaces between the edges of your document (top, bottom, left, and right) and your text. They make your work look professional. The default margin in Word is 1 inch for all sides. There are predefined margins, and you can as well customize your margins.

To apply a predefined margin to your document:
1. Go to the **Layout** ribbon.

2. Choose **Margins** in the **Page Setup** group. A drop-down menu appears.

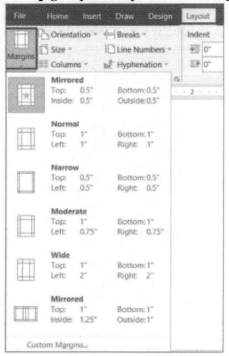

3. Select an option from the list.

To customize your margin:
1. Select **Custom Margins,** and a dialog box will appear.

2. Input your values in the text boxes.
3. Select an option in **Apply to** box.
4. Click **Set As Default** (optional)
5. Press **OK.**

Note: Select the whole document before applying a predefined margin to a document with different sections because Word only applies the predefined margin to the current section.

Page Size

To set Page Size:
1. Go to the **Layout** ribbon.
2. Click the **Size** button. A drop-down menu appears.
3. Select an option from the list.

To customize your page size:
1. Select **More Paper Sizes,** and a dialog box appears.

2. Input your values in the Width and Height text boxes.
3. Select an option in **Apply to** box.
4. Click **Set As Default** if you wish to set the size as default.
5. Press **OK.**

Page Orientation

To change your page orientation:
1. Go to the **Layout** ribbon.
2. Click the **Orientation** command. A drop-down menu appears.

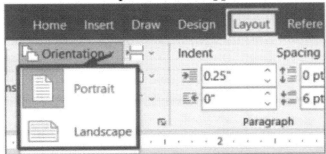

3. Select **Portrait** for a vertical page or **Landscape** for a horizontal page.

Page Breaks and Section Breaks

When working on a document with multiple pages and numerous headings, it might be difficult to format the text so that all chapter heads begin on a new page rather than at the bottom of the previous page. It may also be difficult to add separate headers, footers, footnotes, page numbers, and other formatting elements to some types of documents having several sections, such as an article, report, paper, or book.

Word repeats the headers, footers, footnotes, and the numbering across the document. Document breaks are required to have a separate one.

There are two types of document breaks in Word:
- Page breaks
- Section breaks

Page breaks partition the document's body, while section breaks partition not only the document body but also the headings (or chapters), headers, footnotes, page numbers, margins, etc.

Page breaks are subdivided into:
- **Page break**: This forces all the text behind the insertion point to the next page.
- **Column** break: This forces the text to the right of the insertion point to the next column of the same page when working with a document with multiple columns
- **Text Wrapping break**: It moves any text to the right of the cursor to the following line and is instrumental when working with objects.

Section breaks are subdivided into:
- **Next Page break:** This separates the papers by adding another page with its formatting. This helps divide your document into chapters with various headers, footers, page numbers, etc.
- **Continuous break:** This divides the document into sections that can be independently formatted on the same page without creating a new page. This break is usually used to change the number of columns on a page.
- **Even Page break:** This shifts the insertion point and any text at its right to the next even page.
- **Odd Page breaks** This shifts the insertion point and any text at its right to the next odd page.

To Insert a Page Break or Section Break:
1. Place your insertion point to where you want the break.
2. Go to the **Layout** ribbon.
3. Select **Breaks** in the **Page Setup** group. A drop-down list appears with all the types of breaks.
4. Select from the options the type of section break you want.

Inserting Header or Footer

A header is a piece of text that appears at the top of each document page. On the other hand, a footer is a text put to the bottom margin to provide information about the document, such as the title, page number, image, logo, and so on.

To place a Header or Footer to your document:
1. Go to the **Insert** ribbon.
2. Select **Header** or **Footer** command. A drop-down menu appears with header or footer styles.

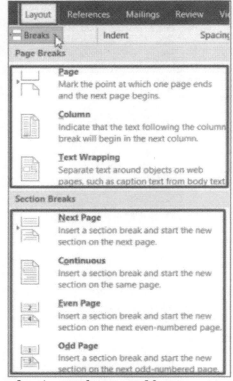

3. Click on the desired style. Word activates the top and bottom margin for your header or footer insertion.
4. Replace the text with your desired text.
5. Click on the **Close Header and Footer** command when you are done.

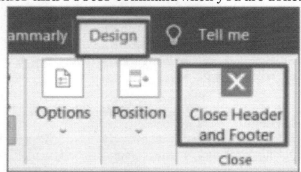

Alternatively,
1. Double-click in the top or bottom margin to activate the header and footer area.
2. Insert your footer or header.
3. Double click outside the margin area or press the **Esc** key to return to your document.

You can always use the above method to edit your header or footer. Also available is a contextual **Design** tab you can use to design your header or footer.

To delete your header or footer, just delete the text and close the header and footer.

Inserting Different Headers or Footers in Word

To insert a separate Header or Footer for a Separate Section:

1. Insert **Next Page** section breaks where you want different headers or footers to start.
2. Activate the headers or footers of each section.

In the **Navigation** group of the **Header & Footer** Tools ribbon:
3. Deselect the **Link to** the **Previous** button to disconnect the sections.
4. Add the header or footer for each section or chapter.
5. To put a different header on the document's first page or a section, Check the **Different First Page** box.
6. To put a right-justified header for some pages and a left-justified header for some pages, check the **Different Odd & Even Pages** box.

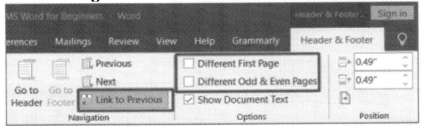

7. Close the header/footer when done with the settings.

Saving Headers or Footers for Later Use

If you frequently generate documents with the same header or footer, it's a good idea to store the header/footer.
To save your header or footer for later use:
1. Activate and select all the header or footer contents you want to save.
2. Click the **Header** or **Footer** drop-down button as the case may be.
3. Select **Save Selection to Header Gallery** or **Save Selection to Footer Gallery,** depending on whether you select Header or Footer. A dialog box appears.

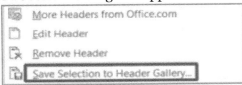

4. Input the name you want to give the header or footer and do any other desired settings.
5. Press **OK,** and your header or footer will be saved.

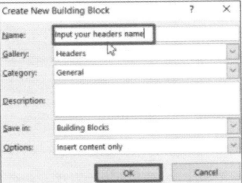

You can access and apply the header or footer at any time in the drop-down list of the **Header** or **Footer** drop button.

To delete your saved header or footer:
1. Right-click on it.
2. Select Organize and Delete. A dialog box appears highlighting the header or footer.
3. Click the **Delete** button.
4. Press **yes** to confirm the prompt that appears.

5. Press **Close** in the dialog box, and your header or footer will no longer be in the gallery.

Page Numbering

To add page number to your document:
1. Click the **Insert** tab.
2. Select the **Page Number** button in the **Header & Footer** section. A drop-down menu appears with the list of where you can insert your page number.

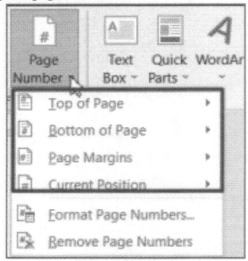

3. Select an option. A dialog box with page number styles appears.
4. Click your desired style. Word assigns page numbers to your document's pages and activates the header and footer areas.
5. Right-click on the page number or Click the **Page Number** command in the **Headers & Footers** ribbon for settings. A dialog box appears.

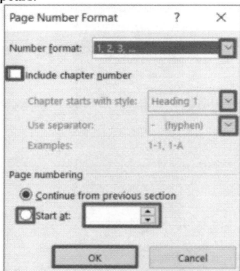

6. Select the drop-down button to select the **Number format** you want.
7. Check the **Include chapter number** box to include chapter numbers, select the **Chapter starts with style** and **Use separator** options (optional).
8. Check the **Start at** button and set the start value if you do not want the numbering to continue from the previous section (applicable for setting different page numbering for different sections).
9. Press **OK**.
10. Double click outside the margin to go back to your document area.

Inserting Different Page Numbers

To insert different page numbers into your document:
1. Insert page number to the entire document first, following the above steps.
2. Create section breaks to the document where you want different page numbers.

Creating Next Page section breaks for each chapter and prefatory sections is advisable if you have different chapters in your document. (Check **section 7.3** for the steps)

3. Double-click the header or footer of the section you want to change the page number.
4. Locate and Deselect the **Link to the Previous** button in the **Header & Footer Tools ribbon's Navigation group if needed**.
5. Right-click on the page number or Click the Page Number command in the Headers & Footers ribbon to set the page numbers as desired.

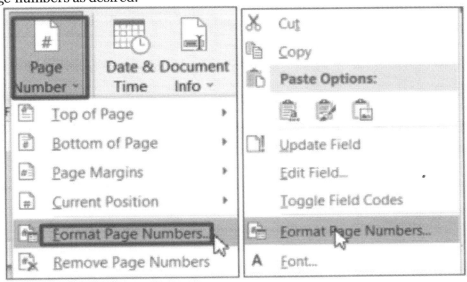

6. Continue **steps 3-5** above for all the sections as desired.

Removing Page Numbers

To remove Page numbers from the entire document:
1. Go to the **Insert** ribbon.
2. Click **Page Number**. A drop-down menu appears.
3. Select **Remove Page Number** from the options.

Alternatively,
1. Double-click on the Header or Footer area.
2. Select the page number and press the **Delete** key.

To remove the page number from the first page of the document or a section:
1. Double-click in the margin of the section or document to activate **Headers & Footers** Tools.
2. Check the **Different First Page** box in the Options group.

You can also check the **Different Odd & Even Pages** box to remove page numbers of alternate pages.

Inserting Automatic Table of Content

Microsoft Word includes a tool that lets you create a table of contents either automatically or manually using simple templates. You must write or prepare your document using the Word built-in headings in the Styles group to automatically insert a table of contents.

To Insert a Table of Contents:
1. Ensure your document headings uses Word built-in headings styles
2. Place your insertion point where you want the table of content to be.
3. Go to the **References** ribbon.
4. Click **Table of Contents**. A drop-down menu appears.
5. Select an option:
   - The first two options automatically insert your table of contents with **all** your available headings.

- The third option inserts the table of contents with placeholder texts and allows you to replace them with your headings.
- Select **More Tables of Contents from Office.com** for more templates.
- Select the **Custom Table of Contents** to customize your table. A dialog box appears. Edit as desired and press **OK.**
- If you already have a table of content in your document, you can delete it by selecting **Remove Table of Contents.**

Updating Your Table of Contents

Word does not update your table of content automatically if you make changes to your document. You will have to update it manually.

To update your Table of Content:
1. Position your cursor in the table of content. Table borders appear with buttons at the top-left.
2. Click the **Update Table** button. A dialog box appears.
3. Click the **Update entire table**.
4. Press **OK.**

Word automatically updates your table.

Alternatively,
1. Right-click on the table of content. A drop-down menu appears.
2. Select **Update Field.** You can also select **Update Table** in the **Table of Contents** group in the **References** ribbon. A dialog box appears.

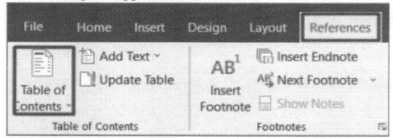

3. Click **Update the entire table**.
4. Click **OK.**

Note: Do not always forget to update your table after making significant changes that affect the headers or page numbers.

Adding Captions to Figures or Objects

A caption is a title or brief explanation of a figure or an object mostly placed below a figure or an object to give information about the figure.

To add a caption to an object:
1. Select the object you want to add a caption to.
2. Go to the **References** tab.
3. Click **Insert Caption** in the **Captions** group. A caption dialog box appears.

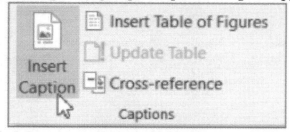

4. Select **Figure** in the **Label** dropdown menu or any appropriate options.
5. Type the object description (it can include punctuations) in front of **Figure 1** in the **caption** text field.
6. Click **OK.**

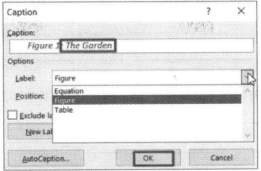

You can **format** your captions in the **Styles** group of the **Home** tab.

To Add a Chapter Number that updates automatically to your Image Caption.

1. Ensure you format your document headings with the Word **Headings** in the **Style** group. (Check **section 7.1** for more information).
2. Use the Word Multilevel list to number your chapter headings or **Heading 1** as the case may be following the steps below:
    *   Select any of your Chapters or Heading 1 style.
    *   Go to the **Home** tab.
    *   Click the **Multilevel List** icon in the **Paragraph** group.
    *   Select **Chapter 1 Heading...**, the last option, and all Headings 1 will be numbered automatically.

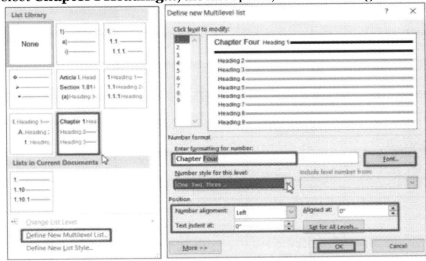

    You can format the numbering in **Define new Multilevel** list. You can change the Chapter to a Section, change the numbers to words, change the font, and so on.

3. Select the object you want to add the caption.
4. Go to **References >> Captions >> Insert Caption**.
5. Select **Numbering** in the **Caption** dialog box. A **Caption Numbering** dialog box appears.

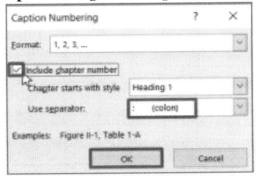

6. Check the **Include chapter number** box, select the desired separator, and press **OK**.

To make your captions stick to your floating object:

1. Select the Object.

2. Go to the **Layout** tab.
3. Select the **Wrap Text** command.
4. Choose any other options aside from the first from the dropdown list as desired. Alternatively, you can click on the Layout button at the top right corner of the object and select an option in the **With Text Wrapping** list.
5. Add a caption to your figure following the above steps.
6. Group the caption and the object.

To Delete a Caption: Select the caption and press Delete.

Note: Word automatically updates the figure numbers as you insert a new caption. You must update the caption or figure numbers whenever you delete or change the position of any caption.

To update the caption numbers:
1. Select all your document using **Ctrl + A.**
2. Right-click and select **Update Field** in the dialog box that appears, or Press **F9** to update the caption numbers.

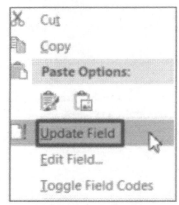

Inserting Automatic Table of Figures

Word has a command to automatically add a table of figures to your work, just like adding a table of contents.
To automatically generate a table of figures, you must have added captions to all the figures used in your document using the Word **Insert Caption** command.

To Insert Table of Figures:
1. Ensure you use the Word caption feature to add captions to your objects.
2. Place your insertion point where you want the table of figures to be.
3. Click the References tab.
4. Select Insert Table of Figures in the Caption group. Table of Figures dialog box appears.

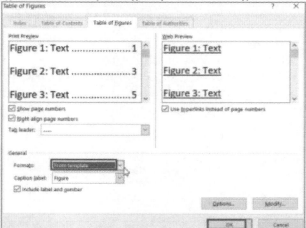

5. Select your desired Format, make other changes, preview, and press **OK**. Your table of figures appears in your document.

Inserting Cover Page

A cover page contains information about the document like the title, author, and other enticing objects or texts.
To insert a cover page:
1. Go to the **Insert** ribbon.
2. Click the **Cover Page** button in the **Pages** group. A drop-down menu appears.
3. Select the desired templates to customize.
4. Edit, format, and the template to your taste. You can add images, text, and so on.

Working with Citations

Citation is a standard technique in academic writing that informs readers about the sources of quotes or paraphrases used in your text. To save you time and frustration, Word provides a tool that assists you with citations.
To insert Citation into your document:
1. Position your insertion point wherever you want to place your citation.
2. Click the **References** tab.
3. Click (Placeholder1) **Insert Citation** in the **Citations & Bibliography** group. A drop menu appears.
4. Select **Add a New Source** option. A dialog box appears.

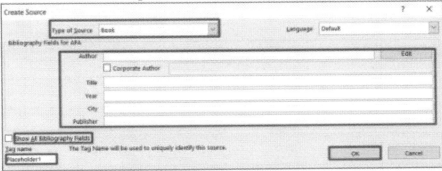

5. Select the **Source type** (e.g., book, journal, article, etc.) using the dropdown arrow.
6. Fill in the source details in the text boxes provided.
7. Check the **Show All Bibliography Fields** for additional information.
8. Input the **Tag name**.
9. Press **OK**, and your citation is inserted.

Inserting References, Works Cited, or Bibliography

A bibliography is an alphabetical list of all sources you consulted for your document, whether or not you cited them. References and works cited are alphabetical lists of all the citations used in your document. In contrast, a bibliography is an alphabetical list of all sources you consulted for your document, whether or not This list is frequently seen towards the conclusion of a text.
The format style utilized distinguishes references from works cited. Different professional and academic groups use a variety of citation styles. When referencing works in APA (American Psychological Association) format, use references, and when citing works in MLA (Modern Language Association) format, use works cited list.
To insert References, Works Cited List, or Bibliography:
1. Ensure you use the Word **Citation** command to cite in your document body.
2. Place your insertion point wherever you want the lists to be.
3. Click the **References** tab.
4. Click **Bibliography** in the **Citations & Bibliography** group. A drop-down menu appears.
5. Select an option, and it appears in your document.
Note: Any time you edit or add to the citations in your document, you must manually update your references, works cited, or bibliography. This can be done from the list or any of the citations in the document.
To Edit and Update your citations:
- Select any of the citations in the document.

- Right-click on the citation or click the drop-down arrow.
- Select **Edit Source** from the menu that appears, edit the **Create source** dialog box, click **Ok,** and click **yes** to the prompt.

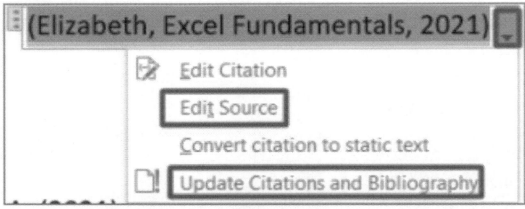

- **To update**, click **Update Citations and Bibliography** instead**.**
  OR
- Select the references or bibliography.
- Click on the **Update Citations and Bibliography** button at the top left corner of the list border.

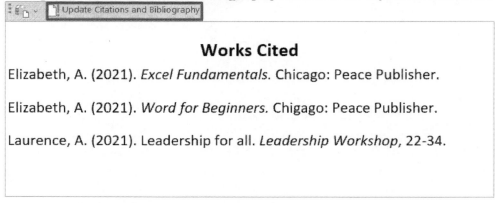

CHAPTER 5:
Borders, Tables, Rows, and Columns

In this chapter, we'll learn how to build, insert, and remove borders, rows, and columns. We'll also go through how to make a table of contents, a bullet and numbering list, an endnote, and footnotes in Microsoft Word, as well as the visuals.

Borders

A border is like a line coupled with a document's text, paragraph, or page. This line can be in a different format, either thin or thick, single, double or triple, dashed, or with various art and color

Insert a Page Border in Microsoft Word 2022

Open a new or existing document on your computer. Then, on the Ribbon, select the Design tab. Then, on the page border, click. Scroll down to the borders and shading section. The dialogue box with the borders and shading appears. Select any type in the options section. Box, 3D, shadow, and so on. Click **Apply to**, which will enable you to select where you want it to appear on the document, and then click **Ok**. You can also change the border's color, style, art, and width.

How to Add Border to a Part of Text

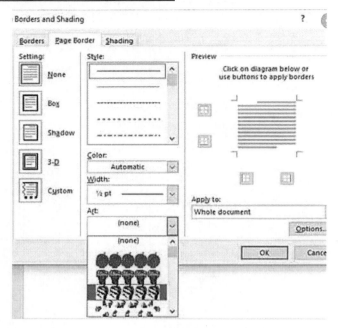

Select the text you want to apply the border to. Click on the **page border** on the design tab and the dialogue box, click on any type and click **Ok**. The border will be added to that selected text in the document. Note you can also edit your border with the elements shown in the figure

How to Add Border to a Paragraph

Select the paragraph. Click on the border on the design tab and click **OK** to apply a border to a paragraph.

To Remove a Border

Click the **None** option on the dialogue box that pops up when you click the page border button on the Design tab.

Tables on Microsoft Word 2022

How to Insert a Table

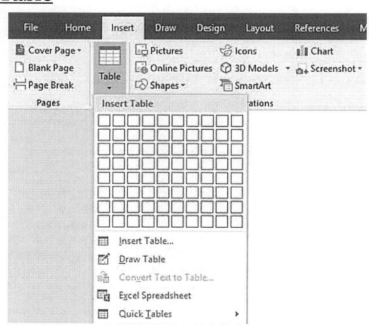

To begin, open a document on your computer. Place your cursor where you want the table to appear in the document. Select the **Table** from the table group from the Insert tab. Move your cursor across and down to select the number of cells in your table that will be grouped as rows and columns. The selected cells will turn orange, then click **Insert Table**.

Quick Table

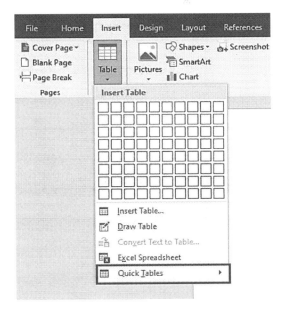

Quick tables are tables that you can change to suit your needs. To begin, place your cursor where you wish the table to be inserted. On the Ribbon, select the Insert tab. As indicated in the figure, select table from the table group, then fast table from the drop-down menu. From the gallery, select the table you desire. Then type over or delete the table example text to fill in your material.

How to Enter Text into a Table

To do this, place your cursor into a cell and type as you normally would enter a text into a table.

Table Styles

Click on the Design tab and then on Table Style. Click on the drop-down button circled in the figure below, and different table styles appear; then, you can select any of them.

Note: You can use the shading menu to add a custom menu to individual rows and columns.

- **Header Row:** Only the header row is colored. The first row is highlighted
- **Banded Rows:** Alternate rows are highlighted
- **Total Row**: All rows are highlighted
- **First Column:** The first column is highlighted
- **Last Columns:** last columns are highlighted
- **Banded Column:** Alternate Column are highlighted

To Create Your Table Styles

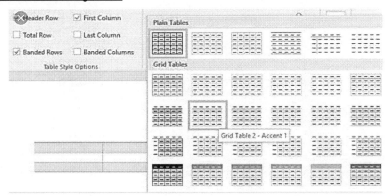

Click on create new table style on the table style group and do lots of formatting on the dialogue box. Click okay when you're done.

Insert Rows and Column

Place your cursor beneath any row to add another row once you've created a table. Select the plus sign. To add a column, go to the layout tab, and select insert left, insert above, insert right, or insert bottom from the drop-down menu. Set your cursor where you want to add the column and click Insert column; then choose any location where you want the column to be placed, and your document will be modified.

Cut/Copy/Paste/Delete Rows and Columns

Click on the row and column on the Layout tab, and you will see delete. Click on it to delete the column or just right-click with your mouse. It displays different options to cut, copy, paste or delete rows and column
To delete a table, select the table selector, a + plus. It will select the entire table. Note that you may have to use the pointer over the table to reveal all the table selectors. Then right-click the table and select the delete table from the shortcut menu,

Resize Rows, Columns, and Tables

Place your cursor in any column, then select the layout tab and cell size group. There is a height choice; click it to expand it, and the column's height will increase, as will the weight.
To make each column the same height, click distribute rows; all rows will be the same height. To get an equal column, do the same thing with the column. Click on distribute column.
Click the resizing lever in the bottom right corner of the table to resize the entire table. You may need to slide your pointer over the table to reveal the handle. Then, using the + sign on the table's bottom side, move the table to the desired size.

Split and Merge Cells

Select all the cells, click on the layout tab and merge cells; while on split cell, place your cursor on the cell, click on split cell, and a dialogue box shows up to type in how many rows and columns you want. Type in the number and click OK. That cell will be split into the number of rows and columns you typed in.
To split an entire table, keep your cursor anywhere you want to split the table. Click on the split table, and it will be split.

How to Convert Text to Table

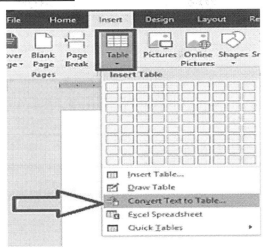

Select your text first. Click the drop-down arrow on the table groupings under the Insert tab. To convert text to a table, scroll down. Select a text separation option from the dialogue box. This is how Word determines what should go into each column. Then press OK.

Placing a Column Break

You can break a column in Word just like you can break a page. Only multicolumn pages can have this column break. It is beneficial for the column's text to halt somewhere on the page and then resume at the top of the next column.

To do this: Click to place the insertion pointer in your document, which will be the start of the next column, and click the **Layout** tab. After that, click on the **break** button on the **page setup group**. A menu appears to click on the column. The text immediately moves to the top of the next column.

How to Create Bulleted List in Microsoft Word

When constructing a list that stands out from the text, bullet lists come in handy. To make a list using bullets. Place your cursor where you wish the bullet list to appear.

Go to the **home** tab and click on the bullet on the paragraph group. On the drop-down arrow, click on any bullet that suits you the best. Then type your first list item. After that, press enter, and the second line starts with the same bullet style. Double-click the enter key to end your bullet list.

To Remove the Bullet and Numbering

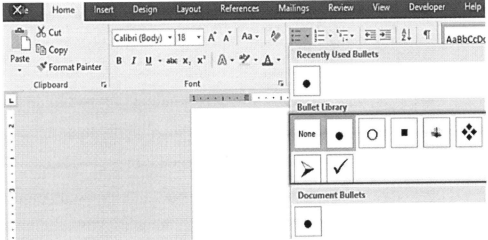

Open the document, go to the home tab, click on the bullet icon, and choose none.

How to Insert Endnote and Footnote on Microsoft 2022

Footnotes are at the bottom of a page, while **endnotes** are found at the end of a document. To begin, place your cursor where the superscript number for the footnote should appear. Select the **Reference tab** and the dialogue box launcher in the footnote group. Select footnote or endnote from the drop-down menu, then select the note's intended location. Other options in the dialogue box, such as number formatting, should be explored. To build your footnote, select insert. After that, type your superscript number, and your cursor will shift to the new spot specified in the footnote and endnote dialogue boxes. Type your note and double-click the number preceding it to return to the body content's matching superscript number. Insert the next note by placing your cursor where the superscript number for the next note should appear, then selecting Insert footnote or endnote from the footnote and endnote group.

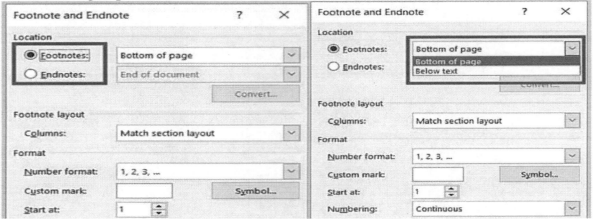

Graphical Works in Microsoft Word 2022

Most graphical tools are found on the Insert tab of Microsoft word 2022. You can insert anything into your document, including pictures, shapes, text, etc.

To Insert Pictures: Place your cursor where you want the image to be inserted and click the Insert tab on the ribbon. The photo tool format tab is one of the commands. It will transport you to areas where you can insert different photos into your work when you click on it. When you've found the image you want, click Insert, and it'll be automatically updated in your document. Use one of the command buttons to select which type of image to add.

Note: You can also insert online pictures by clicking on online pictures from the Insert tab. Then copy the image from the web and paste it into your document

- **To Delete an Image:** click on the image, select it, and click on the delete button.
- **To Copy and Paste an Image:** Select the image you want to copy from another document. Alternatively, press Ctrl + C to copy the image. Then go to the new location where you want to paste that image and click Ctrl + V. Alternatively, right-click the mouse, and options are displayed. Choose the paste option to paste the image

How to Insert Shape into Your Document

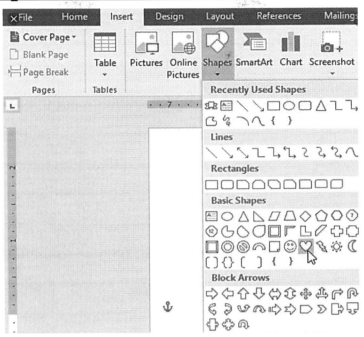

You can Insert shapes into your document. Word has a section that contains some common shapes such as circles, squares, arrows, geometric figures, etc. To do this, Click the Insert tab and click on the shape button. This menu has lots of shapes that you can choose from. Click on your preferred shape, and it is updated in your document. **Note:** you can adjust the shape in terms of size or colors. All you have to do is use the drawing tool format tab. This can be seen on the Ribbon. Just select the shapes to effect those changes. You can use the **Shape Fill button** to set the fill color and the Shape Outline button to set the shape's outline color. You can also adjust the outline thickness (Shape outline button menu), weight, and effect (3D, shadow, or any fancy formatting)on the selected shape.

How to Create Picture Layout on Microsoft Word 2022

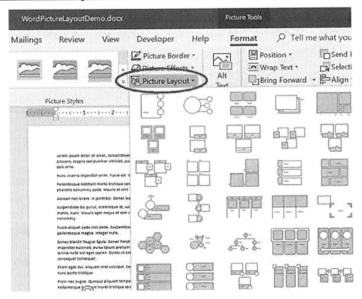

First of all, select the picture, and a new box appears on the selected picture. The picture style group has an option for a **Picture Layou**t. Click on it, and then a list of different Layout will be displayed. Click on the one that suits you and resize it to the box.

How to Wrap Text Around an Image

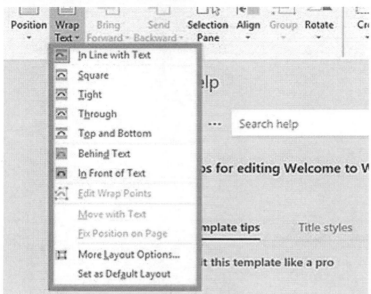

It is crucial to provide a proper layout option to keep all text and images in your document well organized. This layout has three general groups. The **Inline** (where the image is inserted into the text and the image acts as a character), **Wrapped** (text stays around the image), and **Floating** (where the image is seen at the front or behind the text).

To enter an image layout, select an image, then click the Layout Options button, which displays a list of possible layout options. Some alternatives are inline, square, tight, through, behind the text, top, and bottom, front of the text, behind the text, wrap text, and so on. Click on more selections to see more choices. Choose your favorite option and click OK.

How to Resize an Image

When you click to select an image, eight corner handles display as dots around the image. This is how you scale an image to make it bigger or smaller. To rotate the image, use the long top handle circled on the image with the rotate icon.

How to Crop an Image

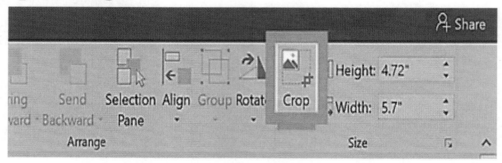

To crop an image, click to select the image, and on the picture formatting tool in the size group, there is the crop button. Click on the button and press the enter to cut out any part of the image.

In conclusion, all images can be edited to suit your choice. You can choose to rotate or change the position of the image. This can be achieved with the picture formatting tool.

CHAPTER 6:
Managing Documents and Word Windows

Saving Your Document

After you've finished producing your document, save it for later use or sharing.
Your document can be saved to your computer, a disk drive, a CD drive, a USB device, or OneDrive. When you save your work in OneDrive, you may access it from any computer that has access to your account.

To save your document for the first time:
1. Click on the **File** tab to go to the backstage of Word.
2. Click **Save As** option in the left-side panel.
3. Select where you want to save your document in the right-side pane. A dialog box appears.
4. Change the document name to your desired name in the **File Name** box.
5. Select the format you want to save your document in the **Save as type** dropdown list.
6. Click **Save**.

You will have to save your work anytime you make changes.

To save your document subsequently,
1. Click on the **Save** icon⊞ in the quick access toolbar or the **Save** tab in the backstage view.
Alternatively,
2. Use the shortcut key **Ctrl + s.**

Note: Using the above methods for the document that has never been saved will initiate the **Save as** command.
Your saved document can be duplicated with the same or different name and in the same or different location by selecting the **Save As** option in Word backstage.

Page Setups for Printing

You can get a hard or paper copy of your document by printing.

To print your document:
1. Ensure your computer is connected to the printer.
2. Ensure your printer is loaded with the right size of paper.
3. Click the **File** tab to go to the Word backstage.
4. Select **Print** in the left side pane. A **print** pane appears on the right side.
5. Input the number of copies you want directly or with the arrows in the **Copies** box.
6. Select a printer in the **Printer** drop-down if your computer is connected to more than one printer.
7. Under **Settings**, the default settings are shown in each box. To make changes to any, click the drop-down in front of the one you want to change and select your preferred option in the drop-down menu.
    - You can print specified page numbers by inputting them in the **Pages** textbox, separated by a comma.
    - The paper orientation, page size, and margins appear as you have set them during formatting. You could adjust them here if you desired.
    - Click on the **Page Setup** for more page settings.
8. Preview your work in the right section of the **Print** pane to see how it will come out. Make use of the scroll bar to go through the pages.

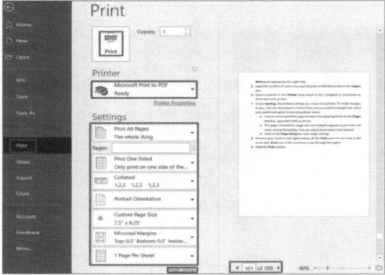

9. Click the **Print** button.

Sharing Documents by Email

Your word document can be easily shared directly as an email body or as an attachment to an email address with the **Send to Mail Recipient** command in Word. **Send to Mail Recipient** command is not available in the Word user interface by default and needs to be added. You can preferably add it to the Quick Access Toolbar by customizing it.

To add 'Send to Mail Recipient to Quick Access Toolbar (QAT):
1. Right-click on the **QAT**. A dialog box appears.
2. Select **Customize Quick Access Toolbar**. Word Options dialog box appears.
3. Choose commands from a drop-down list and **Commands Not in the Ribbon**.
4. Locate **Send to Mail Recipient** in the list. The list is arranged alphabetically for easy location.
5. Click **Add>>** button.
    Word adds it to Customize Quick Access Toolbar.

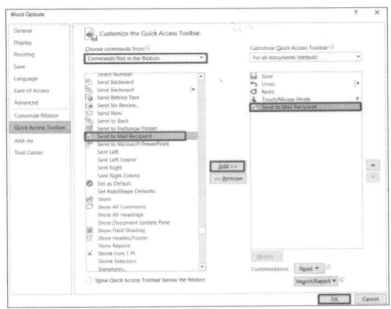

6. Click **OK,** and it appears in your Quick Access Toolbar.

To share your document as an email body:

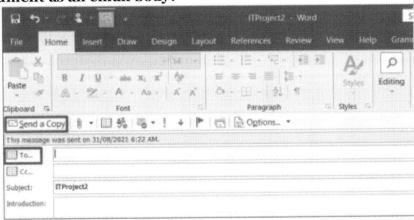

1. Ensure your computer is connected and sign into your email account.
2. Click on **Send to Mail Recipient** command in the Quick Access Toolbar.
   The mail Composing window appears under the ribbon with your document title already added.
3. Add the recipient's email address and other information as desired. You can also change the title as desired.
4. Ensure you have an internet connection.
5. Click **Send a Copy**.

Word sends your document and closes the composing email window. To close the email window manually, click on the icon in the Quick Access Toolbar.

Protecting Your File with Word Security Features

After you've spent time and effort generating your document, you'll need to safeguard it against plagiarism, stealing, accidental alteration, and other security issues.

Depending on its importance, Word has incredible security capabilities that can help you secure your document.

To secure your word document:

1. Go to the Word Backstage by clicking the **File** tab.
2. Click the **Info** tab in the left side pane. Info pane appears on the right side.
3. Click the **Protect Document** button. A dialog box appears.

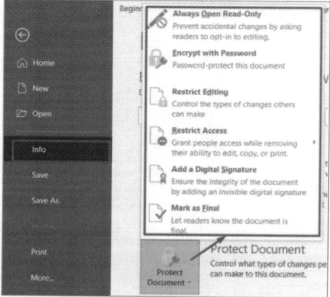

4. Select an option from the list.
   - **Mark as Final:** This makes your document read-only (i.e., typing, editing, and proofing capabilities disabled) with a message at the top of the document screen informing the reader that the document is final. However, any reader can still edit and resave the document by clicking the **Edit Anyway** button in the top message. Select this security feature only if you just need to notify the reader that it is the recommended final version of your document or to discourage editing.
   - **Add a Digital Signature:** Protecting your document with a digital signature has several benefits, like maintaining proof of document integrity, signer identity, and others. You must purchase a digital signature from a verified Microsoft partner to use it. Selecting this option for the first time will prompt you to where you can get one.
   - **Restrict Access:** This allows others to view your document but prevents them from copying, modifying, sharing, or printing it. To help safeguard the document, you'll need to connect to the Information Right Management (IRM) server. If you choose this option, you will be prompted to connect and guided through the procedure.
   - **Restrict Editing:** This is a flexible way of securing your document from editing and gives control over the type of editing that the allowed people can do. This option opens a pane on the right side of the document to set formatting and editing restrictions and **Start Enforcement**.
   - **Encrypt with Password:** Adding a password to your document is a powerful kind of security, and you can only offer the password to people you want access to it. Without the password, no one can open, let alone change, your document. When you choose this option, Word will prompt you to enter and confirm a password.
   - **Always Open Read-Only:** This feature prevents your document from accidental editing by always opening it as read-only. A dialog box appears each time you want to open it, notifying you that the document will be opened as read-only. Press **Yes** to continue and **No** if there is a need to make changes.
5. Follow all the prompts based on your choice and press ok.
6. Close your document for the security setting to take effect.

Closing Your Word Document

To close your document after you are done:
   - Click the **X** button at the top-right corner of the Word window.

OR
   - Go to the **File** tab and select the **Close** option in the left-side pane.

OR
   - Use the shortcuts keys, **Ctrl + F4** or **Ctrl + W.**

Microsoft word closes or notifies you if you try to close your document without saving it.

Recovering Unsaved Document

It can happen that you mistakenly close your document without saving your last changes. The good news is that Word has an **autosave** feature that allows you to recover your file with the last unsaved changes.

To recover your unsaved documents:
1. Go to the backstage view by clicking on the **File** tab.
2. Click the **Open** tab. **Open** pane appears.
3. Click the **Recover Unsaved Documents** button at the bottom of the recently opened document list. The location dialog box appears with the list of unsaved documents.
4. Select the likely document. You can check the date to know the likely document.
5. Click the **Open** button. The document opens.
6. Save the document accordingly.

Alternatively,
1. Go to the backstage view by clicking on the **File** tab.
2. Click the **Info** tab. Info pane opens.
3. Select **Manage Document** dropdown.
4. Click the **Recover Unsaved Documents** menu that appears. The location dialog box appears with the list of unsaved documents.
5. Follow **steps 4-6** above.

Opening Saved Document

You can open your document from the Word application or directly from your device.

To open an existing document from Word:
1. Go to the backstage view by clicking on the **File** tab.
2. Click the **Open** tab. **Open** pane appears.
3. Select the location of your document. An **open** dialog box appears.
4. Select the folder or your document. You can scroll down the left side list of locations on your device to locate your document.
5. Click **Open**.

Alternatively, if you recently opened your document or pinned it to Word, it will be available in the **Recent** or **Pinned** list in the backstage **Home** panel, and you can click on it to open it.

If you often use or work on your document, it will be better to pin it in Word.

To pin your document to the word:
1. Locate the document in the recent list.
2. Move your cursor over the document.
3. Click the pin icon in front of the file.

To open an existing document from your device:
1. Ensure you have the Word application installed on your computer.
2. Locate your Word document on your device.
3. Double-click to open it if it has a Word icon. If not, right-click on the file.

Select **open with** from the menu that appears and select **Word**.

CHAPTER 7:
Word Top Shortcut Commands

Working with Keyboard shortcut commands can reduce your stress, save your time and increase your productivity to a considerable extent. Below are the top shortcut commands you can use to work smartly in Word.

SN	Shortcuts	Functions
1.	Ctrl + A	To select all the content of your document
2.	Ctrl + B	To bold the highlighted contents
3.	Ctrl + C	To copy highlighted text
4.	Ctrl + D	To open a Font dialog box
5.	Ctrl + E	To center align the selected content
6.	Ctrl + F	To open the **Find Navigation** pane
7.	Ctrl + G	To open the **Go To** dialogue window
8.	Ctrl + H	To open the **Replace** dialog box.
9.	Ctrl + I	To italicize highlighted contents
10.	Ctrl + J	To justify aligning selected content
11.	Ctrl + K	To open the **Insert Hyperlink** dialog box.
12.	Ctrl + L	To left-align selected content
13.	Ctrl + M	To increase the Indent
14.	Ctrl + N	To create a new blank document
15.	Ctrl + O	To open an already saved document
16.	Ctrl + P	To go to **the Print** tab in the backstage view
17.	Ctrl + Q	To reset the selected paragraph
18.	Ctrl + R	To right-align selected content
19.	Ctrl + S	To save your current document

20.	**Ctrl + T**	To increase the Hanging indent of the selected paragraph.
21.	**Ctrl + U**	To underline the selected text.
22.	**Ctrl + V**	To paste what you copied last.
23.	**Ctrl + W**	To close your document
24.	**Ctrl + X**	To cut selected content
25.	**Ctrl + Y**	To redo the last action, you undo.
26.	**Ctrl + Z**	To undo your last action
27.	**Shift +Ctrl +A**	To apply the All caps command
28.	**Shift +Ctrl +C**	To copy Format
29.	**Shift +Ctrl +D**	To double underline selected text
30.	**Shift +Ctrl +G**	To open the Word count dialog box
31.	**Shift +Ctrl +J**	To distribute the letters of the selected text evenly
32.	**Shift +Ctrl +K**	To apply the Small-cap command
33.	**Shift +Ctrl +L**	To apply for bullet listing.
34.	**Shift +Ctrl +M**	To decrease Indent
35.	**Shift +Ctrl +N**	To apply the Normal Style of the **Style** group.
36.	**Shift +Ctrl +O**	To open the research pane
37.	**Shift +Ctrl +P**	To open the Font dialog box
38.	**Shift +Ctrl +Q**	To set the Font to symbol.
39.	**Shift +Ctrl +T**	To decrease Hanging Indent.
40.	**Shift +Ctrl +V**	To open the Paste Format window.
41.	**Shift +Ctrl +W**	To underline each word of the selected content.
42.	**Esc**	To cancel an active command
43.	**F1**	To open Microsoft Word **Help**
44.	**Ctrl + Alt + V**	To display the **Paste Special** dialog box
45.	**Ctrl + Shift + F**	To open the Fonts tab of the **Format Cells** dialog box.

CONCLUSION

Personal information is created, edited, formatted, saved, stored, and even printed using word processing tools. Individuals and businesses utilize Microsoft Word, the most extensively used word-processing application tool. It has all the tools you'll need to solve your document development issues. These tools are simple to use and save a significant amount of time.

Microsoft Word is a fantastic program that can be used by students, instructors, and business executives. It has several built-in templates that you can use to create and personalize visually appealing documents that are simple to edit, share, and print.

With the chapters covered above. We can conclude that:

- Microsoft Word is a very useful word-processing tool.
- Its benefits cut across personal and professional assignments.
- It is faster and easier to use than writing by hand.
- It has a lot of formatting choices and styles.
- Documents created can be stored in your computer or any other memory and shared.
- Your document can be printed as a hard copy.

Thank you for reading this book!

BOOK 3: MICROSOFT POWERPOINT 2022

The Most Updated Crash Course from Beginner to Advanced. Learn All the Functions, Macros, and Formulas to Become a Pro in 7 Days or Less

INTRODUCTION

Microsoft PowerPoint 2022 is an up-to-date guide that provides you with all you need to know about Microsoft PowerPoint. In this book, you will learn how to use the amazing features of PowerPoint, design a professional PowerPoint presentation, and make your slides interactive using transition and animation. You will learn how to conveniently insert and format pictures, shapes, tables, charts, videos, and more. This book will also show you how to work confidently and smartly with MS PowerPoint shortcut commands, tips, best practices, and so on.

MS PowerPoint is the most common presentation software first developed by Dennis Austin and Thomas Rudkin of Forethought, Inc. for Macintosh computers in 1987. Microsoft purchased PowerPoint three months after it was developed for about $14 million, and it was incorporated into the Microsoft Office Suite in 1989-1990. The most recent version of PowerPoint is part of Office 2021 and Office 365 suites.

Most of the amazing Microsoft PowerPoint features have been around for a while, and the basics are similar for most versions. So, if you have an older version of PowerPoint, PowerPoint 2021, or Office 365, read on; you will greatly benefit from this book.

Most Essential PowerPoint Features

Microsoft PowerPoint is an easy-to-use software and a powerful tool for giving presentations. It has a lot of unique features for easy communication.

- PowerPoint slides are highly customizable to fit your needs and contents.
- It helps to make your presentation interesting visually with features to add images, audio, video, animations, etc. These illustrative tools will help you to be more improvisational and interactive with the audience.
- PowerPoint has tools like tables, SmartArt, etc., to help you simplify complex and plenty of information into simple and easy-to-understand ones.
- PowerPoint allows you to work collaboratively with its review features, which allow for comments and notes.
- You can share your PowerPoint presentation with your voice to anybody, anywhere, and even on YouTube without losing any of its effects.

PowerPoint has many excellent features you might not know if you do not learn the skill. Learning the skill will make you save time, work smartly, and increase your productivity.

Other impressive features of PowerPoint include:

- Themes for a professional-looking presentation
- Find and Replace
- Paste Special
- Clipboard
- Autocorrect feature
- Spelling checking
- Synonym function (Thesaurus)
- Hyperlinking
- Transition and animation effects
- Security features and so many others

Getting Started

To start using PowerPoint, you must install it on your computer or use it online. Some computers come with Microsoft Office preinstalled, but if you do not have it, you can get it following the steps below:

Buy or Pay for MS PowerPoint

1. Open your web browser, e.g., Google Chrome.
2. Go to the official website: www.office.com.

3. Click on Get Office if you want an office or PowerPoint on your desktop and buy from the available options:
   - **Office 365 Family** and **Office 365 Personal**: You can share Office 365 Family with six people, while Office 365 Personal is limited to only one person. They are both the same in function, and both require continuous subscriptions. Office 365 is the best option for any user who wants access to all the up-to-date office apps and cloud services. It can run on windows 11, 10, 8, 7, and macOS.
   - **Office Home & Student 2021**: This is the latest available for a one-time payment and contains only the essential apps (Excel, Word, PowerPoint, Access, Outlook, OneNote, Team, and Publisher). You can only use it on Windows 11, 10, and macOS.
4. Install Microsoft Office, and PowerPoint is available on your desktop for use.

Use MS PowerPoint Freely

If you are not interested in buying Microsoft office, you can use it for free on the Microsoft official website. The PowerPoint online version is new and does not contain all the features in the desktop version. The website version cannot also work without connectivity, making the offline/ desktop version a good choice.

To use MS PowerPoint freely online:
- Visit their website, www.office.com.
- Sign in if you have an existing account or,
- Create a new one if you do not have one, and MS word will be available for your use.

CHAPTER 1:
Overview of Microsoft PowerPoint 2022

Navigating the Start Screen

The first thing you see after downloading your PowerPoint and launching it is the **Start Screen**. On the **Start screen**, you have three sections: - **Home, New, and Open.**

1. Home Tab

Select the **Home** tab in the first section above **to** select your presentation. You will either select Blank Presentation or choose from the presentations already designed.

Blank Presentation means you will apply background design and font style by yourself, but clicking on one of the available themes means you want a beautiful slide already designed with background and font style. All you have to do is change the background and text.

If you need more themes, you can select **More Themes and** have more themes from Microsoft.

Another option you have is to start your presentation by using **templates**. For example, Type **business templates** in the search box, and you'll find some examples of business templates that you'll work with. Click one of the **business templates** and see already designed business presentations you can edit and work with.

Like the example you made with business templates, you can search for any template relating to the content you will present, click on it, and edit it to your satisfaction.

At the right-down section of the Start Screen, you have: **Recent, Pinned, and Shared with me.**

- **Recent:** Where do you have the recent files you have worked on?
- **Pinned:** If you use a file often, you can pin it, and the presentation will move to **Pinned**. The essence of pinning a presentation or a file is for easy access.
- **Shared with me:** If a file is shared with you on a Microsoft account, it will be available in the Shared with me section.

You can also search for a file by typing the file name into the search button. For example, if you are looking for a file titled **HTML**, you will type HTML into the search button, and it will open.

2. New

The New button has a similar interface to what you have in the **Home** button.

3. Open

To open a saved file, you must select the **Open** button. Here, you'll see your saved presentation files or if you saved them in folders. You could browse locations on your system where you save your file; all you should do is select the file and open it.

If the file was shared with you, you must select the **shared** button, and the file will be available.

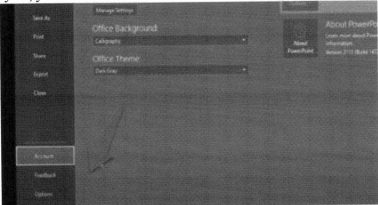

On the left side of the **Start Screen, Account, Feedback, Options.**

- **Account:** This is the place you have your Microsoft account information. Here you see your **Account privacy**. You can change your **office background** or **theme**.
- **Feedback:** You use this to send **information** to Microsoft. You could send a smile, a frown, or suggestions to Microsoft.
- **Options:** Here, you can change your **background or theme**. This is also where you customize your **ribbon**. If a tool is unavailable in your ribbon, you can go to **customize the ribbon** and select the particular tool you want.

For example, select **the main tab** and go to **draw**, select the **plus** tab to display all the tools underdraw, and repeat the same with the main tab on your right. If there's a tool that is not there and you want that tool, click on it from the right tab and add it to the other tab. After that, you could use it within your ribbon.

This is what we do with Microsoft PowerPoint options.

Basic Terminologies in Microsoft PowerPoint

Slide

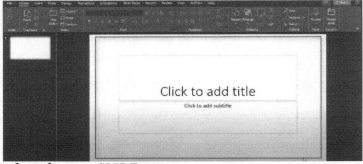

The area in the red line is referred to as a SLIDE.

Thumbnail

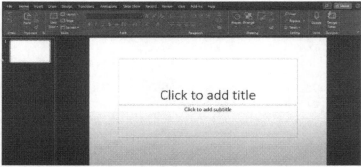

The area in the red line by the left is referred to as a THUMBNAIL.

Status Bar

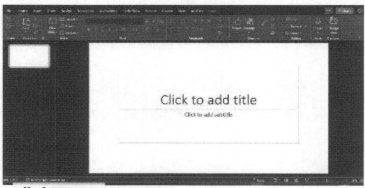

The tools at the bottom are called STATUS BAR.

Ribbon

The tools at the top are called RIBBON.

- **Tabs:** Group of Ribbons.

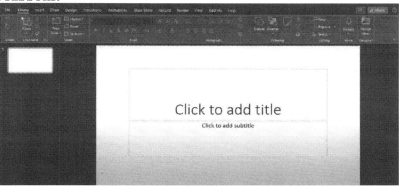

Within the ribbon, we have the TABS.

- **Command Groups:** Group of Tabs.

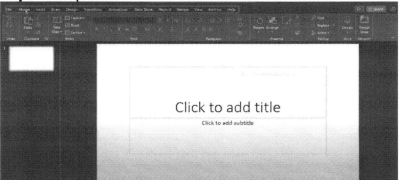

CHAPTER 2:
Slide Master

What is Slide Master?

Slide Master is where you set up your template and all the **configurations** for one **PowerPoint Presentation**.

Here, you can configure many aspects of PowerPoint, including the default font and the palette of colors for your corporate company. Hence, you know your corporate colors, default effects on any object you add to your presentation, the full background color, title, folder information, and many more.

You can add placeholders like content, text, picture, charts, tables, smart objects, media, and other things you could configure into the **slide master**. You could do many configurations with it, and most professionals don't even know these features exist.

Configuring your PowerPoint template, your slide master, saves you tons of time when you create, as you wouldn't need to be concerned about the format anymore. Everything would be already there, already pre-defined, just waiting so you'll create your very nice content and do what you do best. Use your creativity and give the message you have.

Creating Slides

Home Tab

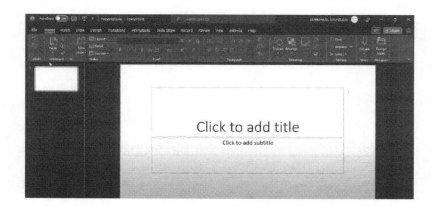

Under the **Home** button, you find command groups like **cut, copy, paste, format painter, undo, and redo**. If you select cut, it moves your words wherever you wish. When you copy, it duplicates it. For example, if you write computer in the text section, copy and paste it, it'll duplicate.

Slides

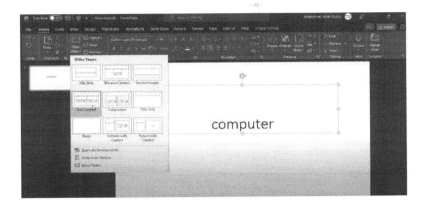

New Slide

It is easy to create New Slides. Click on **New Slide,** and you will find different options to select if your presentation needs a two contents slide. You can select **Two contents** slides. You could select the Comparison slide if you wish to compare two things.

Slide Layout

You use your **slide layout** to transform the layout of the slides. For instance, if you selected the **two content slides** and realize you wish to change the title element, you use the **Slide Layout**. When you want a blank slide, you will select **Blank Slide**. You can **Reset** your slide as well.

Sections

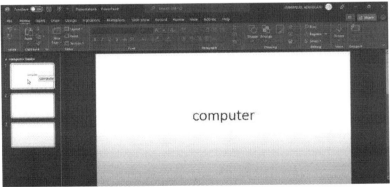

You use **Sections** to add sections to the thumbnail area.

For instance, in the preceding section of your presentation, you wish it to be a topic on computer basics. Simply select the drop-down arrow beside Sections and select **Add Sections**. In it, you will rename the section to **Computer Basics**. The content of Slide 1, Slide 2, and Slide 3, which can be seen in the Thumbnail area, will all be about computer basics.

If you wish for the title of the **second Section** to be **History of Computer**, right-click and select **add a section**, title it History of Computer, and select rename. Then, add slides underneath it by right-clicking. You can also right-click and hit the Enter key. You can go to layout to transform the layout of the slides. Now, you have two sections of thumbnail, **Computer Basics** and **History of Computer.**

Font

If a text is on your screen, use the **Font** command group to **highlight, bold, italics, underline, and text-shadow your texts**. If you wish to, you may change your Font style and increase or decrease your text. For highlights, you use text highlights to highlight a word and text color to replace the color of your texts. You can clear all the formatting on your text using **Font** if you wish to.

Paragraph

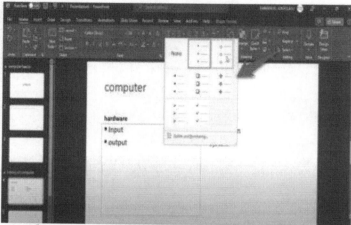

Under the **Paragraph** command group, you have **Bullets**. For instance, typical examples of hardware and software in your slide. Type Input and output as examples of hardware and application software and system software as examples of software.

By default, you will see a **bullet** already used for you, but you can replace it with whatever bullet you like. Click the drop-down arrow beside the Bullet button and make your choice.

You can use **second-level bullets** as well. This is for when you wish to include a text or list under the first one but don't wish for it to be on the same level as the first one.

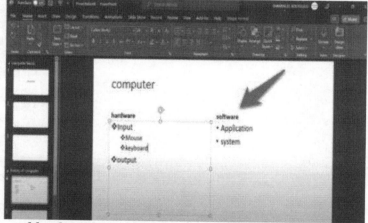

For instance, add a mouse and keyboard as examples of Input. Click the **TAB** key, which will decrease your bullets' size. To take it back to the previous size of the first bullet, hit the **SHIFT** and **TAB** keys.

Shortcut keys can also be used to achieve these or highlight and select **Decrease list level or Increase list level** at the up part of the Paragraph command group.

Still, you will see your different line spacing options and alignment on the Paragraph command group. You can align to the left, center, or right. You may choose your **columns** as well. Your text can be in one column or two columns.

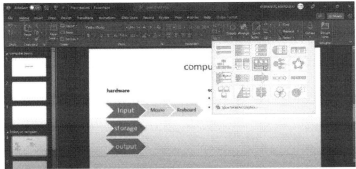

Text direction, you can alter the direction of your write-up. You also have **Align text.**

SmartArt is also available. **SmartArt Graphics** is crucial in creating a beautiful presentation, especially when working with lists. For example, click on your list box of hardware and select **SmartArt**. You will find many beautiful list styles to choose from to give your text an amazing look.

Click on **More Smart Graphics** for more options. You may also change the color and layout of your SmartArt Graphics. **SmartArt** is good at working with lists.

Drawing

Shapes

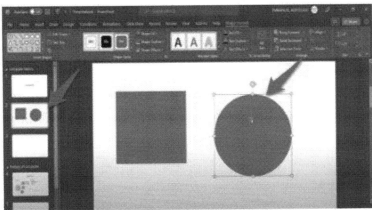

You will still come across shapes under your Insert tab as well. The **drawing** command group has so many shapes to choose from. To draw a shape, select an empty slide, click on shapes and select one. For example, click on a rectangle and a circle.

Once you draw the shape you are working on, you will see **shape formats** among the tabs section. If you click on **shape format,** you have tools that will allow you to format shapes.

Shape fill helps you to change the shape and color. The line around the shape is referred to as **a Shape outline.** You can increase the weight of the outline by clicking on the drop-down arrow beside the Shape outline and selecting **Weight**. In **the Shape effect**, you can include shadows in your drawing.

Arrange

Under the **home tab**, you will find the **Arrange** Command besides the Shapes command.
You can place shapes over each other. For example, place the circle over the rectangle. You can place the circle at the back of the rectangle by clicking the circle, clicking the Arrange tab, and selecting **Send to back.**

How to Combine Shapes

To combine shapes, press the CTRL key and select the second shape to select both shapes. Click on **Arrange** and select **Group**. This will combine the two shapes.

Position Objects

Like text alignment, you can align your shapes to the left, the center, or the right. You can also **rotate** your shapes left 90 degrees, right 90 degrees, flip vertical, and so on.

Quick Style

In **Quick style**, you will ungroup and separate your shapes first. You can **replace the style** of your shapes by selecting any style of your choice. Select the shortcut **fill color** to fill your shape with color, or select **no fill** if you don't want any color in your shape.
To select a color from a diagram or from within a PowerPoint page, click **EyeDropper Fill** and select any color. That is the function of **EyeDropper Fill.**

Editing

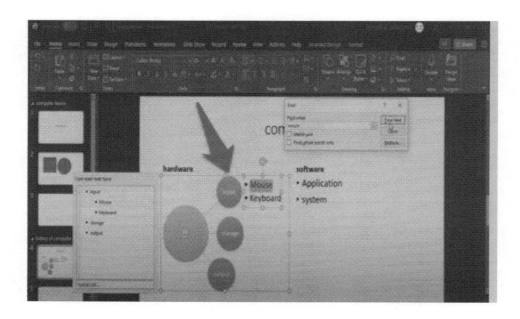

Under the **Editing** command group, you must find, replace, and **Select.** The **Find** section helps you to search for a word in your context.

For instance, tap the **Find** section and type the word **Mouse** into your search box. It will **highlight** the word Mouse in your text if it is within your slide. You can **Replace** a word among your texts on your screen. You can **Select** too, either words or objects.

Voice

In the **Voice** command group, you have to **dictate**. Click on the **layout** and choose a **blank** slide. Select a **text box** in the **Insert** button. You can begin to speak if you click on dictate and have your microphone inserted. Whatever you speak into the microphone will show as words on your blank slide.

To stop dictation, click on **dictate** again. They are the function of the **dictate** tab.

Designer

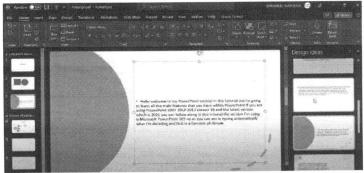

In the **Designer** command group, you have **design ideas**.

Design Ideas gives you an idea of what your slide could look like. So if you like any of the ideas you find in **design,** you can select them and apply them to your screen. You have to be online to access all design ideas and features.

Insert Tab

There are several commands under the Insert tab.

Table

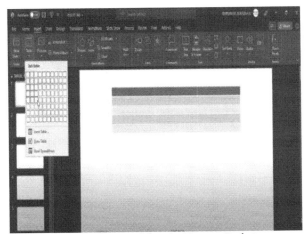

If you select the **table** command, you can produce tables in PowerPoint.

Simply select **Table** to include a table on your screen, or you can select **Insert table** and select the number of **columns and rows** you wish for in your table. **Columns** are vertical aspects of your table, while **Rows** are the horizontal aspect of your table.

For example, click on **Insert table, select five columns and rows for your table,** and click on Ok. You can start typing on your table after that.

Table Design

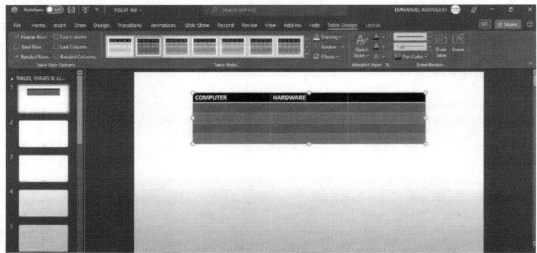

You can transform the styles of your table. Click on **table styles** and choose a style of your choice. If you wish for a light, medium, or dark style for your presentation, simply click it. You may adjust the **shading**, the **borders**, and the **effects** on your table under the **table design**.

Table Layout

In the **table layout** under the **rows and columns** command group, **insert above, insert below, insert left, and insert right** allows you to insert additional columns and rows above, below, left, or right of your table. Right-clicking also allows you to insert additional columns and rows in your table.
You can **merge cells**. If you highlight two cells and select merge cells, it will merge the two cells into one. You can as well split them back. Click on **split cells** to split your merged cells.
Under **table design** and **table layout,** you have many formatting tools that you can work with on your table.

Image Command Group

Under the **Images** command group, we have:

Pictures Format

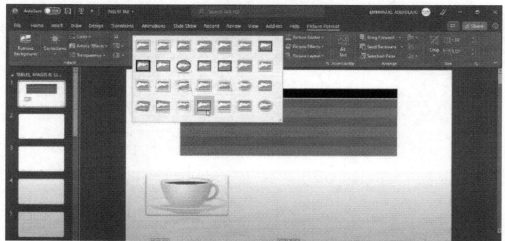

You can get **pictures** from your system if you want to. Click on the picture and select this device to get pictures from your system. This will take you to the locations where you have your pictures. Select an image of your choice and click **insert**.
Just like your table, you have **a picture format**.

Here you may select any **picture style** you wish. You also have **a picture border, picture effect,** and **picture layout**. If you want to, you can remove the background from your picture by clicking on **remove background**. When you click on remove background, you have **mark areas to keep.**

You should mark the areas you would love to keep on your image background. Select the image and click the areas you wish to keep, and it will remove the paint or color covering that area. If you are done, select **keep changes**. You have **color** that helps you replace the color of your image or picture. You have **artistic effects** and **transparency effects** as well. It all depends on what you are designing, your creative ability, and what you are doing for your presentation.

Apart from getting pictures or images from your system, you can get pictures online, or you may get pictures through stock images. Click on the **picture** and select **stock images**.

Your system must be connected online to use the **stock image** feature. You have many images under stock images you can make use of. You can browse the pictures given for your choice or type into the search box what type of stock images you are looking for.

If you type computer into the search box and press **enter**, it will show you pictures of computers you can use.

Still, on the **stock images**, you can get icons, cutout people, stickers, video illustrations, and cartoon people or type directly in the search option what you need.

You may also get pictures online. Select **picture** and click on **online pictures**.

You can choose any options in the **online pictures** and browse for what you wish, or go directly to the search box and search for what you need.

For instance, if you type **animated background** into your search box and click on **Enter**, it will give you animated background images that are online.

You don't have access to stock images if you use a lower version of Microsoft PowerPoint. You may download pictures to your computer to import them to your slides from your system. Go to your browser and type **pixabay.com** in your search box.

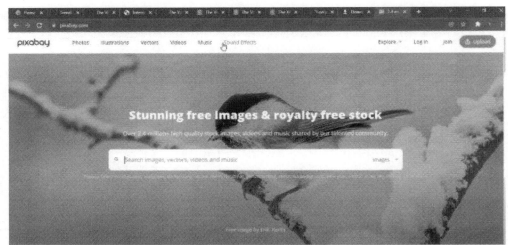

On **pixabay.com,** you have photos, illustrations, vectors, videos, music, and sound effects. You should type what you want into the search box and the area you want it from.

For example, type **computer** under photos, and you will find high-quality images you may use for your presentation. Click on an image of your choice and select download for free. You can bring it to your presentation after downloading it. Then use it for your presentation design.

Screenshots Command

You have a **screenshot** command. If you wish to use the screenshot command, you should first display or open what you wish to screenshot. The file, the webpage, or the particular file you wish to take screenshots from. You should open the page.

Click the area of your desktop you want and snip it

Your snipped area in your Microsoft PowerPoint slide

For instance, if you wish to take screenshots of your desktop background, minimize your Microsoft PowerPoint and go to your background. After that, open your Microsoft PowerPoint and select **Screenshots**. This will bring your screenshot directly to your Microsoft PowerPoint slide. If you see anything in a browser you wish to screenshot, you can use this method.

Photo Album Design

You can design a photo album for your presentation.

All you should do is click on the photo album and insert all the photos you wish to use in creating your photo album.

CHAPTER 3:
Adding Text

Text is vital to any presentation, but too much is lazy and poorly designed. I'm sure you've sat through text-heavy presentations yourself, so you'll know firsthand why I recommend you limit the written word. And don't be one of those presenters that uses text as a dictation aid.

If your presentation NEEDS lots of text, break it up. For example, use headers, short bulleted lists, and bite-sized sentences to summarize the main points.

If you're using the slide master, you've probably used placeholders to designate blocks of text. My advice is to be careful and try not to overdo this. It's too easy to fall into the trap of text-based slides.

My preference is to avoid placeholders in master slides. That way, I have a blank canvas and can add a little text wherever I want, but only as needed.

You can insert text in several different ways, including:

- Text boxes
- Add text to shapes
- SmartArt

And don't forget that you can format text in bold, italic, color, etc. Use all the tools available to help emphasize the points of your presentation.

Text Formatting

Let's do a little exercise using a text box.

Try This

1. Create a new slide and delete any placeholders to give you a blank canvas.
2. Select a text box from the shapes menu from your QAT or the Insert tab and draw out a large text box on the slide.

3. Start typing into the text box. Notice how it automatically resizes the height to accommodate your writing text. As you write, the text box auto-resizes the height to fit all your text. The width of the text box, though, remains unaffected. However, you can drag the handles on the text box to manually resize its width if you need to. Try it now. If you narrow the text box, PowerPoint auto-resizes the height so that the box neatly fits the text.

4. Highlight a word or two in the text box, then select the bold button in the Font section of the Home tab. The highlighted words become bolded. If you click bold again, those words lose the bold format. The same rule applies to *italic*, **underline**, etc. It's one of a few ways to format your text content.

5. Another way to add formatting to text is to select the formatting option before you type. Press the Enter key on your keyboard to start a new line and type "The" followed by a space. Now press the bold button on the toolbar and continue typing more words. Everything you type is in bolded format until you deselect the bold button.

6. Keyboard shortcuts can speed up text formatting as you type. The most helpful are CTRL+B (bold) and CTRL+U (**underline**). And you've probably already guessed that CTRL+I is *italic*. Practice using the keyboard shortcuts as you type a paragraph. If you want to add or remove formatting to words or sentences later, you must **select it/them first**.

7. Press Enter on your keyboard to begin a new line and type a short sentence. Now press the Bullet button on the toolbar to turn that sentence into a bullet point. Pressing Enter again adds a new bullet to the next line.

8. Highlight the sentences you turned into bullet points and click the Numbered List button in the toolbar. The bullet points now become numbers. With the list still selected, press the Numbered List button again to toggle it off. Now press the Bullet button again, and they're back to bullet points. You get the idea.

9. Highlight a paragraph of text in your text box. Next, click the Character Spacing button on the Home Tab Font section to open the menu. Now move your mouse up and down the list of spacing options and watch what happens to the selected text.

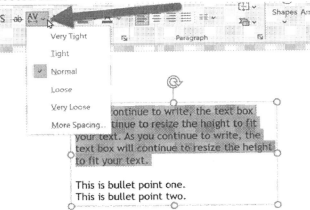

10. Repeat this exercise from the Change Case button with the paragraph still selected. Watch the text change case as you hover the mouse over the options in that list.

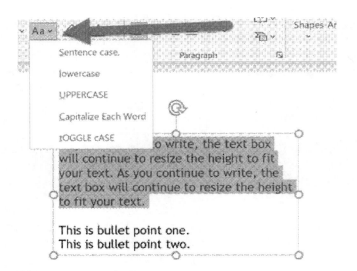

11. Select a few words in your paragraph and click the Text Highlight button. The left side of that button shows the last used color. So, clicking that side of the button reuses that color as the highlight. But you can easily change the highlight color by clicking the little arrow on the right (options may vary between versions).

12. Select a different pair of words, and now click on the Font Color button. This works in the same way. The last used color is shown and ready to reuse with a single click on the left of the button. But you can easily change the font color by clicking the little arrow on the right (again, options may vary between versions).

13. Notice you have an eyedropper tool in the menu. You can click the eyedropper and move your mouse over the slide to select a color you have already used. It's a super convenient tool if you have a color palette in your slide master, like the one we added earlier. It allows you to change the color of any object easily and quickly on your slide to one of those in your custom palette.

14. Add a color palette to the slide master if you haven't done so already, so it's visible on all the new slides you create.

15. Select a word in your paragraph and choose the first color of your color palette using the eyedropper. Then, repeat this for the other four colors in your palette. How easy was that?

16. Select the entire paragraph with all the applied formatting, then press CTRL+Spacebar. This keyboard shortcut removes all the pre-applied formatting from your text. It's a valuable tip to remember if you need to quickly strip formatting from text you added or pasted in from another editor. There's also a Clear Formatting button in the Home tab Font section if you prefer to use that.

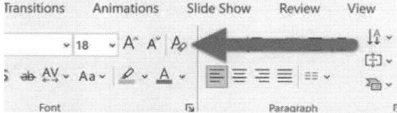

17. To the left of Clear Formatting are two other buttons that change the selected text's font size. Select all the text in the paragraph again, then click the Increase Font Size and Decrease Font Size buttons. After you've played around with this, clear all the font formatting again.

18. Now let's move to the Paragraph section on the Home tab. You can indent text using the Increase List Level and Decrease List level buttons. Select your paragraph text and try them out.

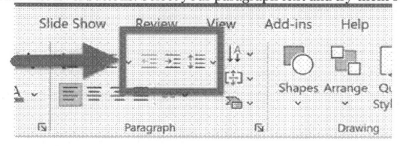

19. You can alter the line spacing using the third button in that row. Select the paragraph and then click the Line Spacing button. Move your mouse down the list and watch what happens to the text. If you need finer control over line spacing, click the Line Spacing Options link at the bottom of the menu to open the Paragraph dialogue box. This option allows you to set alignment and spacing before and after each line. There are also indent options, so try some of those, then click the 1.0 spacing option before moving on.

20. Some interesting ways to pivot the text are using the Text Direction option to the right of these three buttons. First, click anywhere inside the text box and click the Text Direction button. Then, move your mouse cursor down the list and watch your paragraph change. You'll notice that this option affects the entire text box, not just the highlighted text. That's worth remembering if you don't want everything rotated. So, for this feature to work, you only need to click into the text box you want to rotate; you don't need to highlight any actual text. And if you have text you don't want to rotate, create a second text box, and put it there.

21. There is an Align Text button that you can try, but don't expect to see much difference here since text boxes auto-resize to fit the text. Click the final option in the Text Direction menu, More Options. This opens the Format Shape pane on the right. You now have additional formatting tools to exploit your text boxes and their content.

22. The final button in the Paragraph section converts your text box into SmartArt.

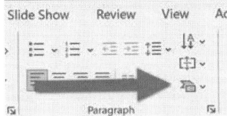

- Have a play with this option to explore the effects available. SmartArt is a great way to spice up your bullet points if you want to be more creative.
- CTRL+Z will undo any changes you make here. Note that on the Insert tab, you can add SmartArt without having any pre-existing text. We will look at the SmartArt features in more detail later.

23. The final option I want to show you here is columns. First, make sure your paragraph doesn't have any formatting applied to it. Select all the text in your box and click the Align Text button. Select More Options at the bottom of the menu to open the Format Shape pane. There are two tab links at the top, Shape Options and Text Options. Click Text Options if it's not already selected. You'll notice three icons along the top. Click the one on the far right, the Text box, if it's not already selected. At the bottom, you'll see a button labeled Columns. Click on that and set Number to 2 and the Spacing to 1. Click OK to save the changes. Your text box now has two columns with a predefined gap between them. If you don't see any difference, use the corner handles to decrease the size of your text box.

SmartArt

SmartArt is an excellent way to make your text more interesting.

1. Create a new slide and add a text box to it.
2. Add three sample sentences as bullet points.

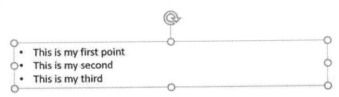

3. Click anywhere inside the text box to select it.
4. Now click the Convert to SmartArt button in the Paragraph section on the Home tab. Then, move your mouse over the options to see how a SmartArt graphic can enhance the look of your bullet points.

5. Click on the More SmartArt Graphics link at the bottom of the menu. It's the same screen you see if you add SmartArt from the Insert tab on the ribbon bar. Here, you have a categorized list of SmartArt you can use to style your text.

Practice Exercise: Adding Text

1. Create a new presentation and delete any placeholders.
2. Add a text box that fills about 1/3 of the slide's width.

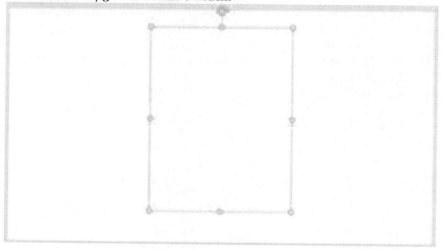

3. Go to Google and search for Ba Ba Black Sheep Lyrics.

4. Copy and paste the first four paragraphs of the rhyme into your text box.

5. Put a line space between each of the four paragraphs to space it out nicely.

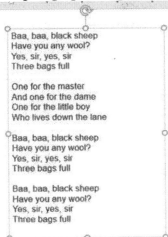

6. Modify the margin of the text box so that there is a 2.5cm (1 inch) margin on the left and right sides.

6. Put a 1.3cm (1/2 inch) margin at the top and bottom.

7. You should find that the text box falls off the bottom of the slide. If it doesn't, increase the top/bottom margin a little until it does.
8. Grab the bottom border of the text box and drag it up to make the box shorter, and see what happens. It won't adjust, right?
9. Right-click inside the text box and select Format Shape from the pop-up menu. Change the text box options in the Format Shape pane by clicking the radio button next to the Shrink text on overflow. You should be able to resize the text box to fit onto the slide.
10. Now click the radio button next to the option, Do Not Autofit, and watch what happens. Some of your text jumps off the bottom of the slide.
11. Click the Columns button in the text box Format Shape pane. Next, adjust the Text box settings for two columns, with two paragraphs in each one.

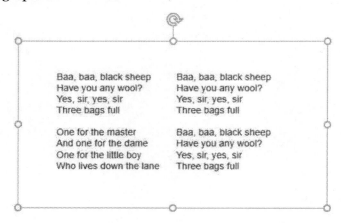

CHAPTER 4:
Creating Shapes, Icons, 3D Models, and Charts

Illustrations are powerful in Microsoft PowerPoint. In illustrations, there are **Shapes, Icons, 3D Models, Charts, and SmartArt**.
There are many shapes and icons you can use for your presentation, depending on your creativity

Creating Shapes and Icons

The first example you will learn is how to create the image below, a SWOT Analysis slide, using different shapes and icons in Microsoft PowerPoint.
SWOT Analysis collects your business's strengths, weaknesses, opportunities, and threats. You lay out all the factors in the appropriate quadrant and devise strategies to address them. For instance, how to build on your business strength, mitigate your business weaknesses, and so on.

Follow the steps below:

1. Create a blank slide

The first thing to do is to open a **blank slide** in Microsoft PowerPoint. You don't need titles and subtitles for this slide so remove them. Click on the **layout** command in the **Home** tab and select **blank layout.**

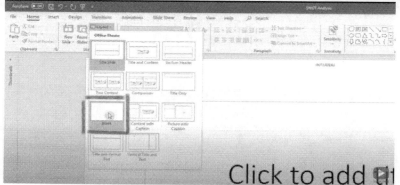
Select blank in the layout command

2. Add Header

Add your **header** by selecting the **text box** in the **drawing** command group. Click and drag the **header** where you want it to be in the **blank slide** and add your text.

You're building **SWOT Analysis** on this slide so that you can use that as your header text. You can add a **subheading** if you wish to. The **subheading** should not be as large as the heading.

You can make your **header** larger and change the font and color to your choice.

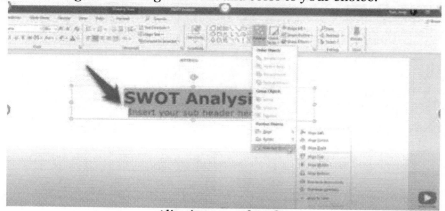
Aligning your header

Center your text within the text box, then uses the **arrange tools** to line the **text box** to the middle of the slide. Make sure **align to slide** is selected, then click on **align center.**

Drag the **text box** up a little bit. Using a mouse might pull the text box off the centreline, so it's a good idea to use the up and down arrow on your keyboard instead.

3. Make shapes

Go to the Insert tab and select the shapes command to start making some shapes. Select a **teardrop shape** and click anywhere on the screen to drop the teardrop shape.

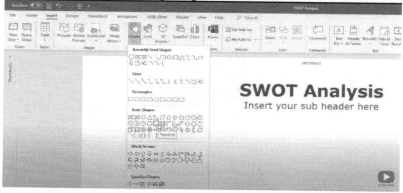

The **teardrop shape** is exactly one inch by one inch. If you want to change the size, drag any of the handles. Always use the **corner handles** to give you more control, and if you hold on to the **shift key** while dragging the handles, it will maintain the shape's aspect ratio.

If you drag on the middle handles or don't hold on to the **shift key** while using the corner handles, it will not maintain the aspect ratio and distort the shape. If you want this shape to be exactly one and a half inches, enter it in the **size section.**

Next, reshape this **teardrop** into a **petal**. Make a copy of the shape by selecting it and dragging it out while holding onto the **CTRL** key. It is a lot quicker than using **CTRL C** and **CTRL V**.

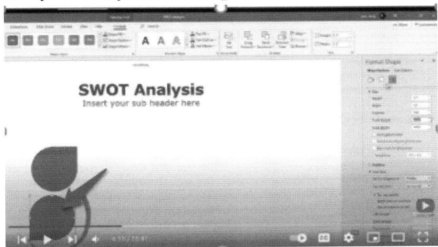

Rotate one of the shapes 180 degrees

Keeping one of the shapes selected, rotate the shape **180 degrees** so that the pointy ends of each shape are facing in the opposite direction. You can use the handle to rotate, but entering the value is more precise and quicker.

Align the two shapes so that they are on top of each other. Select both objects by dragging a selection over the two objects or holding on to the **shift key** and selecting each. Go to the **arrange tool** and select **align**. This time, ensure the **selected object** is checked, choose to **align to the center,** then **align to the middle**.

For quick clarification, if you have **aligned to the slide** selected, the shapes will find the position relative to the entire slide. If **selected objects are aligned**, the shapes will find their position relative to each other.

Merge the Shapes

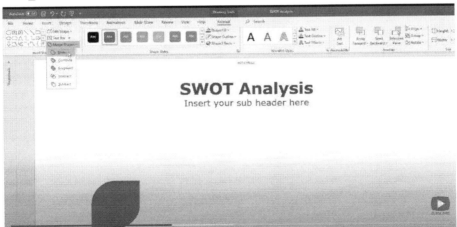

Put the two shapes on top of each other and merge them. Select the two shapes, go to the **Format** tab, **merge shapes**, and choose **union.** This has become a single shape that looks like a leaf petal.

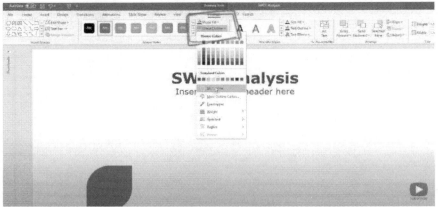
Remove the outline

You need to make four of these petals, but there should be **no outline** in any of the shapes. So, remove the shape outline before you make copies of the shape. While selecting the shape, go to the **shape outline** and select **no outline**.

To copy the petal, select and drag while holding onto the **CTRL** key. Flip the shape horizontally in the rotate tool. Go to the **Format** tab, click **Rotate**, and select **flip horizontal**. Select both shapes, then click **CTRL** and drag to make another copy of the set. This time flip vertically. In the **Format** tab, click **rotate** and select **flip vertical**.

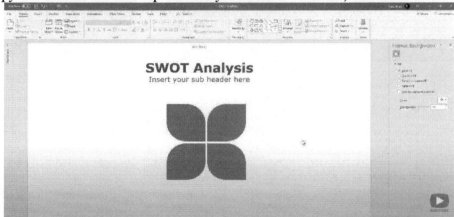
Copy the shapes and flip the first horizontally and second vertically

Next, center the shapes on the slide. The easiest way to do this is to first group them by clicking **Group** in the **format** tab and selecting **group**. Grouping them first will make the shapes not overlap each other. Once they're centered, you can **ungroup**.

Apply some colors to the shapes by selecting the **shape**, then go to **shape fill** in the **format** tab and select an appropriate color. Repeat the process for the other petals as well.

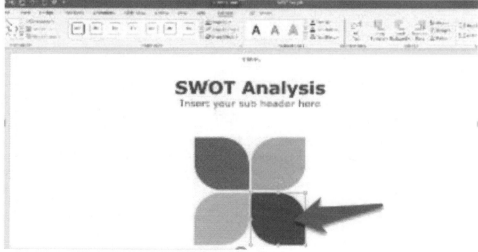
Colour the shapes

Add text to the petals. To do this, go to the **Insert** tab and select **the text box**. Then drag the text box over the entire image of the first petal so that the size overlaps.

In the first petal, type **S** for **Strength**. If the **text box** resizes as you type, go to **format** shape and choose **text options**, then select the **text box shape** and click **do not autofit**. You can now resize the text box properly.

If the text box resizes, select do not autofill

Change the **font**, make the letter **S** larger, and choose white for **the font color**. You can then center the letter and also **align the text vertically**. Copy the **text box** over to the other petals. If you make a mistake and the text boxes are not fully aligned, you can use the **alignment tool** to correct it.

Copy the text boxes to the other shapes and change the letters

Change the letter in each petal using the **SWOT** initials.

- **Add Icons**

To add some icons, go to the **insert** tab and select **icons**.

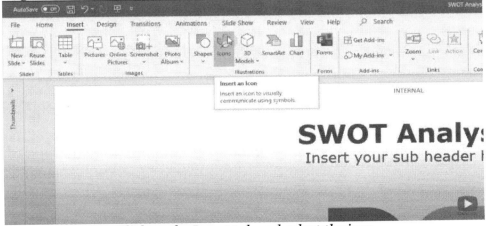

Click on the Insert tab and select the icon

When choosing an **icon** for **strength,** go to the **sports** section and choose the figure of a **person lifting barbells.** For **weakness,** type **links** in the **search box** and select the **icon** of a **line in between two circles.** Notice that the insert button tells you how many you have selected as you select the icons.

For **opportunities,** click on **nature and outdoors,** then select the **figure of a hand holding a leaf.** For **threats,** click on **signs and symbols,** then select the **triangular figure with a danger sign.**

When you select all the appropriate icons, hit **insert,** and all **icons** will be inserted in the center. They will all be clustered together.

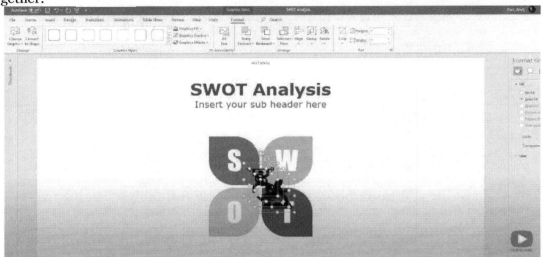

The icons clustered together

Rather than separating them one by one, use the **arrange** tool to separate them evenly across the slide. The **icons** will need a little formatting to make them look more refined.

Add a halo behind each icon. Select the **home** button and click the **oval** tool from the **shape selection** tool in the **drawing** command group. Click on the **slide,** so the **circle** appears on the screen. Alternatively, you can do this by clicking the screen and dragging the circle while holding the shift key.

Make three more copies of the circle by clicking **CTRL** and dragging the circles from one another. Remove the outline from the circles by clicking on the **circle,** going to the **Format** tab, selecting **shape outline,** and clicking on **no outline.**

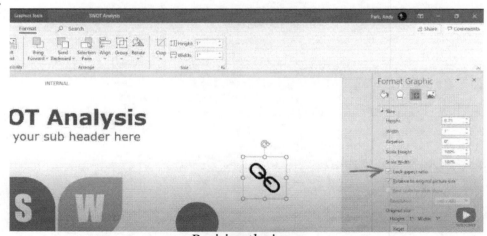

Resizing the icons

The **size** of the circles must be about an inch and if the icons are too big, reduce them so they fit into the circle. Reduce the size of the icons by **selecting all the icons,** hold onto the **shift key,** go to the **size** tab and ensure the **lock aspect ratio** is checked, then change either the **height** or the **width.**

Next, layer the icons over each circle using the **arrange** tool. Select one of the **icons,** then one of the **circles,** and click on the **format** tab. Select **align** and ensure selected objects are checked, then align to center and **middle.**

When you do this, the **icon** seems to have disappeared, but it's hidden behind the **circle.** Select the **circle,** right-click your mouse and then **send the circle to the back.**

Repeat these steps for the other sets.

Layer the Icons into Each of the Circles

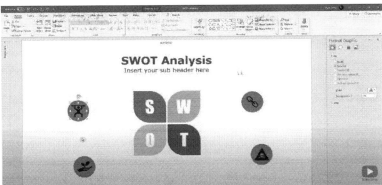

Format the icons next. If you want the **icons** to be **white** and the **circles** to match the **corresponding petals**, **select all four icons** together, select shape fill, and click **white** for the icons.

You can click on shape fill for the circles and select the **eyedropper** tool. Then **sample** the colors of each **corresponding petal**, copy the appropriate color and place it on each of the circles.

Once you are done, you can group each set to make it easier to move them around together. Select the **icon** and the **circle** in the set, click on **arrange** and select **group**.

Next, select each set and position these grouped icons in their respective quadrants. You can use the **lines** above the **icons** to position the top two icons. You can adjust the vertical positions for the bottom ones and then use the **align** tool to **align** with the top two icons.

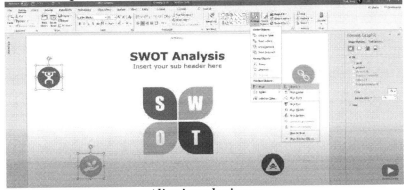

Aligning the icons

Select the **two left icons**, go to **arrange** in the **Home** tab, click on **align** and select **align left**. For the right icons, click on **arrange**, select **align** and choose **align right**.

- **Add text boxes**

The last thing you have to do is to add the **text boxes**. Draw a **text box** around the first quadrant and **align** the top and bottom to the petal.

If the box doesn't want to retain its shape, go to the **text** options in the Format tab, click on the **text box,** and select **do not autofit**.

Copy the **text box** over to the other quadrants, and for the bottom two text boxes, you can align the text to the bottom for symmetry. In each **text box**, you can write whatever you want.

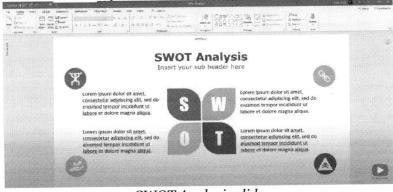

SWOT Analysis slide

This practical example should help you learn how to work with shapes and maybe even give you some ideas for your next presentation design.

How To Create Images with Shapes, Icons, And 3d Models

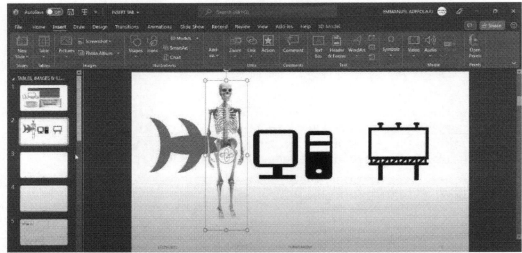

Below is another example of illustrations in Microsoft PowerPoint.
In this example, you'll learn how to create the image below using **Shapes, Icons, and 3D Models.**

Using Shapes

- **Fish Shape**

The first shape is going to be a fish shape.

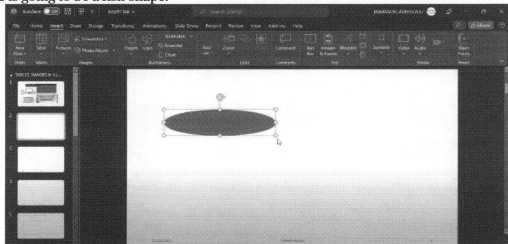

Select an oval shape and drag to draw and enlarge it

Go to **shapes** and select an **oval** shape, **drag** to draw, and enlarge it. Still, in the **shape** command, select a **moon** shape and **drag** to draw a moon shape at the left side edge of the oval shape. Turn the **moon** shape upside down. Click on **CTRL D** to duplicate the moon shape, place it in the middle of the oval shape, and then increase it.

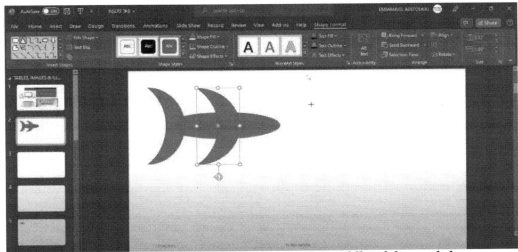

Duplicate the moon shape and place it in the middle of the oval shape

The next thing is to create the mouth of the fish. Select a **triangular** shape, turn it to the left and place the **tip** of the triangle on the **right side** of the **oval** shape.

Click the **fish's body**, hold your **CTRL** key and click on the **triangular** shape. Go to **shape** format, click on the **drop-down arrow** beside **merge shapes** and select **subtract**. This will create an opening at the **edge** of the triangular shape.

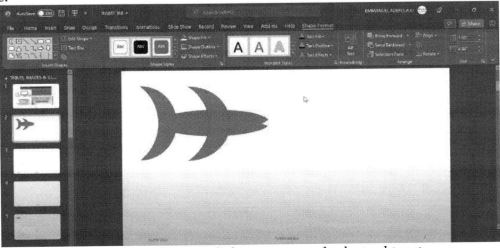

Go to shape format, click on merge and select subtract

The last thing to create in the fish icon is the eyes. Go to the **shape** icon, select an **oval** shape and draw a **circle** on the right side of your fish, close to the mouth. Select **shape fill** and fill the circle with the color **white**.

Select another **circle** in the **shapes** command and fill it with the color **black**. Make sure the **black circle** is smaller than the **white** one. Then move the **black** circle into the **white** one.

Hold your **CTRL** key, select all the shapes you've created, click on **merge shapes**, and select **union**—next, group them all. **Highlight** everything, **right-click**, select **group**, and click on the **group**.

- **Computer Shape**

To draw a computer shape, go to the **Insert** tab, click on **shapes** and select a **rounded corner rectangle**. Next, select a **rectangular** tool and drag it to increase it within the first rounded corner rectangle. The second **rectangle** should be smaller than the first.

Click on the first **rectangle**, select **shape fill**, and change the color to **black**. Change the color of the inner rectangle to **white**.

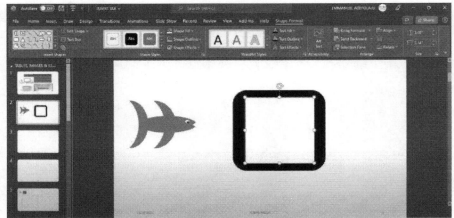
Place the second rectangle into the first one

Select another **rectangle** in the **shapes** command group and drag it below the rounded corner rectangle. This new rectangle should not be as large as the others. Select **shape fill** and fill with the color black. Select **shape outline** and click on **no outline**.

Select another **rectangle** for the **keyboard unit**. Place it below the last rectangle and drag. Fill it in with **black** color. Click on **shape outline** and select **no outline**.

Select another rectangle for the keyboard unit

You have your computer shape.

- **System Unit Shape**

To create the **system unit** shape, select a **rounded rectangle** and drag to enlarge it beside the computer. Fill it with the color black by clicking on **shape fill** and selecting **black**.

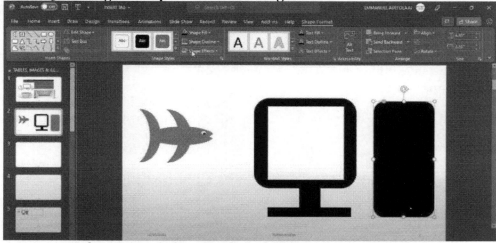
Select a rounded rectangle and fill it with the color white

Select a **rectangle** and drag it into the system unit box. Select **shape fill** and fill it with the color **white**. Press **CTRL D** to duplicate the shape and drag the duplicate under the first one.

Select an **oval** shape and draw a little **circle** at the down part of the system unit for the power button. Fill the power button with white.

Group everything (the computer and system unit) by **highlighting**, then **right-click**, select **group**, and click on **group**. Then **resize** and make everything smaller.

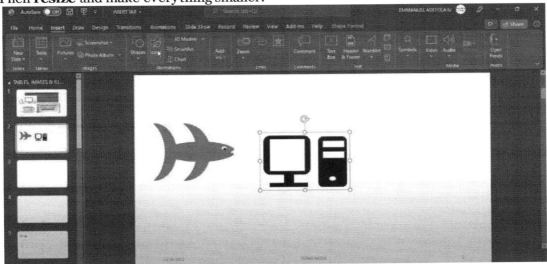

Group, then resize and make everything smaller

Using Icons

Go to the **insert** tab, then select **icons**. If you click on the **icon** command, you will see several icons you can use for your presentation.

Go to the insert tab and click Icons

Choose whatever icon you need and select **insert**. It is going to download it into your slide.

Using 3D Models

Go to the **insert** tab, then select **3D Models**. Make sure you are connected to the internet.

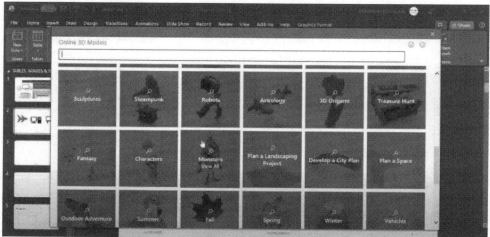

You will see many **3D Models** you can use in your presentation. You can also type whatever you are looking for in the **search box**, which will show you.

For example, if you are looking for a human skeleton, type **Human Skeleton** in the **search box,** showing you different examples of the human skeleton.

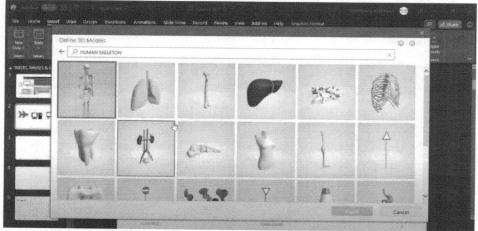

Type Human Skeleton in the search box

Select the first one and click on **insert**. It is going to download it onto your slide. When you have your **3D Image** downloaded on your slide, there is a **symbol in the middle of the skeleton**. You use this **symbol** to rotate the skeleton clockwise, anti-clockwise, to the back, and even 360 degrees. You can show any part of it you want. That is why it is **three-dimensional**.

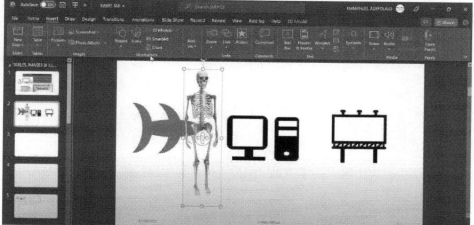

There is a symbol in the middle of the skeleton for rotation

Using Charts for Illustrations

In the **Insert** tab under **illustration** are charts. If you want to use **charts** to illustrate points within your presentation, you have all kinds of charts you can pick from, depending on your content.

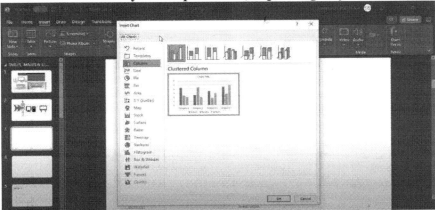

Go to the Insert tab and click on charts

For this example, use **pie charts**. All you need to do is select **charts** and click on a **pie chart**. Then click **Ok.**

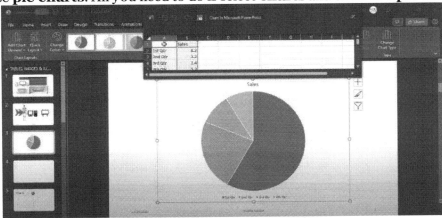

Select charts and click on pie charts

An **excel sheet** will appear at the top of your **pie chart**, allowing you to enter your **data**. To prepare a computer sales report, you will type products in the first box. Type **mouse** below it then here. **The keyboard** comes next, followed by the **Monitor** and **Printer**.

You can change the values that are already there as well. For this example, change the values to 560 for the mouse under sales, 446 for the keyboard, 378 for the monitor, and 589 for the printer.

You can increase the **excel sheet** if you wish to and even perform **calculation**s. Once you enter your data, you can close the excel sheet.

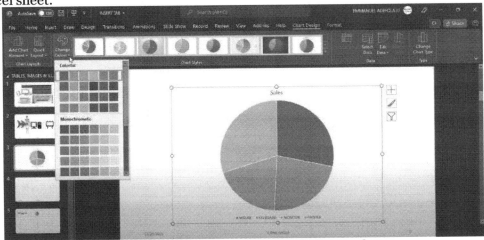

Close the excel sheet after entering your data

We have chart style under chart design if you want to format your chart. We have **charts color** if you want to change your chart's color.

You can add **chart elements** as well; an example is **chart title.**

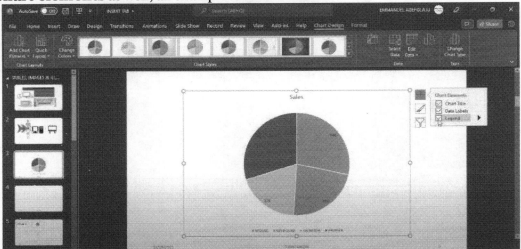

Shortcut at the right side of your slide

There is a shortcut on the right side of the slide. The shortcut includes **chart elements, chart style, and chart filter.**

The **chart elements** include your **chart title, data labels, and legend. Chart title** is for when you want to add or remove a title for your chart. Double click on the title above the chart to change it to whatever title you want.

CHAPTER 5:
Animation and Transition

Transition and Animations are beautiful PowerPoint features that give life to your presentation. Transition is a visual effect when you change from one slide to another during a presentation. On the other hand, Animation is a motion effect that you can apply to the slide objects like text, images, charts, tables, etc. Transition is applied to slides, while an animation is applied to slide objects.

Adding Transition to Slides

To add a transition to your slide:
1. Select the slide you want to add the transition to.
2. Go to the **Transitions** tab.
3. Click the drop-down arrow in the **Transition to This Slide** gallery to see the list of all the available transition effects.
4. Select your desired transition effect.

Transition Effect Options

For some of the transition effects, there are different effect options that you can choose from. The effect options available depend on the type of effect you choose.

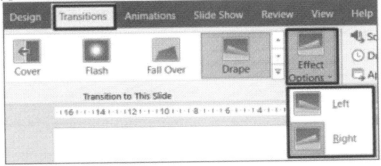

To change the transition effect options:
1. Select the slide you have added a transition.
2. Go to the **Transitions** tab in the **Transition to This Slide** group.
3. Click on the **Effect Options**. A drop-down list appears.
4. Select your preferred transition effect.

Any transition effect you select will apply to your current slide only. Click the **Apply To All** button in the **Timing** group to apply the effect to all the slides or selected slides.

Transitions Settings

-   **Duration:** All transition effects have their default duration, which might be too fast or slow for you. To set your desired effect duration, click the **Duration** text box, input your value directly, or use the up or down arrow.

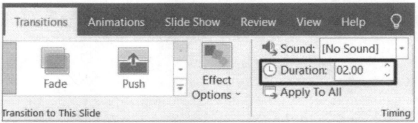

-   **Sound:** You can add a sound effect to your transition in the Sound drop-down button during the presentation. There are some available sounds you can select from and choose any sound from your computer. To choose a sound from your computer, click the **Sound** drop-down button and select **Other Sound...** A dialog box appears. Navigate through your computer to locate the sound, select it, and press **Open.**

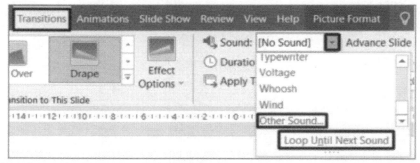

-   **Trigger:** Slides changes on mouse click during the presentation by default. If you, for any reason, want the slide to change automatically after some set time, uncheck the **On Mouse Click** box, check the **After** box, and put the time in the text box directly or use the up or down arrows. If you check both boxes, the first occurrence will change the slide, i.e., if you click the mouse before the set time, the slide will change, and if there is no mouse click, the slide will change at the specified time.

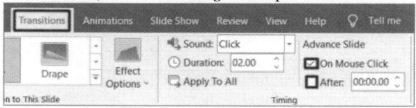

146

Transitions Preview

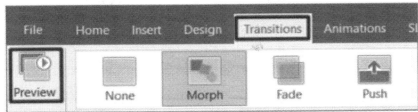

Anytime you apply a transition to your slide, you can see the effect live on your slide by default. You can always replay the preview with the **Preview** command in the **Transitions** tab.

Animating Text and Object

PowerPoint animations are in four categories, namely:
1. **Entrance**: These animations determine the way an object appears on a slide.
2. **Emphases**: These animations affect an object or text on the slide, usually used to draw attention to the object or text.
3. **Exit**: These animations determine the way an object leaves the slide.
4. **Motion Path**: These animations determine how an object moves around on a slide, e.g., an objection can move from left to right.

To add animation to an object or text:

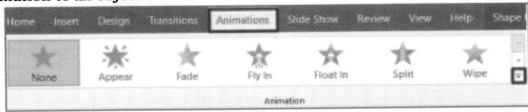

1. Select the text or object you want to animate.
2. Go to the **Animations** tab.
3. Select your desired animation effect in the **Animations** group. Use the animation gallery drop-down arrow for more options. For even more options, click on the **More --- Effects** at the bottom of the lists.

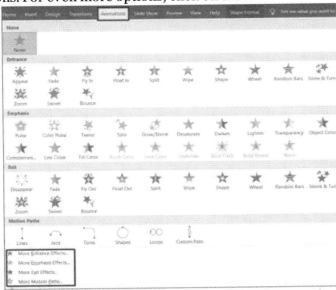

Select your preferred option from the dialog box that appears and simultaneously see the preview on your slide.
4. Press **OK**.

Animation Effect Options

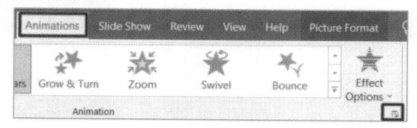

You can choose from different effect options for some of the animation effects. The effect options available depend on the type of effect you choose. For example, the default **Fly In** effect option allows the object to fly in from the bottom. You can change this setting from the top.

To change the animation effect options:
1. Select the object you have added an animation.
2. Go to the **Animation** tab in the **Animation** group.
3. Click on the **Effect Options**. A drop-down list appears.

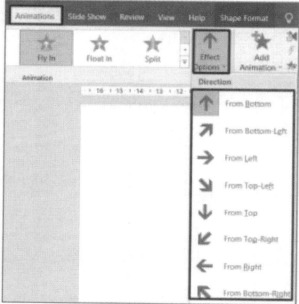

4. Select your preferred animation effect.

For more animation effect options, click on the dialog box launcher in the **Animation** group.

Animations Preview

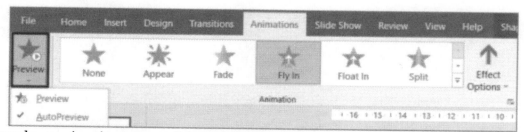

Anytime you apply an animation to your slide, you can see the effect live on your slide by default. You can always replay the preview with the **Preview** command in the Animations tab. Click the Preview drop-down button and uncheck the AutoPreview command to turn off the auto preview.

Tips:
- You can always tell the object with animation with a small number that appears on their left-top side, one for each effect. The number indicates the effect position on the mouse click in the slide.
- The slide's thumbnail with an animated object(s) will also have a star icon.
- You can preview a slide animation and transition by clicking the star beside the slide left side thumbnail.

148

Adding Multiple Animations to an Object

You can apply only one of the animation effects in the **Animation** group to an object. Any additional effect you choose from the main menu will override the initial effect.

To add multiple animation effects to an object:

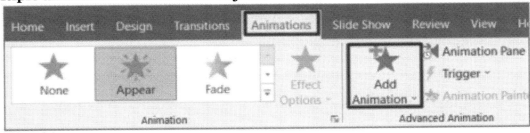

1. Select the object.
2. Go to the **Animations** tab.
3. In the **Advanced Animation** group, click **Add Animation** Button. The Animation gallery appears precisely like the one in the **Animation** group.
4. Add as many effects as you desire. Repeat the above steps to add multiple effects.

Animation Painter

When you want to apply animation effect(s) to an object just as you have applied to one, instead of going through the stress of applying the effects repeatedly, PowerPoint has a special command called **Animation Painter**. **Animation Painter** copies the animation effect(s) of one and applies it to the other.

To use an Animation Painter:

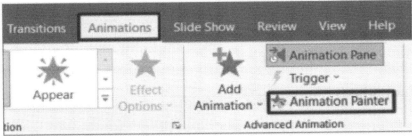

1. Select the object that has your desired animation.
2. Go to the **Animations** tab and in the **Advanced Animation** group.
3. Click the **Animation Painter**.
4. Your cursor turns to a paintbrush. Move the cursor to your slide and select the object you want to add the animation.

PowerPoint automatically adds the animation to the object like the one you copied.
Animation Painter turns itself off after each use. To keep it active for continuous use:

*   Double-click on it.
*   Press the Esc key or click on the icon when you are done.

Animation Pane

You can do your slide animations' complete and advanced settings in the animation pane. You can order, set duration, set delay, repeat, trigger, and do so many settings in the pane. Opening the animation pane for easy settings will be advisable if you have many animations to keep track of. Given below is a screenshot of an animation pane and all its elements:

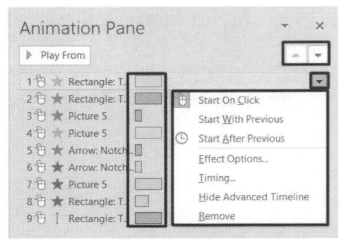

The animation pane consists of all the animation effects on the selected slide.

- The list consists of numbers arranged in the order of effects occurrence on mouse click
- The effect category color symbols
- The names of the objects that have the effects
- The advanced timelines of the effects (i.e., the effects durations)
- A drop-down arrow in front of any selected effect for advanced settings
- Two arrow up and arrow down buttons to move the selected effects up or down
- **Play From** button to preview the animation, from the selected effect to the last effect

Tips:
- Hold down the Shift key to select multiple animation effects for settings and click on the effects one after the other.
- An effect that occurs automatically (i.e., not by mouse click) does not carry a number.
- Use the drop-down arrow to access more options and to fine-tune the effects.

Animation Start Options and Trigger

Animation Start Options

By default, animations are set to start when you click your mouse. You can change this setting and make some animation effects start automatically after or with the previous one.

To start the animation effect automatically:

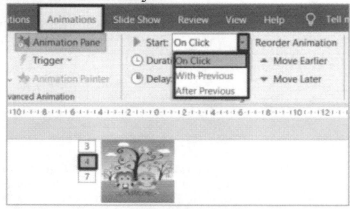

1. Select the object that has the animation and click on the effect number you want to start automatically.
2. Go to the **Animation** tab.
3. Click the Start drop-down button in the **Timing** group.
4. Select **With Previous** to start the effect at the same time as the previous effect or select **After Previous** to automatically start the effect after the occurrence of the previous effect.

Alternatively,

1. Open the **Animation Pane** in the **Animation** tab.
2. Select the animation effects you want.
3. Click the drop-down button in front of the effect.

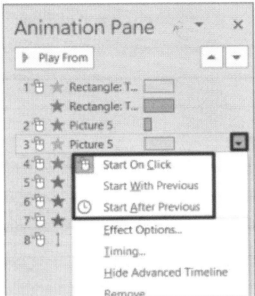

4. Select the desired option from the drop-down menu.

The first animation effect, set to start after the previous, automatically begins after the slide appears or after the transition effect of the slide, if any.

Trigger from the Same or Another Object

Apart from starting the animation of an object with a mouse click, you can also trigger the animation effect by clicking on the object with the effect or another object.

To trigger animation by clicking an object:

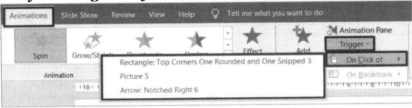

1. Go to the **Animation tab.**
2. Select the object and click the animation effect number you desire to trigger when you click an object.
3. Click the **Trigger** button in the **Advanced Animation** group. A drop menu appears.
4. Select the **On Click** command. The list of all the objects on the slide appears, including the object that bears the animation effect.
5. Select an object you wish to click to trigger your selected effect.

Ordering Animation

If you apply more than one animation on a slide, the animation will be arranged in the order you inserted them, i.e., the first animation you apply will be numbered one, the second one will be two, and so on. You can rearrange the animation order after you have applied them.

To reorder the animations on a slide:
1. Select the object you want to reorder its animation and click on the number you want to change.
2. Go to the **Animation** tab in the **Timing** group,
3. Click on either **Move Earlier** or **Move Later** buttons as desired, which order the animation with a level earlier or later. You can click the buttons several times until you get your desired number.

Alternatively, to have more control over your ordering,
1. Select the **Animation Pane** command in the **Advanced Animation** group.

The animation navigation pane appears on the right side of your window with the list of all the animation effects on the slide, starting from the first effect at the top to the last at the bottom.

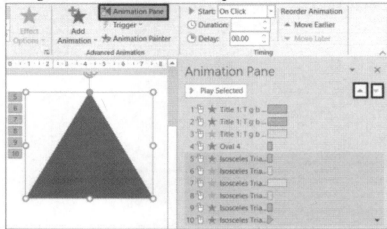

2. Select, Drag and Drop any effect to the desired level or use the arrow key up or down after selecting the effect

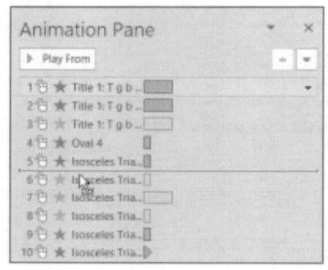

Setting Animation Duration and Delay

PowerPoint animation effects start immediately after it is triggered and play for the default duration. You can choose to delay the effect for some seconds after it has been triggered or play the effect slower or faster than the default settings.

To adjust the animation duration:

1. Go to the **Animation** tab.
2. Select the animation effect number you want to adjust its duration on the object.
3. Set your desired duration in the **Duration** textbox in the **Timing** group.

OR

1. Go to the **Animation Pane,** click, and drag the right side of the effect's **Advanced timeline** to the desired position. As you drag the timeline, use the box that shows you the **Start** and **End** time of the effect to set your desired position.

To add delay to the animation effect:

1. Go to the **Animation** tab.
2. Select the animation effect number you want to adjust its duration on the object.
3. Set your desired delay in the **Delay** textbox in the **Timing** group.

OR

1. Go to the **Animation Pane,** click, and drag the whole effect's **Advanced timeline** to the desired position. As you drag the timeline, use the box that shows you the **Start** and **End** time of the effect to set your desired position.

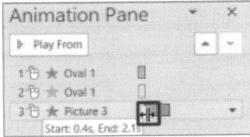

Note: The animation effect duration will be affected if you click and drag the left side of the Advanced Timeline.

Make Text Appear One by One During a Presentation

PowerPoint animation can reveal your text paragraph by paragraph during a presentation. It can be a helpful feature as it can display your points as you want to discuss them by clicking.

To reveal your text paragraph by paragraph:

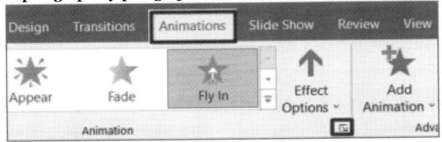

1. Select the text box that contains the point you want to display one by one.
2. Go to the **Animations** tab.

3. Click the **Animation** group dialog box launcher.
4. Click the **Text Animation** tab in the **Effects Options** dialog box that appears.
5. Click the **Group text** drop-down button.

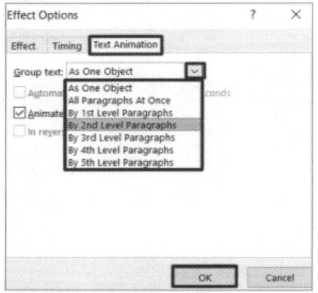

6. Select an option from the drop-down list as desired.
   - **By 1st Level Paragraph** will bring a paragraph with its sublevels at once.
   - **By 2nd Level Paragraph** will bring a paragraph first and all its sublevels next.
   - **By 3rd Level Paragraph** will bring a paragraph first, its first sublevel next, and all other sublevels next. Etc.
7. Press **OK** when done.

Repeat Animation

At times and for a particular reason, you may want your animation effect to repeat several times or continuously until you take action.

To set your animation effect to repeat:

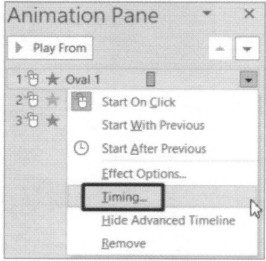

1. Go to the **Animation** tab.
2. Click the **Animation Pane** in the **Timing** group.
3. Select and click the drop-down button of the effect you want to repeat in the animation pane.
4. Select **Timing**... from the drop-down menu. The effect dialog box appears.

154

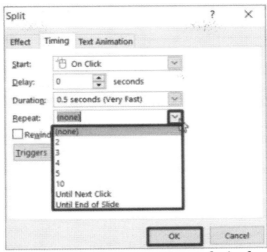

5. Click the **Repeat** drop-down menu and select an option as desired.
6. Press **OK.**

Remove Animations

To remove animation from an object:
1. Select the object you want to remove its animation effect
2. Go to the **Animation** tab.
3. Set the animation to **None.**

OR
1. Select **Animation Pane.**
2. Select and click the drop-down button of the effect.
3. Select **Remove** in the drop-down list.

Animating with Morph Transition

Morph transition is used for a smooth animation when moving objects from slides to slides during a presentation. It is a fantastic PowerPoint feature that can make your communication easy and classic. For Morph transition to work perfectly, you must have at least two identical slides, i.e., the slides must have at least one object in common. You can duplicate the slides or copy the objects from slide to slide to achieve this.

To animate with Morph transition:

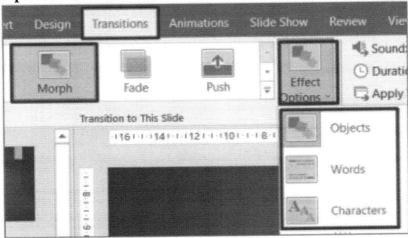

1. Prepare a slide with all the elements you want.
2. Right-click on the slide Thumbnail pane on the left. A drop-down list appears.
3. Select **Duplicate** to reproduce the slide. Duplicate the slides as often as you need a smooth movement of objects between slides.

155

4. Reposition the objects in the duplicated slides as desired.
5. Select all the slides you duplicated except the first slide.
6. Go to the **Transitions** tab.
7. Select **Morph** in the **Transition to This Slide** gallery.
8. Select the **Effect Options** to choose how the transition should work.
9. Click the Slide Show to preview the effect.

Notes:
- **Morph** transition creates an appearance of movement of objects in different locations from one slide to the other; therefore, you do not need to add animation to the object you want to morph. Animation effect overrides morph transition.
- Objects like text, shapes, pictures, SmartArt graphics, and WordArt **Morphs.** However, Charts do not morph but disappear from an initial position to reappear in the new position from slide to slide.

Tips:
You can morph one object into a different object in another slide by renaming the two objects with the same name and with **!!** in front of the names.

To rename an object:

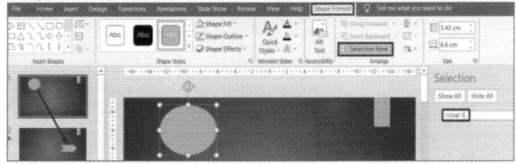

1. Select the object.
2. Go to the object contextual **Format** tab (or **Home** tab and click the **Select** button in the **Editing** group).
3. Click the **Selection Pane.**
4. Double click on the object name in the selection pane to activate the edit mode.
5. Rename the object starting with **!!**
6. Go to the second slide with the second object and rename the object with the same name as the previous one.
7. Apply **Morph** transition to the second slide.
8. Go to the Slide mode and preview how the first shape morphs smoothly into the second shape.

CHAPTER 6:
Managing Slides and PowerPoint Window

Saving Your Presentation

After creating your presentation, you need to save it for subsequent use or presentation. You can save your presentation on your computer, disk drive, CD drive, USB drive, or OneDrive. Saving your work in OneDrive allows you to access your presentation anywhere you can log in to your account. To save your presentation in OneDrive, you must be connected and signed into your account.

To save your presentation for the first time:

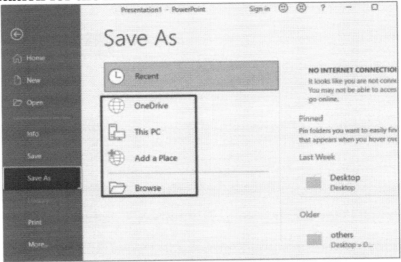

1. Click on the **File** tab to go to the backstage PowerPoint.
2. Click **Save As** option in the left-side pane.
3. Select where you want to save your presentation in the right-side pane. A dialog box appears.
4. Change the file name to your desired name in the **File Name** box.
5. Select the format in which you want to save your presentation in the **Save as type** dropdown list or leave it as **PowerPoint Presentation (.pptx)**
6. Click **Save.**

You will have to save your work anytime you make changes.

To save your presentation subsequently,

1. Click on the **Save** icon 🖫 in the quick access toolbar or the **Save** tab in the backstage view.

Alternatively,

2. Use the shortcut key **Ctrl + s.**

Note: Using the above methods for the presentation that has never been saved will initiate the **Save as** command.

You can also duplicate your already saved presentation with the same or different name and in the same or different location by selecting the **Save As** option in the PowerPoint backstage.

Tips on file formats:

- You can run your presentation as a video on many media players by saving it as **MPEG-4 Video** or **Windows Media Video.**
- You can also turn your presentation into a graphic with an animation effect for use on a web page by saving it as **GIF.**
- PowerPoint Show opens your presentation in Slide Show view when clicked.

Slide Setup for Printing

You can get a hard or paper copy of your presentation by printing.

To print your presentation:

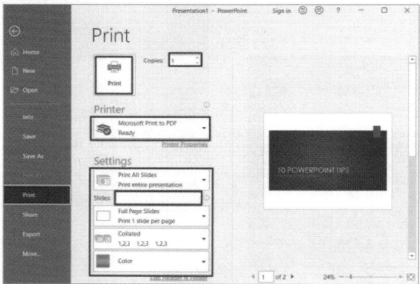

1. Ensure you connect your computer to a printer.
2. Ensure you load your printer with the right size paper.
3. Click the **File** tab to go to the PowerPoint backstage.
4. Select **Print** in the left side pane. **Print** pane appears on the right side.
5. Input the number of copies you want directly or with the arrows in the **Copies** box.
6. Select a printer in the **Printer** drop-down if you connect your computer to more than one printer.
7. Under **Settings**, each box shows the default settings. To make changes to any, click the drop-down in front of the one you want to change and select your preferred option in the drop-down menu.

   - You can print specified slide numbers by inputting the numbers and separated by a comma in the **Slides** textbox.
   - Collated style is applicable when you want to print more than one presentation copy.

8. Preview your work in the right section of the **Print** pane to see how it will come out. Make use of the scroll bar to go through the pages.
9. Click the **Print** button.

Slide Show

Slide Setup for Presentation

After preparing your presentation, PowerPoint has a lot of options for you to set up your slide show preparation for presenting your presentation. For example, you might want your slide show to play on its own continuously until you press the **Esc** key, maybe for advertisement or some other reasons.

To set up your presentation:

1. Go to the **Slide Show** tab.
2. Click the **Set Up Slide Show** command in the **Set Up** group. A dialog box appears.

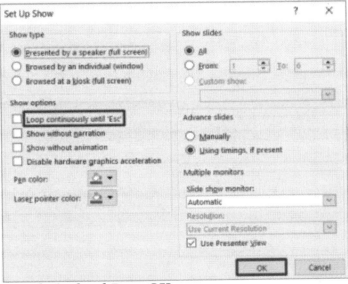

3. Make all your settings as desired and Press **OK**.

Rehearse and Record Your Presentation

Other options in the **Set Up** group of the **Slide Show** ribbon are:

- **Rehearse Timings**

This command, when clicked, takes you to the slide show view and allows you to present your presentation while it records the time. Press the **Esc** key when you are done, and you will see the time it takes you to make the presentation with a prompt to **save** the timing or not. You can use this feature to rehearse your presentation as often as possible to keep up with time during the actual presentation.

- **Record Slide Show**

You can record your presentation and voice with this command for a self-running slide show. Selecting the command takes you to the slide show view, which records your presentation as you present.

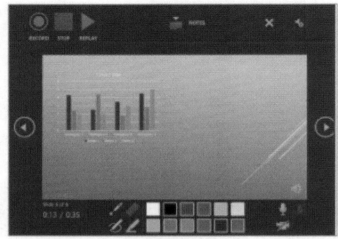

Click the red Record icon on the top-left side of the slide. Start presenting after the countdown number. You can pause, stop, and replay your record with the other buttons on the top-left side of the slide. Also available on the slide screen are drawing tools you can use during recording and some other options for settings before you start recording. Use the arrow keys on both sides to change the slide. Press the **Esc** key and save or share your presentation as a video or PowerPoint file as desired. Your presentation automatically starts playing when anyone opens it and selects play.

Presenting Your Presentation

To Start your Presentation:
There are different ways you can start your presentation. You can:

- Click the **Start from Beginning** icon in the **Quick Access Toolbar** or press **F5**

- Click the Slide Show View in the Status bar.

- Go to the **Slide Show** tab and start the presentation by selecting either **From Current Slide** or **From Beginning.** You can as well access more slide show options from here.

Selecting any of the above options makes your presentation appears in full-screen mode.
Using the Presentation Tools and Features:
Move your cursor to the bottom-left of your presentation in the slideshow view tools and options you can use for presenting.

- The first two arrows are for changing the slide.

- The next icon ⬚ is used to change your cursor to a drawing tool or a laser pointer. You can change the highlighter's color from the menu that appears, select a tool for your presentation, and drag it to draw or highlight as desired. An eraser is also there to clean your marking.

See all Slides/commands that will display all your slides for you to select and jump to the desired slide.

- **Zoom into the slide**/icon, when clicked, will allow you to move to any part of your slide and zoom in.
- **More Slideshow options** icon opens a menu box where you can select any desired option. For example, you can access your computer taskbar during a presentation by clicking **Screen** and selecting **Show Taskbar**. **Show Presenter View** gives you access to a special set of controls (reference slides notes, preview next slide, presentation duration, and much more) on your screen. The audience will not see the control if you present with a second display like a projector.

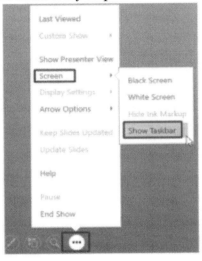

To Move from Slide to Slide:

- Click your mouse or press the spacebar to move to the next slide.
- Use the arrow keys down or right to move to the next slide. Also, use the arrow key up or down to go back to the previous slide on your keyboard.
- Move your cursor to the bottom left of your presentation screen. Click on any of the arrows in the presentation tools to move your slide accordingly.

To Stop your Presentation:

- Press the **Esc** key on your keyboard or
- Click the **Slide Show Option** at the bottom-left of your presentation and Select **End Show** from the pop-up menu.

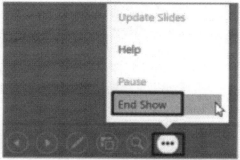

Your presentation automatically stops when it gets to the last slide. You can click your mouse or press the spacebar to return to the Normal view.

Protecting Your File with PowerPoint Security Feature

After devoting your time and energy to creating your presentation, it will be necessary if you protect your sensitive presentation from plagiarism, stealing, indeliberate editing, and so many forms of security threats.
PowerPoint has impressive security features to help you secure your presentation based on how sensitive the presentation is.

To secure your PowerPoint presentation:
1. Go to the PowerPoint Backstage by clicking the **File** tab.
2. Click the **Info** tab in the left side pane. Info pane appears on the right side.
3. Click the **Protect Presentation** button. A dialog box appears.

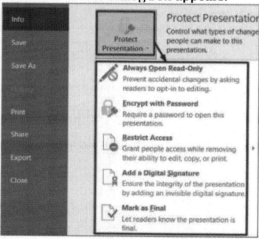

Select an option from the list.

- o **Mark as Final:** This makes your presentation read-only (i.e., typing, editing, and proofing capabilities disabled) with a message at the top of the presentation screen informing the reader that the presentation is final. However, any reader can still edit and resave the presentation by clicking the **Edit Anyway** button in the top message. Select this security feature only if you just need to notify the reader that it is the recommended final version of your presentation or to discourage editing.
- o **Add a Digital Signature:** Protecting your presentation with a digital signature has several benefits, like maintaining proof of presentation integrity, signer identity, and others. You must purchase a digital signature from a verified Microsoft partner to use it. Selecting this option for the first time will prompt you to where you can get one.
- o **Restrict Access:** This gives people access to your presentation but restricts them from copying, editing, sharing, or printing it. You will have to connect to the Information Right Management (IRM) server to help you secure the presentation. This option will prompt you to connect and lead you through the process.
- o **Restrict Editing:** This is a flexible way of securing your presentation from editing and giving control over the type of editing that the allowed people can do. This option opens a pane on the

right side of the presentation for you to set formatting and editing restrictions and **start enforcement**.

- o **Encrypt with Password:** Adding a password to your presentation is a strong form of protection, and you can give the password to only those you want access to your presentation. Without the password, nobody will be able to open your presentation, not to talk about editing. Selecting this option, PowerPoint asks you to enter a password and to re-enter it for confirmation.
- o **Always Open Read-Only:** This feature prevents your presentation from accidental editing by always opening it as read-only. A dialog box appears each time you want to open it, notifying you that the presentation will be opened as read-only. Press **Yes** to continue and **No** if there is a need to make changes.

4. Follow all the prompts based on your choice and press ok.
5. Close your presentation for the security setting to take effect.

Closing Your PowerPoint

To close your presentation after you are done:
- Click the **X** button at the top-right corner of the PowerPoint window, Or
- Go to the **File** tab and select the **Close** option in the left-side pane, Or
- Use the shortcuts keys, **Ctrl + F4** or **Ctrl + W.**

Microsoft PowerPoint closes or notifies you if you try to close your presentation without saving it.

Recovering Unsaved Presentation

It can happen that you mistakenly close your presentation without saving your last changes; the good news is that PowerPoint has an **autosave** feature that allows you to recover your file with the last unsaved changes.

To recover your unsaved presentation:
1. Go to the backstage view by clicking on the **File** tab.
2. Click the **Open** tab. **Open** pane appears.
3. Click the **Recover Unsaved Presentations** button at the bottom of the recently opened presentation list. The location dialog box appears with the list of unsaved presentations.

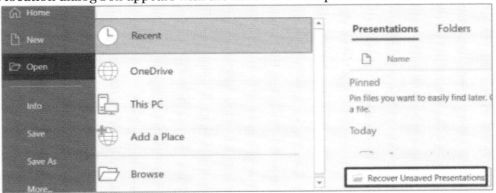

4. Select the likely presentation. You can check the date to know the likely one.
5. Click the **Open** button. The presentation opens.
6. Save the presentation accordingly.

Alternatively,
1. Go to the backstage view by clicking on the **File** tab.
2. Click the **Info** tab. Info pane opens.
3. Select **Manage Presentation** drop-down.
4. Click the **Recover Unsaved Presentations** menu that appears. The location dialog box appears with the list of unsaved presentations.

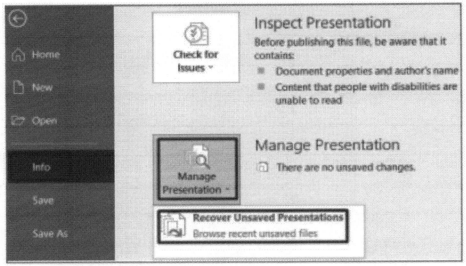

5. Follow **steps 4-6** above.

Opening Saved Presentation

You can open your presentation from the PowerPoint application or directly from your device.

To open an existing presentation from PowerPoint:
1. Go to the backstage view by clicking on the **File** tab.
2. Click the **Open** tab. **Open** pane appears.
3. Select the location of your presentation. An **Open** dialog box appears.
4. Select the folder or your presentation. You can scroll down the left side list of locations on your device to locate your presentation.
5. Click **Open**.

Alternatively, if you recently opened your presentation or pinned it to PowerPoint, it will be available in the **Recent** or **Pinned** list in the backstage **Home** panel, and you can click on it to open it.

If you often use or work on your presentation, it will be better to pin it in the PowerPoint.

To pin your presentation to PowerPoint:
1. Locate the Presentation in the recent list.
2. Move your cursor over the presentation.
3. Click the pin icon in front of the file.

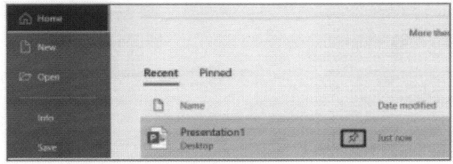

To open an existing presentation from your device:
1. Ensure you have a PowerPoint application installed on your computer.
2. Locate your PowerPoint presentation on your device.
3. Double-click on it, and it opens.

CHAPTER 7:
MS PowerPoint Keyboard Shortcut Commands

Working with Keyboard shortcut commands can reduce your stress, save your time and increase your productivity to a huge extent. Below are the top shortcut commands you can use to work smartly in PowerPoint.

SN	Shortcut Keys	Functions
1.	**Ctrl + A**	To select all the contents of a slide or text placeholder
2.	**Ctrl + B**	To bold the highlighted texts
3.	**Ctrl + C**	To copy the selected item
4.	**Ctrl + D**	To duplicate the active slide
5.	**Ctrl + E**	To center align the selected text
6.	**Ctrl + F**	To open the **Find** dialog box
7.	**Ctrl + G**	To group selected items
8.	**Ctrl + H**	To open the **Replace** dialog box.
9.	**Ctrl + I**	To italicize highlighted text
10.	**Ctrl + J**	To justify aligning selected content
11.	**Ctrl + K**	To open the **Insert Hyperlink** dialog box.
12.	**Ctrl + L**	To left-align selected text.

13.	Ctrl + M	To insert a new blank slide
14.	Ctrl + N	To create a new blank presentation
15.	Ctrl + O	To open an existing presentation
16.	Ctrl + P	To go to **the Print** tab in the backstage view
17.	Ctrl + Q	To close the presentation
18.	Ctrl + R	To the right, align selected text
19.	Ctrl + S	To save your presentation
20.	Ctrl + T	To open the Font dialog box
21.	Ctrl + U	To underline the selected text.
22.	Ctrl + V	To paste what you copied last.
23.	Ctrl + W	To close your presentation
24.	Ctrl + X	To cut selected item
25.	Ctrl + Y	To redo the last action, you undo.
26.	Ctrl + Z	To undo your last action
27.	Ctrl + Shift +C	To copy Format
28.	Ctrl + Shift + G	To Ungroup Selected items
29.	Ctrl + Shift + F	To open the Fonts tab of the **Format Cells** dialog box.
30.	Ctrl + Shift + >	To increase the selected text font size
31.	Ctrl + Shift + <	To decrease the selected text font size
32.	PgDn	To move to the next slide
33.	PgUp	To go to the Previous Page
34.	Shift + F3	To toggle the selected test cases
35.	Shift F10	To display the context menu
36.	Esc	To cancel an active command
37.	F1	To open Microsoft PowerPoint **Help**
38.	F5	To go to the slideshow view of the presentation
39.	F7	To open the Spelling checker pane
40.	Alt + F4	To Exit your presentation

41.	**Alt + W + Q**	To open the Zoom dialog box.
42.	**Alt + Shift + V**	To paste formatting only to another Shape
43.	**Alt + Ctrl + Shift + >**	Superscript selected item
44.	**Alt + Ctrl + Shift + <**	Subscript selected item
45.	**Alt + F**	To go to the **File** tab
46.	**Alt + H**	To go to the **Home** tab
47.	**Alt + N**	To go to the **Insert** tab
48.	**Alt + G**	To go to the **Design** tab
49.	**Alt + T**	To go to the **Transition** tab
50.	**Alt + A**	To go to the **Animation** tab
51.	**Alt + S**	To go to the **Slideshow** tab
52.	**Alt + R**	To go to the **Review** tab
53.	**Alt+ W**	To go to the **View** tab
54.	**Alt + Q**	To search item

CONCLUSION

If you are reading this part of this book, you have successfully gone through this user guide. I commend you for your patience and time invested in seeing this through until the end.

No doubt, I am sure you have been able to acquire new knowledge as a beginner and more knowledge as an advanced learner. However, if this is not done yet, you can go online to get more knowledge to increase more and more in proficiency with the use of Microsoft PowerPoint.

Finally, do not forget to recommend this user guide to your family, friends, colleagues, and counterparts.

Thank you for reading!

BOOK 4:

MICROSOFT ONE NOTE

2022

The Most Updated Crash Course from Beginner to Advanced Learn All the Functions to Become a Pro in 7 Days or Less and Be More Productive and Organized

INTRODUCTION

Microsoft OneNote is a tool that automatically syncs and saves your notes so you can access them anywhere, whether you're on your phone, PC, or any device with access to the web. So if you're using it on a computer and accessing it across any of your devices, you could go to your phone, install the app, log into your account and access the same information from there

OneNote is one of the best note-taking apps in the universe, and you can gather as many collaborators as needed via the program. Microsoft creates beautifully designed programs with top-notch inbuilt quality that brings users closer to technology via a better interface that establishes a user-gadget relationship. Furthermore, with OneNote, Microsoft brings the best note-taking program to users worldwide.

Microsoft OneNote is a workbook that can always contain more. Capable of performing the functions of all supplies in your desk drawer, OneNote is the perfect organizer. By familiarizing yourself with this software application, you can relieve stress by systematizing all your notes, graphs, links, etc. Take advantage of the many functions with the help of these Microsoft OneNote tips and tricks.

The OneNote software application will allow you to carry out various activities easily as you enjoy the latest technology. You can, for instance, scribble down ideas, write loosely structured notes, make digital notes that you can, later on, organize and bind

Besides being a great digital notebook, OneNote can be a very effective information organizer. You do not have to go through the hassle of organizing important information all the time since this software will make things very easy for you. It is the best digital idea processor you will use by far.

Take notes, brainstorm ideas, create lists, and store articles on the web for later reading - collecting all this information can lead to disorganized clutter. We need a place to store everything to find it when needed. The best note-taking applications consolidate all your ideas, regardless of the format they take, making them searchable and searchable.

Microsoft OneNote is one of the best options on the market. It is designed to keep all your information in one place and make it accessible to you, regardless of the device you have on hand because it offers Android, iOS, macOS, Windows, and web applications.

CHAPTER 1:
Understanding Microsoft OneNote

In other words, this app helps one with a hectic schedule to be more organized and to ensure that all their marvelous and intriguing ideas are captured for later reference. It is usual for humans to forget, and we tend to forget a lot. More often than not, you get an idea, and since you did not put it down on pen and paper, you try as hard as you can to remember what the idea you had at the time was, to no avail. By learning how to use OneNote, those days are as good as behind you. Read on to discover everything you need to know to create a paperless life with OneNote.

When it comes to OneNote, you can expect to capture, organize and share all of the notes you will be placed in your notebook. Truly, this innovative software will be the help that you need.

Who Should Use OneNote?

OneNote is most welcomed by the majority of people who hate paper trails. Having a desk full of piles and papers is just unsightly and can also mess with your morale to work, considering you have to go through the papers. With OneNote, one need not worry about that mess as the app is more organized, giving you a clear head and leaving you refreshed as you decide where to start. When your mind is clear, your work becomes a tad easier, which is why you should learn how to use OneNote.

Why Use OneNote

When shopping for an application, you have in mind what you want the app to help you do. However, in most cases, you will come across numerous apps that can perform the simpler functions that you need to be done. With the wide variety of note-taking applications available in the market today, it is hard to decide which of them will meet your note-taking needs best. The truth is, all the apps out there can help you take notes the ordinary way. However, there is much more to taking notes than just typing what you want to capture and saving it on your device. One element distinguishing OneNote from other note-taking apps is its unique features that add value to the note-taking process. These features are discussed in detail later in this guide, but here are some of the things that the OneNote app enables you to do:

- **Organize lists**: Notes taken on OneNote can be shared with other people, and any changes made by other people in your circle become visible to everyone in the group. This feature decreases the chances of forgetting to purchase something you need or a last-minute requirement for a project.
- **Create recipe lists**: If your recipe book takes a beating due to over-use, you can transfer your recipes to OneNote. You have the option to organize them based on the main food items that you use.
- **Locate favorite news items**: You may not realize it yet, but as you browse the internet and add content to your OneNote, the app allows you to list the content in the order of your favorite items. This makes it easy to reaccess them so you can read them whenever possible. This feature works well for articles and recipes.
- **Make audio/video recordings**: When using the full version of OneNote, you can record audio and video notes to attach to your notes.
- **Convert Images to Text**: This is probably one of the best features of OneNote. It allows you to take a picture of a page in a book you love, and it will quickly be converted to text as long as it is easy to understand. You need not transcribe it one by one.

All these capabilities and much more make OneNote a practical and easy-to-use application. As you go through this guide, you will discover many essential features of OneNote that make it the ideal application for note-taking. If you are wondering how other people use OneNote, you will be pleased to know some of them use it the same way you want to. They use the application to take notes about lessons they learn in school, deliberations from a work meeting, and capture reminders of things they do not want to forget. Some people use Microsoft OneNote to improve their lives in a significant way.

For example, schools want to be able to show video clips and enable students to listen to audio clips without duplication. Finding software capable of doing that became an easy task when they tried out Microsoft 365 equipped with OneNote. They realized that this software makes organizing, sharing, and note-taking easier.

Various schools started by testing the effectiveness of Microsoft 365 in different groups and departments. The initial results of these tests were favorable, with most group members showcasing their creativity. As time passed, the teams started learning more about the stuff that this suite of applications allows them to do. These test outcomes informed the schools' decision to use OneNote for overall note-taking.

Besides students, some teachers use OneNote to connect with their classes. For instance, some teachers create shared notebooks so students understand the lessons better. At the same time, the notebooks also contain necessary details on upcoming quizzes and examinations. The use of OneNote is taking note-taking to a whole new level.

How OneNote is Organized

OneNote is organized by Notebooks, sections, and pages similar to printed, spiral-bound notebooks.

- **Notebooks**: These are the major organization category.
- **Sections in the current Notebook**: Sections let you organize notes by activities, topic, or people in your life. You start with a few in each notebook.
- **Pages in the current section**: Create as many note pages in each section as you want or as necessary.

After understanding how OneNote is organized, it is time for you to advance to the next level as you need to learn how to create your notebook.

The Design and Basics of OneNote

The great thing about the OneNote is its ability to look similar to the physical notebook. This design is perfect for users who are not ready to let go of their notebooks yet but would like to have the convenience of using an application.

Expect to Have Multiple Notebooks

This is similar to having a lot of subjects in school. You cannot expect that all the lessons you have learned in Science will also be in the same notebook wherein you would place all your notes in Math. You need to have separate notebooks to know what to get.

With OneNote, there will be available tabs for each notebook you have. As you can already guess, each tab refers to a section of the notebook that you possibly would like to pay attention to. For example, if one tab refers to your grocery list and you need to do your grocery, you can click on this and scan through it instead of having one long list of not only your grocery list but also the other things that you plan on doing.

If you have created new tabs but cannot find them in the multiple notebooks that you already have, simply go to Quick Notes because this is where the new notes are placed.

Share Your Notebook

If you would like other people to have input about the notebook you have made, you can simply share it with others. After some time, you can also see their creative input on the notes you have placed.

Understanding Different Versions of OneNote

OneNote has a variety of versions depending on the operating system. The complete OneNote version runs on Windows.

Windows Version

If you use Windows on a touch screen enabled laptop or computer, you can use OneNote in the best possible way. The application allows you to take notes with a stylus; if you wish, you can convert them to text so that they are there the next time you want to refer to them.

You can use the inking tools to highlight text for emphasis. You may add circles or squares depending on how you think the details should be highlighted. You may also embed files that you already have in Microsoft Office to OneNote, so you access this data fast whenever you need to. It is possible to embed excel sheets, though of smaller sizes.

Keeping data in separate files might be challenging without using an application like OneNote. Your data would get all mixed up. With OneNote, you have the power to keep your items in separate files and update them regularly. Though a Windows phone is designed to do all these things, installing the OneNote application enhances its ability to organize data.

iOS Version

The iOS version of OneNote comes with handwriting features that convert written notes to text. A user can convert the text or leave it as it is. This may then be linked to personal or business accounts. It is ideal for capturing good moments or sharing funny images with other people without mixing them up with other work-related items. Previously, it was challenging to use OneNote on iOS devices due to small screens. However, this has changed significantly as larger iOS devices became available in the market.

Android Version

Android offers the latest version of OneNote. It is a direct competition to GoogleKeep, which offers seemingly similar functions. Unlike iOS, OneNotecan creates different widgets that allow you to immediately access the notes you need by simply scribbling or placing a code. You can also take pictures with your phone and add them to the application. In case you opt to be reminded of your notes and own an Android watch, you may choose to access such notes on your watch. This OneNote feature on Android platforms makes everything highly accessible.

Mac Version

Though the Mac version is somewhat similar to OneNote'sWindows version, a few noticeable differences are observed. The Mac version allows for sharing of notes with other people but does not allow users to add multiple accounts. This means that one has to choose whether they only want to create a personal notebook or a work notebook.

Now that you know the various OneNote versions available, you can decide which version is most helpful to you and make an informed choice. Depending on your platform, you will find it easier to tackle problems that come your way. Not to mention, the work is saved seamlessly and can be accessed through any device that you are already signed in.

CHAPTER 2:
Saving, Syncing, and Sharing

After working on your notebook, several actions can be taken to ensure you keep track of your note. This section covers those actions which you can take to keep your notebooks secure. You can decide to share your notebook, a page, or a section with others, export, or just save them. To know more about how you can achieve these, let's go.

Sharing

If you want to share your "Personal" Notebook with anybody, you need to move it to OneDrive. To do this, open your "Personal" Notebook, navigate to "File," and then go down to your share option; what you'll see in there is it says to share this notebook, so you'll need to put it in OneDrive or SharePoint. You're going to put that in OneDrive by selecting it. You could also browse for it if you don't have it listed here. You can name your notebook and choose "Move notebook." You will get a message saying the notebook is now syncing to the new location; click on "OK." Now that you've done that, you'll see that you now have all of your share options because you've now put it in a location where sharing is available.

It's not necessary to always share the entire notebook; if you prefer, you can only share a single page from the notebook. So, if you want to share a page from your notebook, make sure you've clicked on the page that you want to share, go up to the Home tab, and you'll see you have an option here to "Email page," keyboard shortcut Ctrl + Shift + E. What it does is it will open up an outlook email, and it's going to attach the contents of that page. You can select who you want to share this with and send that email. The user receives an email with the notebook's name and an open button. If they hit that, it'll open up the notebook in the browser, and if that user changes, it will sync that change, and, in your notebook, you'll see the difference, with a little marker indicating that the user added it.

Syncing and Saving

One important thing to remember when sharing notebooks is that multiple people can access and edit a notebook anytime. So, your notebook must be synchronized to ensure data is updated immediately.

To do this, go to the File tab and ensure you are in the "Info" area. What you'll see over on the right-hand side is you have a button here to view sync status, which will show all of the notebooks you have and whether they're synchronized, and the last time they were updated.

The option automatically selected is to sync automatically whenever there are changes. So, if you've shared this notebook with five other people and they're all in this notebook making changes, any changes they make are automatically synchronized so that you can see them.

However, if you prefer to sync manually, you have the option as well, and as soon as you do that, it puts a cross over each of these notebooks just to let you know that they're not currently synchronizing, and you can choose which one you want to sync.

So, if you click "Sync Now," the icon will change and any updates made since the last sync will be updated. If you have a lot of notebooks in here, to make this easier, you have a single button at the top to "Sync All."

Password Protection

Another thing you might want to do when sharing your notebooks is password-protect notebook sections. This prevents unauthorized access to specific sections of your notebook that you don't want people to see. If you want people to see everything in one section but not another, you must right-click and select "Password protect This section," click "Set Password." Now, if you share this notebook, people aren't able to see what's in that particular section.

To unprotect, right-click, go back into "Password protect This Section," select "Remove password," and type it in to remove that protection.

Exporting Notebooks

Many of us use OneNote notebooks to organize our lives. It is important to know how to backup your OneNote because technology can fail and when it does, you want to make sure your materials are safe and secure, so it is necessary to backup your work. It is highly recommended that you do this at some point, especially as you get towards the end of the school year and leave for the summer or work with other team members. Backing up your notebook in OneNote is a great idea.

There are cases where you may not have access to OneDrive. Let's say you're getting a new job, moving to a different district, for some unforeseeable reason, your server goes down, or you need access when you're not online, you need to export your OneNote. To do this, go to your "Files" tab, and instead of choosing "Save," you're going to choose "Export." You'll get several options. You can export a page, that's handy if you just want to share a page with somebody; you can share a section, or for your use, you can export your entire OneNote notebook, and you will have file types to choose from. You can export them as PDFs but can't edit them in the future. To export your OneNote as a package so you can upload it into OneNote in the future as its full functioning self, you'll need to select "OneNote Package," and then you just click the export button.

You're going to tell it where to save on your device, and you have your OneNote notebook saved on your hard drive for loading whatever you want, wherever you want, whether you are online or not.

This can also be done for group notebooks, so if you're in charge of your group's notebook, this is a good idea to do every once in a while, but it's also handy for individual notebooks.

CHAPTER 3:
How to Get Started

OneNote is a free digital note-taking app from Microsoft that you can use to capture ideas and thoughts. You can use it to create notes and add content to them, and it stores your notes in the cloud. This is great if you're in a classroom taking notes, in a business meeting, or just for everyday life, family life, planning a vacation, and want to put all these ideas in one spot.

How to Get OneNote

You may be thinking of how to take advantage of OneNote and how to get to OneNote. Well, the good news is OneNote comes with Windows 10, so if you have a Windows 10 device, you already have it.

How do you get OneNote? You can go down to the search field and type in **"OneNote,"** What you'll see happen is that OneNote will show up as the best match on the list. You can now click on it, and the OneNote app will open up. If you are a Windows 11 user, unfortunately, this application doesn't come pre-installed. You need to visit Microsoft Store; there, you can find OneNote.

Another way you could also get OneNote is from your web browser. You could simply open up your web browser and then go to **office.com**. This is how you're going to access OneNote. Click on **sign-in,** and if you have a Microsoft account, you sign in with your Microsoft account. If you don't have a Microsoft account, you could create one accessible by clicking on the create one button.

As earlier said, OneNote stores all your notes in the cloud, and because they're in the cloud, it can sync those notes between all the devices you're using. So if you create a note on your phone, you'll immediately see it on your desktop. For the syncing to work, you need to log into OneNote, and to do this, you need a Microsoft account; this could be one that you use at work or school with office 365 or from another Microsoft service like Outlook and so on.

Once you sign in, you'll land on office.com and see that you can access OneNote by clicking on the OneNote icon. In addition to OneNote, you could also get Word, Excel, and PowerPoint through office.com, and if you have a phone, whether an Android device or an iOS device, you can also download the OneNote app from the App Store or the Google Play Store and you can install that on your phone.

The Hierarchy

A great feature of OneNote is that you can create your hierarchy structure. There are three primary levels, the highest level Is the Notebook, and just like the physical notebook, it can hold many pages. The next level down is Sections. Think of this like chapters in a book. And finally, there are Pages. These hold your actual notes.

You can cluster multiple sections into a section group if you need more hierarchy levels. After you create a group, you can drag sections into the group. Another level you can create is Sub-pages. You need at least two pages in a specific section to use them.

For example, let's say you have a page with your meeting notes from Excel Conferences. You can create sub-pages with the notes for the individual sections. So you have a piece called Session Notes Excel Conference and sub-pages for each section.

To create sub-pages, click on the page you want to turn into a sub-page and select "Make subpage." It's going to indent the title. You can even have another level for a sub-page that says sub-page of a sub-page. You don't have to use these as much, but if you have a lot of notes and need a detailed structure, they can be beneficial.

So to summarize, these are the different hierarchy levels you can have: Notebook, section group, section, page, sub-page one, and sub-page two. Start with a structure that makes sense to you. You can always change it or add to it later.

The Interface

So, you have got Microsoft OneNote installed, what you have to do next is to click on the application, and if you are starting this application for the first time, you need to **sign in** with your Microsoft account. If you don't have one, then you can click on "**Create one,**" and it will take you to the Microsoft website, where you can create your brand new account from Microsoft.

The beauty of this application is that whenever you log into your Microsoft OneNote, it will automatically sync and download all the notes you have created. Still, if you are doing it for the first time, you won't see any notebook, and you would have to create one.

The first thing I want to introduce in OneNote is its appearance. If you go up in the left-hand corner, you have this thing called "**Show Navigation**." Go ahead and click on that; that way, you can organize your notes. The three main elements of OneNote are the **Notebook**, the **Section**, and the **Page**.

Pages are stored in sections, and sections are stored in notebooks. At the top, you can see the notebook account; then, along the left-hand side, the sections consist of Events, Meetings, Projects, Quick Notes, and Research.

You will see all your notebooks if you click on the top bar. You could think of this as an actual physical notebook, and you can have many different notebooks. If you want to create a new notebook, you come up to the notebook section at the top, and you can see your current notebook if you have any and also the option to look for more existing notebooks. Then you can come to the bottom and click on "**Add new notebook,**" which will give you the chance to give your notebook a title, after which you'll have a second notebook you will see at the top.

To switch between notebooks, all you need to do is press on them, choose the other one, and it will take you back to the other notebook.

Within a notebook, you could set up what are called **Sections**. Under the notebook, you have one section, and next to that, you can see the **pages** within the sections.

If you want to create a new section within this notebook, you go to the "**Add section**" button, give the section a title, and then you can add new pages to it by pressing "**Add page**." If you've already got a page, when you press "Add page," it adds another, and you need to type the title in over on the right side to name it.

What you will do next is to rename the section as your Chapter One. Let's say this Unit has two chapters. You can create one more section and give it the name of Chapter Two. What you may likely do next is to place these two chapters inside Unit One; for that, you will drag them and drop them inside. So, you can easily place these chapters inside this unit, and if you click on the drop-down arrow under Unit One, you can see how these chapters are hiding inside this subgroup section.

Not only can you create subgroups sections, but you can also create other groups. For that, simply right-click and create a "**New Section**." Here you can see that you have created one Subgroup, and inside that subgroup section, you have added two sections, and then you have created the next Subgroup, and inside it, you can have another section. So, whenever you want to move it, you can easily do that by dragging it upwards or downwards.

On each page, you can make a note. You can not only type there but also have several options to draw, write or create handwritten notes and add images, links, and videos. We will look at these in detail in the next section.

Let's say you create a notebook to hold all your recipes. You can either right-click and select New Notebook or click on the Add notebook. The sections in this notebook could be the different types of dishes. So, you can create a section for appetizers, one for main dishes, one for vegetarian dishes, one for desserts, and so on. Within the sections, you add separate pages for the actual recipe. Using the example below is a recipe for wild rice and mushroom burger. You can see that it has the ingredients, the directions, pictures, and even a link to where the recipe was gotten from.

Apart from recipes, you can have notebooks for ideas for videos with different sections depending on the progress, like brainstorming, research, or scripting. You can also have a notebook for private things like shopping lists, vacations, etc.

So you could organize your notebook as much or as little as you want, but you have a lot of tools where you could set different hierarchies to your organization for OneNote, so quite a bit of power there.

Outstanding Features in the Different Versions of OneNote

This section summarizes the amazing features and benefits you can get with OneNote, giving you the specific versions where these features are available.

The feature of Copy Text from Pictures. This is only available in the version of OneNote that comes with Microsoft office. Remember that you can get this for free. To copy text from pictures, first, bring a picture into your OneNote file, and when you click on the image, you can extract the text by simply right-clicking on the image, and then there's an option you'll see that says "Copy Text from Picture." It will use OCR to extract all of the text from this image, and you'll see all of the text from the image was extracted and pasted into OneNote.

Microsoft OneNote makes it easy to consume content using the Immersive Reader. It improves the reading experience and can also have OneNote read to you. This is only available on the OneNote for the Windows 10 app, and this is the app that comes pre-installed with Windows 10. To use the immersive reader, go to the toolbar on top and select "View." Within the View ribbon, click on Immersive Reader, which opens up your text. First, it removes all of the distractions around the text, increases the font size, and makes the spacing a lot better, making it easier to read the content. You can change my text preferences, highlight different parts of the speech, and you can have OneNote help you focus on each line.

Another feature is the ability of OneNote to read to you. At the bottom of the Immersive reader, there is a play button, and next to that, you'll see some voice settings. Here, you can set the voice speed and choose whether it's a female or a male voice.

You can create Sticky Notes in the OneNote mobile app and have them automatically synchronize and show up on windows 10. First, you need to get the OneNote app. You can get that through the app or play store; it's free to download and install. Along with typing text, you can insert a photo or change the color of the sticky note. On your Windows 10, go to the taskbar, and type in sticky notes. This is an app that comes pre-installed and comes with windows 10, this launches the sticky notes app, and you will see your notes are in synchrony with your mobile app. This is a very nice way if you want to add sticky notes on the go and then get them onto your Windows 10 PC and vice versa. You can also add sticky notes on your Windows 10 PC, which will appear in your OneNote app.

You can have Microsoft OneNote help you write meeting notes. This is handy if you've agreed to take notes for a meeting that's taking place. It is available in both versions of OneNote, and you need to use Microsoft Outlook to take advantage of it. This inserts all of your meeting details; you can see the subject, date, location, and participants, and once the meeting takes place, you can start typing in your notes.

You can easily take tasks from your Microsoft OneNote, and you could add them to your Microsoft to-do task list. Click over on the left of the text, and there's your cursor, then go up to the Home tab, and over on the right-hand side, there's an option for Outlook Tasks. When you click on that, it opens up a menu, and you can now choose when the task is due. Once you pick your desired action, it adds a flag next to the item within your OneNote, and this will now be synchronized over to Microsoft To-do and tasks within Outlook. If you go to your Microsoft To-do task list, you'll see the task you just added from OneNote. So, it synchronizes in both places and your Microsoft Outlook. You will see that same task in your task list synchronized over OneNote. This functionality is only available in the version of OneNote that comes with Microsoft office.

You could tag items in your OneNote to help you get back to them more easily in the future. This is available in all versions of OneNote. To make sure you remember something so you can return to it in the future, a tag can help you with that. Go to the Home tab; in the middle, you can see all the different tag options. You can even add your tags. Once you add the tag over on the left-hand side, you'll see it added an important marker next to the item. If you want to return to this tag in the future, right up above in the same area, you can click on find tags. This now opens up a pane on the right-hand side, and you see a summary of all your important tags. So this makes it easy to get back to the item. You can also see other tags used in the document and a category for tasks or dates those items are due.

Microsoft OneNote makes it very easy to collaborate with others. If you want to share a page with others, you can right-click on that, and there's an option to copy a link to this page. Not only are you limited to copying pages, but you can also copy sections. Right-click at the top of a section, and you can copy a link to the entire section. Within outlook, now you can simply go in and paste a link to the meeting notes, and then other people can click on this, and they'll be able to see your OneNote and then work on your OneNote with you. This is available in both versions of OneNote.

You can easily password-protect a section of OneNote. This is available in both versions of OneNote. If you don't want anyone to be able to see a part of your section, when you right-click on the section, you have the option to password-protect this section. While using this feature, please note that if you forget your password, you won't be able to get back your data, so be very careful and remember your password.

You can easily convert handwriting into text that you can edit on your computer. This works in both versions of the OneNote app. Doing this is extremely simple. Go up to the top toolbar, click on Draw, and over on the far right-hand side, there's an option to turn Ink to Text. Clicking on that converts your hand-drawn text into editable text on your computer.

Did you know that you can set it, so your OneNote window always appears as the topmost, especially when taking notes? You might have multiple windows open, and your Note canvas within OneNote falls to the back. It would be nice to keep it always on top. Within OneNote, click on the View tab, and over on the far right-hand side of the ribbon, there's the option to always keep OneNote on top. When you select this, you can click on your browser window or other content, and your Note canvas will stay on top. This is only available in the OneNote app that comes with Microsoft office.

You can convert your OneNote into full-screen mode to help you with note-taking. This is available in both versions. When you click on it, this removes the ribbon and all the chrome of OneNote, so you only see the canvas. Together with staying on top, this is an excellent way to take notes on your PC.

You can easily translate text in OneNote, which is available in both versions. To access "Translate," go to the bar on top, go over to Review, and in the middle of the Review ribbon, there is the option to translate. You could translate the selected text and open up a mini translator.

You can now choose what language it starts in and what language you want to translate. After that, you have two options; you could insert it as is, which will replace the English text I have over there. Alternatively, you can copy it and paste it into your page.

To use the Mini Translator, click on "Translate" within the Review ribbon and then activate the Mini Translator. With the Mini Translator activated, when you hover over a word, you'll see a text box appear over there, and when you move your mouse over it, it'll show you the translation for this specific word.

Did you know you could access previous versions of a OneNote page, especially if you're storing your OneNote in OneDrive or SharePoint? This is available in both versions of the app. When you right-click on the translate option on a page where you have to translate, there is the option to Show Page Versions at the bottom of the list. When you click on this, you see a previous version of this page where you just had the English text, and if you go to the current version, this version now has the translated text. As you work on a page over time, you'll see more versions stored.

If you start taking a lot of notes, sometimes it's nice to have multiple instances of OneNote open. If you currently have one copy of OneNote open and want another one, it's easy to do that. Simply navigate down to your taskbar and right-click on the OneNote icon, and then you can click on OneNote, which will open up another copy of OneNote. This, too, works with both versions of OneNote.

You can use OneNote to solve math equations. This is only available in OneNote for Windows 10. First, you highlight the equation. Next, you go up to the top toolbar and click on "Draw." Within the drawing ribbon, all the way over on the right-hand side, click on the option that says "Math." When you click on Math, this shows you your equation over here, and below, you have a drop-down list where you can select an action. When you click on this, you can solve the equation. Another nice feature here is another drop-down menu; when you click on that, you can view the steps for solving the equation.

You can dictate to OneNote, which will type up everything you say. Click on the Home tab, and if you go to the right-hand side, there's the option to "Dictate." Click on that, and you can now start speaking. This is available in the OneNote for Windows 10 app.

CHAPTER 4:
Typing and Writing

Typing

To type on OneNote is the same process you would do on Word. You click anywhere and type. The key to these features is the word 'anywhere.' Unlike word, where invisible margins and rulers bind your typing, in OneNote, you can click and type anywhere on the page.

Doing this will create a small container that expands as you continue to type. This is because once the note is written, you can pick it up and move it anywhere on the page, any section of the notebook, or any other notebook. For note-taking purposes, you don't have to be aware of where the note is being written compared to others. Once you have finished making the notes, you can move and pair them with similar ones.

Writing

If typing isn't your thing, OneNote allows users to physically write and take notes by hand. Now, if you have a tablet that allows you to use a pen on the screen, then all the better. If not, then that's OK too.

A tab called 'draw' is located at the top of the OneNote screen, and here, you will find options for everything from line thickness to color. The real beauty of OneNote comes in its ability to transcribe the drawing once you are done.

Pictures

Importing pictures into OneNote couldn't be simpler. You will see an 'Insert Picture' option in the' Insert' tab. Click this, open the relevant file, and that's that. Like a container, the picture can be picked up, moved, and resized as you see fit.

One more terrific function in regards to pictures. If there is a word in the picture, this word is searchable. So if you have saved a picture of a pie recipe and later search for the word 'pie,' this recipe should come up.

Voice Records

Another great feature of OneNote is its ability to audio record. The process is relatively simple too. All you need do is hit the 'Audio Recording' button, found in the 'Insert' tab, and it begins to record automatically.
This will appear as an audio file in the relevant section and page.
Another great feature about this audio function that needs to be mentioned is that the audio is searchable. So let's say that the word 'dog' is spoken and recorded. The user can type the word 'dog' into the search bar, and the audio file will pop up.

Videos

OneNote is a do-all program. The team at Microsoft has made it their mission to make the gathering and organizing of notes as simple and effective as possible. Nowhere else is this more evident than its ability to play video.
Say you find a great Youtube video that goes perfectly with the notes you are trying to make. All you need do is copy the link to the video and paste it onto the page. It will then appear as a regular Youtube video on the page. You don't need to open the web browser again as OneNote does for you.

Tags

Tagging is a crucial aspect of OneNote that should be utilized where possible. You will see an entire section dedicated to tags in the Home tab. These are little pictures that represent features of note-taking. For example, a light bulb represents an idea you might have for later, whereas a check mark represents something you need to do.
All you need do is click and drag the tag to each relevant note to help it stand out more.
Another great feature, and a recent addition as of 2022, is the ability to search the tags. Next to the add tag location, you will see a small icon labeled 'Find Tags.' clicking on this will bring up a menu that lists all the tags you have used and where to find them.

Grids, Tables, and Equations

Grids and tables can be made just like in a word document. And then it too can be picked up and moved. The unique thing about OneNote is that it allows you to convert this table or grid into an excel spreadsheet. This will then allow you to use it in excel. You can convert the information into any number of graphs and charts as Excel allows.
OneNote also has a very simple calculator function. Again, in the 'Insert tab,' you will see an option for 'equations.' This creates a small dialogue box for you to type simple equations into.

Webpages and Hyperlinks

The first thing is first. Hyperlinks can be copied and pasted into OneNote. It's simple and reasonably effective. But there is a better way to store the information on a webpage for later use.
The first thing you will need to do is to download the add-on. Downloaded, this add-on should insert itself into your taskbar (this varies depending on the web browser that you are using).
Once you are on the page you wish to add to OneNote, simply hit the clipper button. This will redirect you to a new menu which will give you the option of either inserting the whole page into OneNote, clipping just a fragment of the page yourself, or whether you want the clipper to do it for you. If you are clipping a page with a food recipe, the clipper function will convert the page so that only the recipe and photo of the food are shown.
The final product will then be downloaded to your default notebook, and all you need to do is move it to the relevant section and page.

Personalization

One final thing you will want to do is personalize your notebooks and sections. Again this is simple to do and usually done to make your work more organized and accessible.

With OneNote, you can personalize everything from the color of your notebook (this option is presented when you first create a new notebook) to the color of each section. You can also choose if you want each page to be lined, drawn up as a grid, or just a blank page. And to take it even further, templates are available to add a flair to the background of each page, too, such as flower drawings and doodles. OneNote is dedicated to making this working space personalized and adaptable to your needs.

CHAPTER 5:
Section Groups

Section groups attempt to implement the concept of a section and subsection. Suppose you have a notebook for recipes and find you have too many dessert recipes (can one have too many dessert recipes?). In that case, you might want to reorganize your sections, so you have a section for cakes and another section for pies and another section for ice cream, and then you can put all of those sections under a section group of desserts. The problem with section groups is that they are implemented very oddly. On PCs and Macs, section groups look very odd. On mobile devices, section groups look how you expect them to look, but there is only one very minor thing you can do with a section group on a mobile device.

What Can You Do with a Section Group on a PC or Mac?

Create a New Section Group

Once you've selected your notebook, you're presented with a tabbed display of your sections. Right-click to the right of the tabs, and then click on New Section Group. This will create a section group named New Section Group (with a number after it if you already have a section group named New Section Group). The name of the section group is highlighted, so if you just start typing, that will change the name of the section group.
You can also create a section group within a section group. Once you select your section group, you are presented with a tabbed display of your sections within that section group. If you right-click to the right of the section tabs, you can create a new section group within this section group, just as you do within a notebook.

Select a Section Group

Once you've selected your notebook, click on the section group name (section groups are those multi-tabbed items to the right of the section tabs) you wish to select.
As a side note, section groups are always listed in alphabetical order, and you cannot change the order in which section groups are displayed.

As a further side note, if you attempt to change the order in which section groups are displayed by dragging and dropping a section group, you may find that what you have done is moved a section group to now be within another section group. Go ahead, ask how this was discovered.

Delete a Section Group

Right-click on the section group you wish to delete, click on the Delete menu item, and then confirm you wish to move the section to Deleted Notes.
To see your Deleted Notes, click on the History menu, click on the down arrow associated with Notebook Recycle Bin, click on the Notebook Recycle Bin menu item, right-click the section you wish to restore, and then click on the Move or Copy menu item and tell OneNote where you wish to restore your deleted section.
WARNING: Deleted section groups are permanently deleted 60 days after you move the section group to the Deleted Notes.

Change the Name of a Section Group

Right-click the section group, click on the Rename menu item and then type the new name into the tab.
Unlike a section, you cannot double-click on a section group to rename a section group.

Move a Section Group

You can move a section group from one notebook to another notebook or a section group.
Right-click on the section group you wish to move, then click on the Move... menu item. In the Move Section Group dialog, click on the notebook or section group to which you want to move this section group, and then click on the Move button.
Once the section group has been moved, the section group will now exist in the target notebook (and target section group, if you chose one), and the section group will no longer exist in its original location.

What Can You Do with a Section Group on a Mobile Device?

Viewing the sections within your selected notebook, you can see section groups with their sections under them. In the dessert example above, you see the Desserts section group with Cakes and Pies and Ice Cream listed as indented sections underneath Desserts.

Sync Section Group

On the page that lists your sections, long-press the desired section group, then press the "Sync section group" menu item.
While OneNote will automatically synchronize your notebooks, sections, and section groups in the background when it detects you've made changes, you can manually force the synchronization of a section group between your device and OneCloud right now if you feel you need to do that for some reason.

CHAPTER 6:
Using Add-Ins

OneNote is a strong productivity tool but has much more potential if used with other third-party tools. Many of these are free, which makes it even better to experiment.

The following tools mainly focus on the desktop version, but some may also work on the mobile and web versions.

OneNote might not offer an "Insert" feature like many other note-taking programs, so to start using Add-ins, you need to go to "File, Options, Add-ins" to add or remove each add-in.

Some downloads require a 32-bit or 64-bit version of OneNote. To find out which version of OneNote you have, go to "File, Account, About OneNote." The information should be displayed at the top of the page. This will help you always download the version of the right add-in and prevent errors.

Here are some recommended add-ins for you to try.

Learning Tools Add-In

This learning tool will help improve both your reading and writing skills. Whether you are a student, office worker, writer, or have dyslexia, this tool has all the features that may benefit you.

The tool includes many features, such as Focus mode, Font spacing and short lines, Enhanced dictation, Immersive reading, Parts of speech, Syllabification, and Comprehension mode. For more detail, visit the official website: https://www.onenote.com/learningtools

Onetastic and OneCalendar Add-In

With Onetastic, you will be able to replicate some Word or Excel features in OneNote through the use of Macros. For example, tools include search and replace, table of contents, function, favorites, image crop and rotate, custom styles, text select, etc.

There is a slight learning curve on macros, but tons of tutorials will get you started and are definitely worth the effort.

Onetastic also gives you access to OneCalendar, a standalone tool that provides a calendar view.

Navigation in OneCalendar is easy and has plenty of useful features. You can:

- Switch to a different month/year, previous/next day, week, and month without having to toggle.
- Customize your week to start on a Sunday or Monday.
- Hovering over OneNote titles will give you a preview of the page.
- Search on the calendar.
- View pages by the day it was created or modified.
- Display only the notebooks of your choice.
- Click on the number of the day to get a view of the day. You can also switch between day, week, and month views by navigating to the button at the bottom right.
- Customize it further by using the Settings View or Keyboard and mouse shortcuts.

Send to Sway Add-In

This tool will let you export data to Sway, which can then be used as a presentation in Microsoft PowerPoint or just to give your work some visual appeal. It allows you to present the information in fluid, dynamic ways. Sway is included in many Office 365 accounts, so if you have a subscription already, you can start using it immediately.

Class Notebook Add-In

Class Notebook is designed for teachers and professionals to help manage work groups and classes more efficiently. The add-in creates an additional menu tab with all its new features. This includes:
- Page and section distribution to a selected group of students
- An easy and fast review of work
- Assignment and grading integration with many Learning Management or Student Information systems
- Create assignments and set due dates
- Post student's scores for an assignment

Windows 10 and mac users don't have to download the add-in, as it is already built into OneNote.
There is also a OneNote Staff Notebook where teachers can share information and work together by planning lessons, taking notes, or discussing other developments.

OneNote Web Clipper

This is an extension for your web browser, allowing you to capture information into your OneNote notebooks. It differs from the Send to OneNote add-in, which is included with the desktop application. Where sending to OneNote lets you capture files on your desktop computer, Web Clipper records from the Internet, making research faster and easier.

Gem Add-In

This add-in combines over 400 features across six tabs to make OneNote more like other Office programs or products such as Evernote. This includes table features, batch tools, reminders, anchor tools, batch tools, sorting, commonly used functions, etc.
Visit the official website for a list of all features: https://www.onenotegem.com/gem-for-onenote.html

Office Lens Add-In

Office Lens is a standalone app or built-in feature on Android or iOS devices. It allows you to take pictures of documents, business cards, or whiteboards, then enhances the photo to look like a scanned image like the Evernote app. The picture is then saved as a note, making the image's text searchable.

OneNote Publisher for WordPress

If you run a blog and do most of the work in OneNote, then OneNote Publisher for WordPress will come in handy. This tool lets you export your OneNote pages directly into your WordPress blog, thus eliminating the process of copy-and-pasting content yourself and re-doing all the formatting.

Customize the OneNote User Interface

The OneNote interface can be customized in many ways to enhance your experience with the program. The desktop version lets you change the default font for notes. Changing to your desired font or color each time you launch a note-taking program can grow tiresome, especially if you take notes a lot. Like many other Microsoft programs, OneNote has several pre-installed fonts but allows you to add your custom fonts.

To import a new font:

- Download and unzip the specific font.
- Then, search for Fonts in Control Panel, locate the file you have downloaded, and save it.

Not only can you change default fonts, but OneNote also allows you to adjust the default size of pages. This is a great way to make notes appear as they would on a smartphone or tablet. The option can be found on the View Tab under "Paper Size." The desktop version also has a few themes and backgrounds for you further to customize the look and feel of the program. This won't make any changes to pages and will have to be customized on its own. Page colors can be found on the View tab. If you don't like the plain colors, add a background to a page by either adding a picture from the "Insert" tab or simply dragging and dropping the image into the page. Right-click on the inserted image to set it as a background.

Just like a paper notebook, sections can be categorized with different colors. Organizing sections by color will make your notes easier to find and more attractive. Simply right-click on the section and choose "Section Color" to choose among 16 colors.

If you feel overwhelmed by the number of tools shown on the screen or do not need certain ones, you can always choose which tools to display and how you want them displayed by going to Options under the File Tab. For example, choose if you want Page or Navigation tabs to show on the left or right side of the interface.

Also, customize the Ribbon area and Quick Access Toolbar by showing or hiding the tools of your choice to have a more organized and less cluttered appearance. Having control over the tools on the interface will help you take notes easier and make your work more efficient.

Example: If you use handwriting, stylus, or other drawing tools, pin your preferred pen styles to the Quick Access Toolbar for easy access.

If English isn't your main language, you can change the default language to one you prefer. This is found in the Options menu. You might need to download and install the additional language depending on the language.

OneNote pages have a broader width than other Office programs. If this bothers you, change the setting by using the "Fit Page Width to Window" in the View tab. To create a zoom effect, select the "Page Width" setting. This will match the page width to the window width.

OneNote has a Dock to Desktop feature, which will dock the program to one side of your desktop. This handy feature for easy access to your work if you always use multiple programs. Dock the whole application or several OneNote windows by choosing "Dock to Desktop" or New Docked Window" in the View tab.

Opening more than one window makes it easy to compare notes. But multiple open windows can also be annoying sometimes if the smaller windows keep disappearing behind the larger ones. Luckily OneNote has an "Always on Top" feature in the View tab, which will always focus on the selected window.

OneNote pages are a white blank by default. If you need to fit images or other objects a certain way and need lines to guide you, there are a few different rules or grid lines to enable under the View tab. You can also customize them by changing the color. Just note that the lines won't appear on printouts, so use them only to plan drafts.

If you don't want to see the title of a note, or the displayed time and date, remove it by clicking on the "Hide Note Title" in the View tab. Be aware that this option completely removes it, not just hides it from view.

Use shortcuts, widgets, or live tiles for people who want to access notes faster to save time and be more productive. On your smartphone, for example, you can either set a shortcut on the home screen or use the very useful screen widget to make quick notes. If you are using Windows 8 and up, set live tiles on the start menu or pin them to the taskbar.

CHAPTER 7:
Ways to Use OneNote for Project Management

After spending more than 15 years in IT project management, I appreciate the tools that make project management easier and more efficient. OneNote (yes, OneNote!) is such a tool. Today I want to emphasize how a project manager and project team members can utilize and receive OneNote when overseeing ventures inside an association.

It is imperative to note that OneNote is not a project management software. However, OneNote, combined with SharePoint Site, Office 365 Group, or Planner, does this. So when I talk about the features of OneNote below, the software is more of a help/facilitation tool that complements the other tools in the Office 365 ecosystem.

Storing and Sharing of Agendas

OneNote can be ideal for storing calendars for gatherings. You can make a page for each gathering and name it accordingly.

Because OneNote is standard on all SharePoint sites and Office 365 groups, you can use it to collaborate and create together and easily ask your team members by adding items to a calendar.

Keep the Minutes of the Meeting

Another great piece of content owned by OneNote is minutes. You can utilize the equivalent OneNote page where you have saved the above agenda items and save meeting notes, actions, and other meeting results so that everything stays in one place. You can also create another meeting minute page and organize it with the calendar page above in a section.

If you manage your projects using the Agile method, OneNote can become a great tool to keep track of these daily Scrum meetings.

Save the Lessons Learned

Another excellent method to utilize OneNote is to catch exercises learned about a project. When I led projects in the business world, I held lessons for lessons learned for each project I managed. This helped me prevent errors in future projects.

And then, you can allow users to write together and contribute to the document by creating a database of lessons learned.

Organization of Risks in a Risk Register

Another interesting way to use OneNote is to record project risks. In general, the risk register is built in Excel, I also recommend using a custom SharePoint list for this, list for this, yet you can likewise utilize OneNote and embed an Excel table or document directly on the page.

WikiProject

What makes OneNote great - is that it can become an easy dump (repository) for all content (images, audio, video, tables, handwritten notes, etc.) that would otherwise not be stored in a SharePoint document library. You can use the sections and pages of OneNote to create a fun Wiki project! OneNote is accessible, so you can generally find what you are looking for.

Status Reports

Oh yes, situation reports! Who doesn't love them? Well, the truth is that nobody does it except senior management. I remember that when managing projects in the business world, I disliked having them in the same place. You dedicate a lot of time to a thing that would take senior managers 1 minute to read, only to make a stupid and unreasonable decision. Sorry, I wandered a bit. Either way, OneNote tends to be an incredible tool to accelerate the development of these weekly status reports.

List of Methods

Action Items is one of the many contents that could be perfect for OneNote. This can be ideal for quick task lists that are not part of the formal task list/planning. The checklist (To-Do functionality in OneNote) is excellent!

E-Mails

Have you received an important e-mail inviting you to be part of a project file? You can copy the entire e-mail to every OneNote notebook with one click on the button.

How One Note is Efficiently Use by Project Calendar And Insurance Organizing

OneNote is a fantastic Microsoft program that often goes unnoticed and is underused. It is a great productivity tool because it focuses on taking typed and handwritten notes, audio recording, and search tools and integrates with the rest of Microsoft Office programs. Until recently, I was still in the old school and wrote all my notes in a spiral-bound notebook, but I discovered OneNote. It is as if you have a digital notebook that organizes pages for you, makes sharing information with your colleagues much easier, and does the job much more efficiently. Below you will find only a handful of options that OneNote offers to improve your experience taking notes.

What Makes OneNote Special?

Trusted Interface

OneNote uses a trusted interface already part of other MS Office tools, such as Word, Excel, and PowerPoint. It has a horizontal ribbon on the top, where you can access all the usual commands and operations.

Logical Hierarchy

OneNote follows a "paper" notebook approach to organize and store notes electronically. Just like the traditional paper notebook, where you have different pages and sections, OneNote follows the same terminology and methodology. In OneNote, you can create the following:

Pages

The pages are your usual pages in a notebook. For example, you can create a page for each meeting where the meeting agenda and minutes are saved.

Sections

The pages are then organized into sections. The part is how you usually split your paper notebook, right? So you can have a role for meetings, apart from project problems, business requirements, etc.

Integration with Outlook

OneNote has cool coordination with Outlook. You can extract the meeting details in OneNote from Outlook. Similarly, clicking a button can include notes in your appointment invitation. No more attachments, and users can ask them to send a plan!

Mobile-Friendly

Much the same as SharePoint, OneDrive, and different MS Office instruments, OneNote additionally has a portable application. This makes OneNote effectively available from the "field," where there is no opportunity to make formal records.

Online Edition

Like the rest of the MS Office tools, OneNote can be edited in the browser. This indicates that there is no need to download the file or even install OneNote if you want to make changes to OneNote quickly 'on the fly.'

See Microsoft OneNote as a Digital Version of a Physical Laptop

This means that you can take digital notes and keep them organized. It also means that you can add images, diagrams, sound, video, etc. Use OneNote with other Office package programs on your desktop or mobile devices.

Useful Tips and Tricks for Microsoft OneNote

Extract Text from Images

Unknown to most and easy to learn, with this feature, you can create an image with a recognizable font and copy the text to your page. This handy item can save you from retyping sentences or paragraphs, perfect for screenshots and extensive images. Here's how you can extract text from images in Microsoft OneNote.

Search in All Your Notes

OneNote is a great organizational tool, but sometimes things can get lost. Instead of clicking on all your sections and pages, search your notes to find that missing item.

Integrate OneNote with Outlook Tasks

If you want to control online ordering, this tip is for you. Synchronize your Microsoft OneNote task list with your Outlook e-mail and ensure all tasks are before you. Avoid switching windows and learn how to integrate Microsoft OneNote tasks with Microsoft Outlook.

Perform Simple Calculations without a Calculator

The ability to make calculations without a calculator or preprogrammed formula is smart and useful. You can perform calculations on the spot by applying the simplest mathematical functions. So don't take your calculator out of your house. Let OneNote take care of your computing needs.

Make a Digital Note

Microsoft OneNote is there for you if you are busy at work and have a random thought to be noted. Clicking on WINDOWS + N opens a digital note on your computer. You can type, draw, insert attachments, or record audio with this note. Simply close, and the note will be saved in your quick notes.

Integrate Documents and Spreadsheets into Your Notes

Constantly switching between Windows on your computer can be annoying. Fortunately, Microsoft OneNote has a solution: you can integrate any saved document or spreadsheet into your notes. The inserted file is then treated as an image so that you can only refer to the content and cannot change it. You can embed documents and spreadsheets in your Microsoft OneNote notes.

Work Together via Microsoft OneNote

If you want someone else to view parts of your OneNote notebook, share it with him. Sharing notes makes collaboration easier because you and your colleagues can maneuver through organized plans and ideas. You can share your notes in Microsoft OneNote as follows.

Microsoft OneNote is a great tool to use. By using the many possibilities, your organizational skills will certainly improve considerably. Therefore, apply these seven tips and tricks from Microsoft OneNote to get the most out of this practical and flexible software.

How Organizations Use OneNote

The great thing about OneNote is that it can be used differently due to its nature (informal notes). Here are some examples I have seen from my experience:

Project Meeting Management

OneNote is ideal for project management. I even blogged about OneNote, which is widely used in project management. You can use the OneNote pages to communicate meeting calendars, meeting minutes, and project status.

User Comments/Informal Requirements/Wishlist

OneNote can also be an excellent tool for collecting, for example, a business requirement for software or user wish list/feedback items. Until you have an official document, OneNote can also become a "dump" for users to enter and type what they want. This can be a quick way to collect user feedback without having to set up complex surveys or structures.

CHAPTER 8:
Pros and Cons of OneNote

Applications like OneNote are created, and features are added, considering the user's evolving needs. It is thus fair to say that such applications, including OneNote, are not exactly perfect. While this application is designed to offer users a wide array of features that they look for, they must be aware of its limitations, so they know what to expect. Here are the pros and cons of OneNote applications.

Pros

The Stack Interface

Whether you have been using OneNote for a long time or are just getting started, you can tell that the interface makes the whole application user-friendly. No matter what platform you run the app on, you can be assured that it will be easy to figure out.

Color Divider

If you want everything color-coded, the OneNote app can do this and enhance your ability to keep things organized. The app also enables you to organize individual tabs using color codes, making them easy to find based on their colors.

Easy to Run on All Devices

You can run the OneNote app with a Windows-powered laptop or even a Mac-powered one. The app also runs on all phone platforms available in the market. Though the features may differ a bit depending on the platform designs, most tend to be more compatible with the Windows version of OneNote. However, the app can generally run on any platform.

Elegant Look

Everyone wants to use an application that looks good. OneNote comes with a simple but elegant look that appeals to most users.

<u>**Easy to Integrate with Other Documents**</u>

If you want to place a portion of content from word files to notebooks you have created or vice versa, OneNote allows you to do this with relative ease. The latest versions of OneNote are integrated with MS Word and Excel, an aspect that will enable users to add Excel files to OneNote and review them from the app.

Cons

<u>**Newbies May Find OneNote Hard to Understand in the Beginning**</u>

New users will likely find OneNote tricky to understand. This is especially true for the Windows version with a wide variety of improved features. It might be a bit complicated initially, but after spending time interacting with the application, one becomes accustomed to it and finds it easier to use.

<u>The Application is Not the Same for All Platforms</u>

OneNote does not use the same design across all operating systems and phone platforms. The features vary from one platform to another. Each operating system has its design, which challenges people who want to use it on different platforms. Users can do more with OneNote than Mac or iOS platforms on the Windows operating system. For instance, the Mac version is less than stellar because of the limited features available.

<u>**Mac Users Cannot Embed Videos**</u>

While it is possible to add files, text, and other details to notes created on OneNote, users cannot add videos to the Mac version of this application. This feature is only available in the Windows version of OneNote.

Comparison of OneNote with Other Applications

<u>Comparison of One Note with EverNote</u>

The release of OneNote was direct competition for another application called EverNote, which is interesting considering how popular EverNote has been. EverNote has dominated the market for a very long time, but it was about time to release a program that would cover up some of its shortcomings of EverNote. The two programs have been designed to work on the same platforms. Still, they have very distinctive features, which makes OneNote much better than the popular EverNote and EverNote better than OneNote in the other sense.

OneNote is a great way to get organized, something EverNote does not offer its users. With OneNote, you can create simple to complex notes from the beginning, organize them into notebooks that can be searched and browsed, and even make them accessible through different platforms through synchronization. You can easily access your notes, plus all their details, from OneNote, with little or no effort.

OneNote's note creation tools are much more advanced than those of EverNote. If you are the kind of user that needs software that will create great quality notes and help you organize them, you will be much better off using OneNote. However, it cannot clip notes from the internet like EverNote, which is its main shortcoming.

OneNote gives its users access to many different kinds of features, and this means that it is much more useful than its counterpart. If you are looking for software that will give you more benefits between the two, it is best to go for OneNote but always remember that there are features from EverNote that you may not get from OneNote. However, if you are looking for software that will allow you to find, capture and organize content from the internet, OneNote will not be great for this, but EverNote.

EverNote and OneNote are note-taking tools, but their features make them so different in what they offer their clients. You will choose what to go for depending on what you want to achieve. The good thing is that you can always use both of them for their different features to ensure that you achieve more every day and make things easier for yourself.

Why is OneNote Better Than EverNote?

OneNote and EverNote are two applications that compete to become market leaders in the note-taking space. These two notetaking applications often compare because they appeal to various users, each with features that give it an edge. Most importantly, there are functions that OneNote can perform that EverNote currently cannot. Such functions include adding text to files, images, doodling, and writing ideas that come to mind. A lot of the functionality in OneNote depends on a user's ability to personalize it, which makes it better than EverNote. Here are details of what a user can do using OneNote differently than when he uses EverNote.

Integrating Office

Unlike EverNote, integration with Office is possible with OneNote. This is perhaps because EverNote is not connected to other software like OneNote is to Office. Users cannot include Word documents with the former, but this is easy to do with OneNote.Adding Videos to Notes

When using the OneNote for Windows, one can take notes differently than they take down notes using traditional methods. Instead of drawing comic strips to keep things interesting, you can easily add videos to your notes and make things work well for you. This is not the case with the EverNote app.

Keep To-Do Lists Organized

You can expect that aside from your OneNote notebook, there is much more to do with the app, like ensuring lists are organized. This is easily achieved by adding tabs to pages of a notebook. Users can also compare their lists using sticky notes if they so wish. On OneNote, sticky notes may be placed just like they are added to a typical notebook.

Get Additional Storage for Free

For those who take notes on different things and need plenty of space, OneNote comes in handy. The app offers users free storage space of up to 15 GB with ease. This amount of space is not bad when considering how much text and images you need to generate to fill it up.

From the things mentioned above, it is evident that OneNote offers a lot of things that the EverNote app cannot.

Comparison of OneNote with Google Keep

While people never thought that Google Keep would be revived by Google again, the app was coming back to the market to compete with EverNoteas well as OneNote. The Google Keep app is free for users when used online and for download on Android-powered devices.

On the other hand, OneNote is part of the Microsoft Office 365 subscription. It can come as part of the package when purchased alongside other applications that are useful in devices. Like Google Keep, OneNote can be used for free online. A free version of the app is also available for users who do not wish to spend money on it. The OneNote Office version is better than other versions because it can take screenshots that can be printed directly. So far, Google Keep does not have applications that can be used on Android and iOS devices. This means that users can only access and use it online with a laptop or desktop computer. Eventually, Google might release something similar to what OneNote is already offering to the general public. Still, for now, OneNote is the perfect choice for people looking for an efficient note-taking application.

When it comes to text editing, it is easy to tell that the OneNote app is superior mainly because of the rich text formatting features that come with it. These features allow users to organize the text appropriately they place in their notebooks. With Google Keep, it is not possible to do this. Instead of organizing text, pressing the enter button creates a new file on Google Keep

GoogleKeep tends to be a choice for people who want to keep things simple. However, if you are not just looking at simplicity but want to experience a wide range of ways to get things done completed while exploring different features that enhance your ability to keep notes intact, OneNote is your best choice.

Other Applications Similar to OneNote

EverNote and GoogleKeep are two other applications that are considered to be very similar to OneNote. However, others offer similar features. They include the following:

- **CintaNotes:** As its name suggests, this application allows you to add notes easily. Though this application is pretty simple and easy to use, it does not come with most features that OneNote offers. Compared to OneNote, its features are fundamental and limited.
- **EverNote**: This was initially created to run on Linux operating system, and it was only after some time that it became available for Windows platforms. While Evernote serves more as a response to EverNote than OneNote, it is not very functional.
- **TiddlyWiki**: If you have been looking for apps to enable you to organize your documents better, you may have come across this application before finding it. While it does much of what OneNote can do, OneNote can still do those things much better. One has to learn many shortcuts before using the TiddlyWiki application more quickly than OneNote. OneNote does not require users to learn numerous shortcuts to use it, an aspect that makes it distinct from TiddlyWiki

Different applications and software are available for note-taking running on various platforms. Comparing all these applications, OneNote still emerges as the best choice. This is mainly due to the options in terms of features that it offers users that build their confidence in organizing their personal and work-related things based on their needs.

CONCLUSION

Today, things have changed. Using physical notebooks is not the only way people can capture ideas, thoughts, or points worth remembering. With the continuous advancement in computer technology, the note-taking process has significantly simplified. With the option of using technology, people no longer have to bring physical pens and papers everywhere. Software companies have creatively developed note-taking applications that are much easier and fun to use and more efficient in preserving and protecting information captured by note-takers. These applications have also increased the range of things users can do with their technological gadgets.OneNote is one application that has replaced age-old note-taking tools.

OneNote application is compatible with most of the mobile devices currently in use; whether you are using android, iOS, or Windows-powered mobile phones, you can surely download this application and use it for your needs. Devices with PC-style interfaces, for instance, Windows XP and Windows Vista operating systems, can also work well with the software.

OneNote is believed to be only useful for tablet PCs, which is not the case. If this were the case, it would mean that only a few people would benefit from this software's features. OneNote can perform very well on any platform, particularly on Windows-powered machines. The use of OneNote should not be limited to taking notes and organizing them only. You can see many other things you can do with this eBook, including integrating media files and photos into your messages. As you continue using the program, you will realize that you will achieve a lot from its features.

OneNote can be used on various platforms, and although the type of things it can do may vary a bit, it does not change the fact that it is beneficial for note-taking. It is something that can be used anytime, anywhere.

BOOK 5:
MICROSOFT ONE DRIVE

Top Tips to Finally Master and Efficiently Use Microsoft Onedrive Software on Windows, Mac, and Phone

INTRODUCTION

Microsoft is one of the best software giants, and it has been at the top of its product since its inception. Microsoft OneDrive is one of the Microsoft web-based stores that offer free storage for its users, and it's a hard drive in the form of a cloud with which you can store and share your files.

OneDrive is a web cloud storage system that allows you to store your files and your photos, and it allows you to access your files and photos from any device anywhere. If you lost your phone or device and stored your files on OneDrive, rest assured that you won't lose them because they are stored on OneDrive.

Microsoft OneDrive is stored in a cloud which can be accessed with any device that contains it. It enhances the easy storage of files and documents without much stress. Microsoft OneDrive assists you in keeping the proper arrangement of files and the ability to access your relevant documents, photos, and any other related files from a different device. It also does much work on how to share those documents or photos with friends, family, and co-operators. Microsoft OneDrive can be opened on your PC, website, and mobile phone. It also assists in the proper updating of every file on your PC. Any documents being edited or added in OneDrive will be synced through the cloud to people or devices you have shared with previously.

As of today, you must not store your files in physical flash drives. You can do that digitally with what is called OneDrive. You cannot just store your files in OneDrive compared to flash drive days. OneDrive has some features that flash drives do not have. With OneDrive, you can store files, share, and sync different files across different devices you use. Is that not great development?

Microsoft OneDrive has become a very interesting storage folder because of its easy accessibility. One important thing you will understand is how to share files and create documents on Microsoft OneDrive without stress. Sharing files via OneDrive solves the problems of sending massive files through emails.

It is very simple. When you have already installed the app, find the OneDrive folder on your PC, and then drag and drop the file in the folder. In the case of a mobile phone, you can add files using the OneDrive app. You will turn on camera upload for you to save every photo and video taken, and it will facilitate quick and easy views of the files on other devices.

This book will discuss everything about OneDrive. Even if you buy a new phone or device, you can still access your files on your new phone, provided it is stored on OneDrive. With OneDrive, you can always connect to your families and friends through file sharing. There is no need for large email attachments. All you need to do to share your photos or file is to send an email link for them to click.

Many people may find OneDrive hard to use, even though it is a good thing to happen to the web storage system. OneDrive does what Google Drive and other Cloud storage apps do regarding web storage. This is because, with OneDrive, you ultimately have a place to put or store your files on the web. Just like other storage cloud apps, you have to sign in to your Microsoft account for you to be able to access your data or files.

Microsoft made the OneDrive more suitable for those that have a Microsoft account. With a Microsoft account, you automatically have OneDrive storage in your account. One does not know whether this is a Microsoft business strategy to get more users to their cloud storage.

CHAPTER 1:
What is OneDrive?

Microsoft OneDrive is a storage system that was launched in the year 2007 by Microsoft. It is a file hosting service, and it is also a synchronizing file service that gives you the ability to store and synchronize at the same time. Microsoft built it to enable you to store your data and files. The data ranges include photos, documents, pictures, etc. The Microsoft OneDrive allows you to synchronize your data to system settings, visual customizations, themes, app settings, and Microsoft Edges tabs. It also gives you the browsing history ability and allows you to use a password.

Microsoft OneDrive allows you to store everything in its web cloud storage services and will enable you to share your files and folders and everything you want to store in its web Cloud app. With OneDrive, it's quite easy to share files with just a click and get a shared link easily. The Microsoft OneDrive allows you to receive and share files with others, including family, friends, and work colleagues. It also gives you complete access to all the contents of your files and folders.

Microsoft gives the privilege of having a free 5GB of OneDrive to all those with a Microsoft account. Though this offer is limited to 5GB of free storage, you can still get 50GB of storage on a subscription.

OneDrive is an online-based storage platform with a significant amount of space offered for free by Microsoft to anyone with a Microsoft account. It can be likened to a hard drive in the cloud, which you can share with a few extra beneficial features. Although OneDrive is cloud-based, you can still access your files and folders without ever having to open your browser. OneDrive provides a more personal experience for end-users to store private files or collaborate with others inside and outside the organization. There is a personal drive and a business drive. Microsoft OneDrive is a straightforward and intuitive interface that requires little guidance, and the comprehensive and responsive support available can assist with anything more complex.

OneDrive is an online Microsoft cloud that stores files and documents on its platform. OneDrive was first known as *SkyDrive*, but it was later rebranded earlier in 2014 due to a trademark problem brought up by a United Kingdom local broadcaster. OneDrive assimilated into Windows 10 and as an application on Android phones, Windows phones, iOS, and on the internet through any web browser. Operators can store their photos, videos, music, and other relevant documents on this platform.

Microsoft cares a lot about your security and ensures your files are well protected. The system OneDrive web cloud storage keeps your file secured, and it is a Windows built-in software that gives you 100% sure of the safety of your files when it comes to online storage. This means that you can store and use your files without the danger of security breaches or leaks to your files. Microsoft, because of a security breach, built Microsoft OneDrive with *OneDrive Personal Vault* to give you further security to your sensitive files on the OneDrive cloud storage system. This superb technology assures you 100% secure data in their storage system. This means that all doubt on whether files and data stored on OneDrive are 100% safe is wholly erased, knowing the quality of security Microsoft attached to its OneDrive. With this security, you can safely assume that your files are secured and protected by the Microsoft OneDrive software.

Advantages of Using Microsoft OneDrive

- OneDrive allows you to have your different kinds of files stored on their cloud storage system, and you can at the same time have the ability to access them from your windows computer or any of your mobile devices.
- Provided you have a Microsoft account, you can store up to 5GB of your data for free.
- Microsoft OneDrive allows you to store your files without much difficulty. It was made that people can go to your shared files by just clicking on the link you're provided with.
- The OneDrive sync client enables users to download their content from their workstations, and they can be able to work their content offline without the internet.
- The OneDrive gives you Files on Demand Syncing, in that users can decide not to sync their OneDrive entirely but can sync the files they prefer to use.
- Because it is OneDrive, it enables you to work with Microsoft office applications. This is because it is from the Microsoft platform, and because of this, when an application is launched, it will show you a list of your documents, including those you stored on OneDrive.

Signing Up for Microsoft OneDrive

There are procedures you follow when signing up for Microsoft OneDrive.

1. Enter the website *OneDrive.live.com*. The interface below will be displayed, and you select "Sign Up for Free."

2. Choose the account type. In this case, you will decide whether to create a personal or a business account. For business accounts, the features there are not free. You have to pay to be able to access them.

3. Key in your email address. There is space to enter your email address; if you don't have an email address, you can create a new one for yourself.

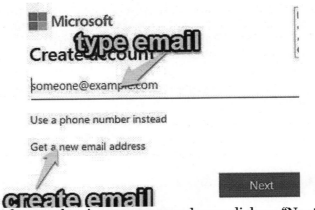

4. Enter a fresh password. After you key in your password, you click on "Next."

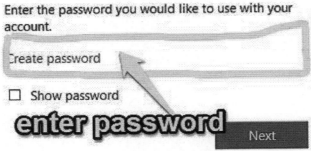

5. Other details: You must indicate your country and date of birth at this stage.

Create account

We need just a little more info to set up your account.

Country/region

Nigeria

Date of birth

Day	Month	Year

Next

6. Verification of your email address: After all these processes, a code will be sent to your phone number or email for proper confirmation to ensure you are the email or phone number owner. Then you will type in the code for it to be confirmed.

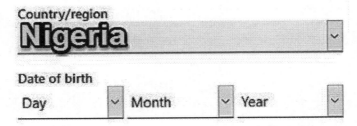

☐ I would like information, tips and offers about Microsoft products and services.

Choosing Next means that you agree to the Microsoft Services Agreement and privacy and cookies statement.

Next

7. Final confirmation and account creation. You must indicate that you are human by correctly entering the captcha code. After then, your account will be created, and you can now upload your files and documents to your account.

Create account

Before proceeding, we need to make sure that a real person is creating this account.

	New
	Audio

Enter the characters you see

enter code here

Signing Into Microsoft OneDrive

You can sign in to OneDrive through the web page or the application. If you already have the app on your system, you will *sign in* with the following procedures below. But if you don't have the app on your system, you will either install the app or log in through the web page (OneDrive.live.com).

1. You will click on the Start search case and type "*OneDrive*." Then you will see OneDrive showing in the search outcomes and click on it.

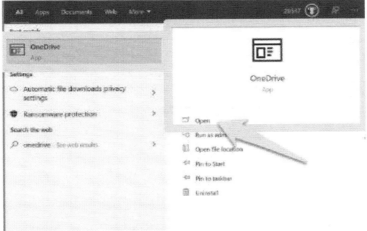

2. When you already have an account with OneDrive, you will just enter the email address you used in signing up for the account. Then you will click on "*sign in*."

Put your files in OneDrive to get them from any device.

Enter your email address

3. After that, enter your password on the next page. Suppose you have formerly set up another form of authentication for your Microsoft account. In that case, you must enter an additional code sent to your email or phone to confirm account ownership properly.

4. You must trail the directives to select the OneDrive folder you want. If you have signed in on this system, you may already have the OneDrive folder. You can click to *use this folder*, or you will select *choose a new folder*.

Signing Out from One Drive

1. Signing out is very easy. Click on where the initials are shown below.

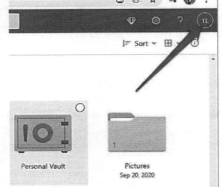

2. Once you have clicked on the initials of your name, it will bring out a list with your name showing my profile, my account, and sign-out, as shown below.

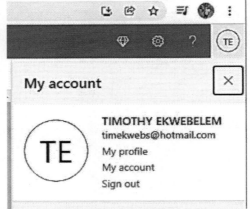

3. Choose the sign-out from the list and then click on it. You will be signed out.

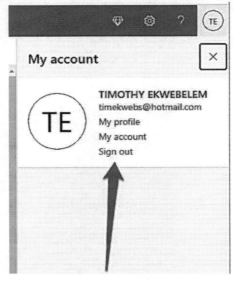

CHAPTER 2:
Downloading OneDrive in Different Devices

Technology has gone far in our world today. The evidence can be seen in OneDrive usage on different device types. You can have OneDrive on both your Personal Computer and on your smartphone as well. The phone may be running Windows OS, Android, or even iOS. All can run the OneDrive cloud storage app.

Using OneDrive Online (Web)

The first step is to use your phone or any computer to log on to your OneDrive account through the web. Just visit OneDrive web URL, which is *https://onedrive.com*. When you visit that URL in any browser, it will open a page that looks like the one I have in the photo below.

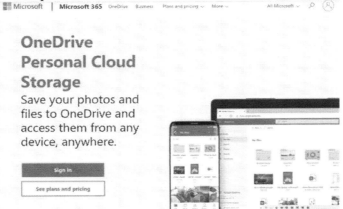

**Organized. Protected.
Connected.**

OneDrive homepage

Click on the *Sign in* button. Sign in with your Microsoft account details. Once successfully, you will be landed on the Files section of your OneDrive cloud storage. This will look the way you see it when you just open the OneDrive folder of your computer. What you can do when you visit the folder on your computer is the same as when you log in via the web platform. That is the reason I am continuing my teaching from the online platform. Irrespective of the channel you choose to access OneDrive cloud storage, you can carry out the tasks the same way.

The photo below is what your OneDrive cloud storage app will look like when you log in through the web using a browser on your computer.

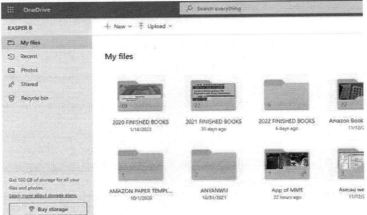

The OneDrive web page, when logged in

As you can see in the above photo, you are directed to the My files folder when you log in for the first time. You can carry out some tasks from that place.

If you want to view your recent actions on your OneDrive cloud storage platform, just click on the *Recent* tab. This will display the recent actions carried out on your account.

On the other hand, you may like to view all your photos on OneDrive. It is something simple to do. To achieve that, just click on the *Photos* tab. This will display all the photos you have uploaded on OneDrive so far.

Another thing you may like to track is the files you have shared with others since you started using OneDrive cloud storage. This finding is easy. Just click on the Shared tab positioned at the top-left to achieve that, just like the other main tabs.

And lastly, on the main tabs, you may feel like finding out the files or documents you deleted from your OneDrive account in the last 30 days. It is something simple to find out. Click on the *Recycle bin* tab positioned at the top-left, like the other tabs. It will give you an instant result based on the request.

How to Download OneDrive on Your Computer

The device you use determines how you will get OneDrive on your system. The windows you are using will be considered in the case of a personal computer. For example, if you are using *Windows 7,* you need to Download OneDrive. My computer is *Windows 10,* and it already contains OneDrive. Just click on OneDrive and follow the instruction to install the app.

Set up OneDrive

Put your files in OneDrive to get them from any device.

Enter your email address

Create account   Sign in

Open and follow the instruction to "install" the app. Click on *get started* and follow the commands.

Clicking "Get started" means you agree to the Microsoft service agreement and privacy statement. OneDrive may also download and install its updates automatically.

Get started

When you have successfully installed the OneDrive on your computer, the OneDrive folder will be added automatically to Windows Explorer.

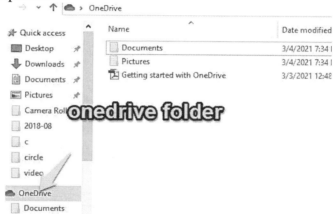

How to Install OneDrive on Older Windows Computer

If your computer does not operate with the recent Microsoft Windows like Windows 10 or Windows 11, you may need to install the OneDrive app on your computer. To carry out that task, you must visit the OneDrive download page on your computer. Visit the web link https://www.microsoft.com/en-us/microsoft-365/onedrive/download in your browser. When you are on the page, you will see the page that will look like the one I have in the photo below.

About to download the OneDrive program on a computer running older Windows OS

As you can see in the above photo, when the link opens in a browser, you will see the two buttons. They are *Start OneDrive* and *Download*. Because our interest is to download and install the OneDrive program, click on *Download*.

After you tap the *Download* button, wait for the program to download. After it is downloaded to your computer, locate the program. By default, it should be in the Downloads folder. So, click the *File Explorer* icon pinned at the taskbar section of your computer and then navigate to the *Downloads* folder.

Look for the program you just downloaded, which usually comes with the name *OneDriveSetup.exe*. If you do not know how to run the program, you do that by double clicking on the *OneDriveSetup.exe* file. You will be asked if you want the program to make changes on your PC. Click *Yes* or *OK,* depending on how your computer is programmed. Agree with the terms and conditions and follow up with the other prompts. In the end, installing the OneDrive app on your computer will be a success.

After the installation, search the app through the Search icon pinned on your computer's taskbar and click on it to open. The next is to enter your Microsoft account details and click the *Sign in* button for you to sign in. I have explained how to go about this in detail. If you do not have any existing account with Microsoft, click on the *Create account* button and create a new account with Microsoft. These are just the steps you are to take to have the OneDrive app up and running on your computer if the one you are using does not operate with the recent Windows or your computer work with Operating System that is not Windows.

How to Install OneDrive on Android Phone

As much as your Android phone can visit the Play store, you can have the OneDrive application installed. First, get connected to Wi-Fi or switch on your mobile data. You are to do that so that your phone will be connected to the internet. Without getting connected to the internet, there is no way you can download any application from the Play store.

As your phone is connected to the internet, click the Play store symbol on your phone. Play store comes preinstalled on all mobile phones that run the Android operating system. The phone below indicates the play store application on my mobile phone.

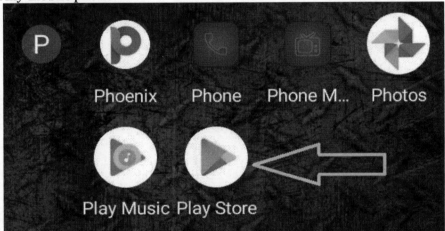

The arrow indicates the Play store application

Click the Play store app on your phone for it to be launched. In the search section, type "OneDrive." This will display OneDrive among the other search results. The photo below shows how the OneDrive application appeared when I searched for it on the Play store.

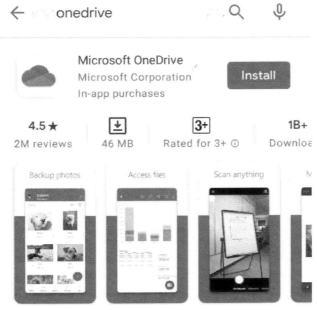

The OneDrive search result

Click the *Install* button to download and install the application on your phone. Please be patient for full installation to take place. Once the installation is over, click the *Open* button for the application to open.

As the application opens, you will see the part that reads "SIGN IN." The photo below shows what appears when the application opens.

Welcome to OneDrive

Access and share your documents and photos anywhere, on any device.

• • • •

SIGN UP

SIGN IN

The first thing you will see after you open the OneDrive Android app

Click the *SIGN IN* button. Enter the email address and password you used when creating your OneDrive account for the first time. When the Application confirms that the details you entered are all correct, you will be logged into your OneDrive account. You will see all the files, folders, and other contents in your account.

Installation of OneDrive App on iPhone

If you are a user of a phone running iOS, you can still download and install OneDrive on it. Like my guide on installing the OneDrive app on Android, installation on iPhone involves the same step.

A store where iPhone users can download applications that run on their device is the one named App store. So, you can get OneDrive software from there. But let me break it down more to your understanding.

Click the App store application on your iPhone for it to open. In the search box, type the word "OneDrive." This will display the OneDrive app among the other applications like it. Click the OneDrive app and select the *GET* button. This will get the OneDrive app downloaded and installed on your iPhone. Click the *Open* button for the installed app to open.

As the application opens, type the email address and password you used to sign up for OneDrive on their website. And lastly, sign into your account. As you sign in, you will be taken to your account dashboard. You will see some commands which you may not know how to use.

CHAPTER 3:
Important Operations on OneDrive

How to Sort Out Your Files

Sorting out your files is more or less managing your files, as we saw in the previous lesson, but we will use a different method here to approach sorting out your files.

Firstly you have to go to your OneDrive app, which is in the middle of your page, and then click on it as shown below.

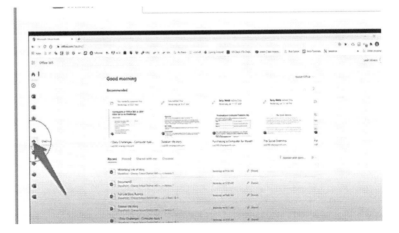

Once the OneDrive cloud is opened, it will take you to a new tab on your browser, as shown below, so that you can see your OneDrive files.

Here, what we are going to do is to go ahead and make a folder. This folder is going to be for our practice file. What we are going to do is to go to the top left and click the *"New"* button, as shown below.

That's going to take us to the following options.

Go ahead and click "Folder" here.

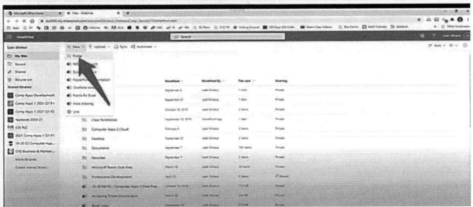

You will notice that *"Create a folder"* will just pop up on the screen, and we are going to name our folder as *"Computer apps1. P1"* and then click on *"Create."*

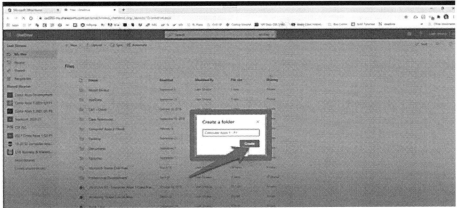

The moment you do that, it will pop up in your files on OneDrive, as shown below.

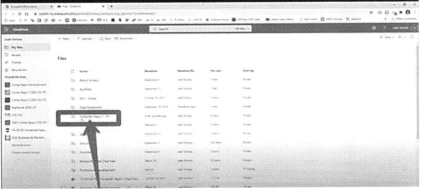

Go ahead by clicking on the newly created folder.

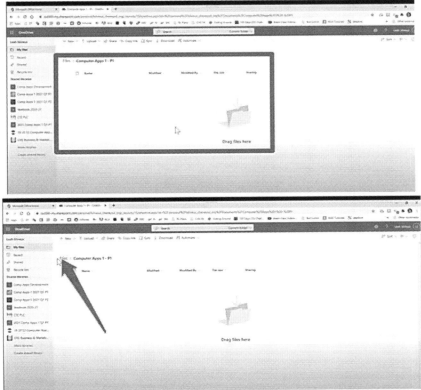

Inside the list of files, you should have the life story there, and all you have to do is to move into your **"computer apps 1.P1."** To move it, click and drag it. You can also click the little triple dot next to it to get many more options.

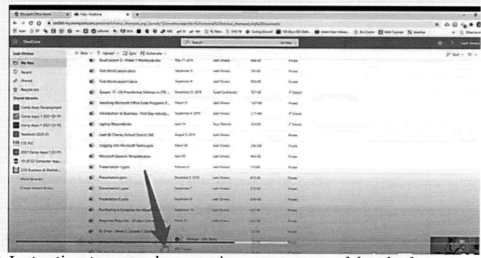

When I click on it, I get options to **open**, share, preview, copy, move, and download.

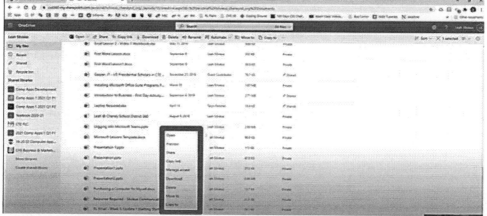

You also have an option to *"Move,"* and as I click on *"Move,"* a little box on the right side of the screen will appear, as shown below, allowing you to view where you're going.

You can see that I **have "computer apps 1.P1"** courses here. These are themes that exist here. These appear here, and it all also appears on the left side of the pane, as shown below.

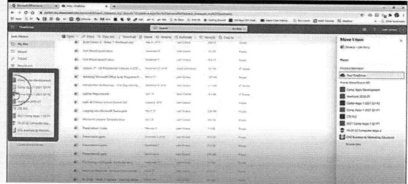

In this case, we are working on my personal "**OneDrive,**" so we will use "OneDrive Your Destination" on the right pane. Click on *"Computer apps 1. P1"* and place it.

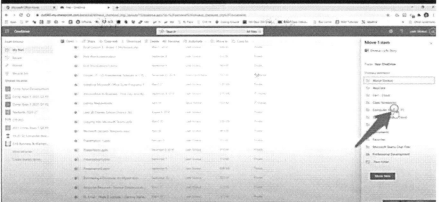

Once you're inside my **"Computer apps 1. P1,"** *click* **" Move here."**

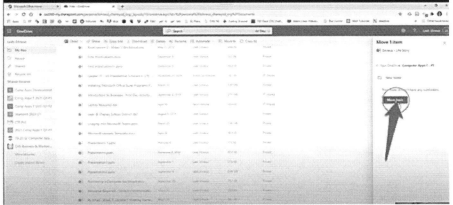

Then it will allow you to move it directly to where other files are. Next, you're going to move up. There is a little circle arrow at the top right. Click on it as shown below.

Go to my **"Computer apps1.P1"** folder as shown below.

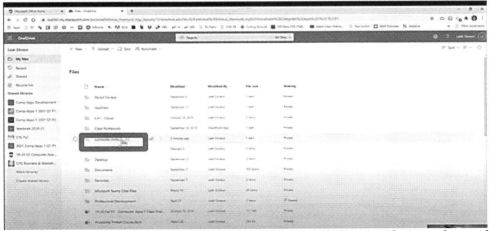

You will then have to click on the file **"Computer apps 1. P1,"** and then inside it, and you should now have something similar to what's shown below.

In addition to that, go ahead and create an additional folder inside of it to control. Go to my folder and put *"Instruction files"* and *"Create."*

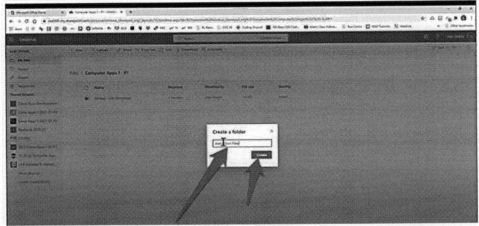

Now, the file is created, and when ready, go ahead and make a new folder. Now, you have your files organized.

OneDrive Keyboard Shortcuts for the Web

Keyboard shortcuts they're handy, quick, and very useful. Here are some keyboard shortcuts for OneDrive's web interface.

Shortcut key – Action:
- ? - Display keyboard shortcuts
- Ctrl+A - Select all
- Ctrl+D - Deselect all
- Up, down, left, right keys - Select the adjacent item
- Spacebar - Select or clear the selection of a file or folder
- U - Upload
- Ctrl + S - Download selected item
- Ctrl+Shift+N - New folder
- Esc - Clear selection
- F2 - Rename
- F5 - Refresh

Viewing Recent Activities on OneDrive

OneDrive software is built with some beautiful features. One of the beautiful features is your ability to view your recent activities on your account. Maybe you were working on something on your account before you left for something urgent. The recent activities section will remind you where you stopped.

To view your recent activities, click the Recent tab at the top left, as shown in the photo below.

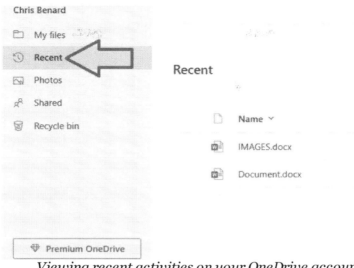

Viewing recent activities on your OneDrive account

Creating Word, Excel, and PowerPoint Right from OneDrive

From your OneDrive cloud storage online platform, you can create Word documents, Excel, and PowerPoint documents within a short time. When the file is created, it is saved automatically on OneDrive without stress. Take, for instance, I want to create a list of some items I may be needed next month using Microsoft Word, and I can do that within a short time. You, as a reader of this nice book, can do that. To complete that task, as you are already logged into your OneDrive account online, click on the *New* command followed by the *Word document*. This is indicated in the photo below.

- **To create a Word document on OneDrive**

The Word document file will load in a new tab. Type what you want to have in the document. When you are done with that, click on the default name given to the Word document(example Document2). The position of the default name is indicated in the photo below.

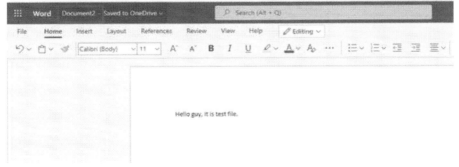

- **To change the default name given to the Word Document**

*T*ype the new name you want the document you created to be identified with and press the *Enter key* of your computer keyboard for the name to be saved. Close the Word document after typing all you want to have inside it, and the document is saved automatically on OneDrive cloud storage. That is the power of OneDrive.

Know that if you want the Word document created inside a particular folder, you need to click on the folder first for it to open before you click on the *New* command followed by the *Word document*.

In the same way you created a Word document on the OneDrive cloud storage and syncing platform, you can also successfully create an Excel workbook document. It requires the same procedure. But for the sake of clarity, let me break it down. The first step is to click on the *New* command, usually positioned at the top-left. Select the *Excel workbook* from the list. This action will open a new Excel workbook. Just type all you want in the spreadsheet. Click on the default name assigned to the file to give it a new name of your choice, and hit the *Enter key* of your computer keyboard for the name to be saved. After creating all you want in the Excel spreadsheet, close the workbook by clicking on the close icon in the top-right-hand corner. In doing that, the file is closed and saved automatically on the OneDrive cloud storage platform. As a piece of additional information, the file is synced across all your devices with the OneDrive app up and running on them.

To create PowerPoint as you are signed into OneDrive via the web or on your computer, click on the *New* command at the top-right corner. From the options that are displayed, select *PowerPoint presentation*. On taking this step, the PowerPoint platform will open in your browser. Create any presentation you want. After creating the presentation, you can change the default name assigned to the presentation file by clicking on the default name. Give it a new name entirely, and press the *Enter button* on your computer keyboard for the name to be saved. You can then close the presentation. As you do that, the presentation file is saved automatically on OneDrive.

Know that you can follow this same procedure to create other files type. You can follow the steps to create a OneNote notebook file, Forms survey, and Plain text document. So, it is possible if you want to create any of those file types while on the OneDrive platform. Just click the *New* command, select the document type and go on with what you want to create. It is just a simple thing to do.

Finding Out Shared Files on OneDrive

One of the properties of the software is file sharing. What if you have already shared some files with people and want to track those files you shared? How do you know those files you shared? It is something simple to find out. Once you click the *Shared* tab at the right of your dashboard, you will see your shared files. The photo below indicates the *Shared* tab you are to click.

The Shared *tab indicated*

File Sharing on OneDrive

To share any file on OneDrive, you need to log in to your account by visiting the OneDrive website through the website www.onedrive.com. On the dashboard, click the *My files* tab and select the file you want to share. If the file is in a folder, click the folder for it to open. When it opens, just select the file you want to share. The photo below shows my selected file, which I want to share with someone.

- **To share a file with someone**

To select any file on OneDrive, you need to drag your point to that file and click the checkbox to select it. Referring to my above photo, as I dragged the pointer to the file, I selected that checkbox designed in a circular shape. The arrow points to that.

After selecting the file you want to share, the next step you need to take is to click the *Share* bottom, which appears at the top. The Share button is also indicated in a rectangular design in my photo above.

The next thing that will surface is a popup that requests you enter the information of the person(s) you want to share your file with, the way you want to share, and the access level the recipient(s) will have. The photo below shows the popup you will see after clicking the share button.

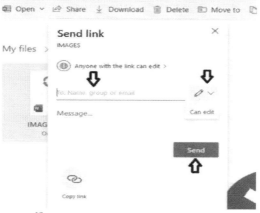

- **To share a file through email**

If you want the file to be sent to the email address of someone, type the email address of the person in the space that reads *To Name, group, or email*. If you share with more than one recipient, type their email addresses in that space. Also, if the person is in your email contact, you can type the name in that section. In the section that reads *Message*, you can just type a short note informing the recipient what the file you are sending is all about. And lastly, click the *Send* button for your file to be sent to the recipient.

But you can change the settings to "*Can't edit*" before sending it to your recipients. To change that, click the pencil-like design I indicated in the photo. As you do that, you will see what I have in the photo below.

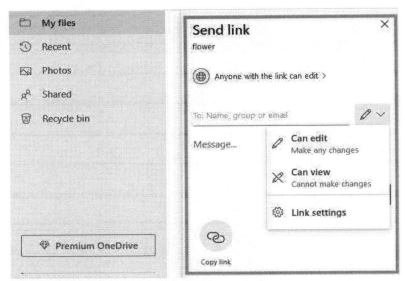

- **To change the file share settings**

You can select the "*Can view*" option by just giving it a click. This implies that the recipient of the file you are about to share can only view the file without having the power to make any changes to the file's content.

If you share links with people and want to set boundaries on what they can do on the link, you just need to click the part that states "*Link Settings.*" As you do that, a new section will open, which I displayed in the photo below.

- **Changing link settings before file sharing**

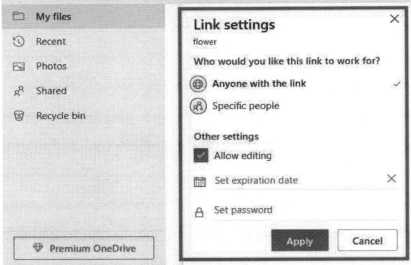

Under the section "*Who would you like this link to work for?*", you can choose *Anyone with the link* or *Specific people*. By default, it is set that anyone with the link can view its content. But if you want to select the second option, just give it a click followed by *Apply* button, and the change is saved.

Take a good look at the *Other settings* section. It contains some additional settings information on the link you are about to share with people. Under that section, you have to *Allow editing, Set an expiration date*, and *Set a password*. By default, the settings are on *Allow editing*. What that means is that anyone that has the link can edit it. The *Set expatriation date* allows you to set a date the link you are sharing will expire. The third option, *Set password*, allows you to set a password someone must type before accessing the link you share with them. It means that without the person inputting the password, they cannot view the link. So, you need to send the passwords to the people you share the link with. When you are done with choosing the settings option, click *Apply* button for the settings to be made effective.

OneDrive Recycle Bin and Files Restoration

Whenever you delete any file from your OneDrive account, the deleted file is moved to the recycle bin folder of your account. That is why you must recycle the bin folder on your PC.

The difference between the recycle bin you have on your PC (personal computer) and that of OneDrive is that the files moved to recycle bin can only stay there for just 30 days before they are deleted permanently. But the deleted files from your computer, which are transferred to the computer's recycle bin folder, can stay there for years. The photo below indicates the recycle bin.

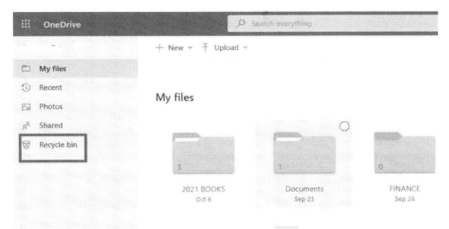

Recycle bin *folder on OneDrive*

When you click that *Recycle bin,* you will see any file you recently deleted from your OneDrive. You can even restore the file and move it to its initial folder of your OneDrive.

It is just a few steps to restore a recently deleted file from your OneDrive. As you are logged into your OneDrive account dashboard, click the *Recycle bin* tab. The *Recycle bin* tab you are to click is indicated in the photo below.

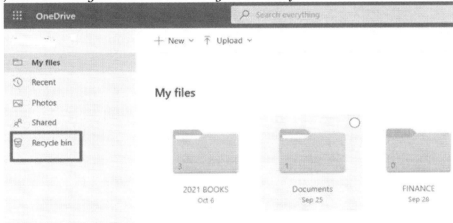

The Recycle bin *tab indicated*

The files you recently deleted from your OneDrive, which are 0 to 30 days, would be there. Select that particular file or files you want to restore. Next, select the *Restore* command I indicate in the photo below.

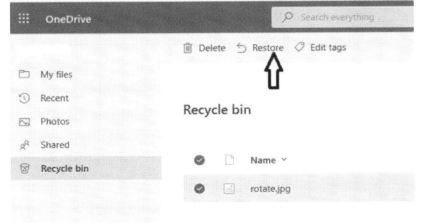

The Restore *command indicated*

Once you click the Restore command, the file is returned to its original location before deleting. These are just the simple steps to restore your previously deleted files.

Searching for Files on OneDrive

A time will come when you will have many files on your OneDrive account. In that situation, you may have more than 10,000 images and documents in your account. With that number of files accumulated in your account, you may not find it easy to find any file of your choice easily. One of the easiest approaches to get to any file you need in that situation will be using the Search box of OneDrive.

The search box is at the top part of your OneDrive dashboard. The photo below shows the location of the search box in OneDrive.

The location of the Search box in OneDrive

If you remember a few texts on the name you gave the file before uploading it on OneDrive, just type it in that search box. The search result will bring up the file based on its name. You can then click the file to have a full view of it.

How to Create a Folder on OneDrive

Folders are essential because it helps you have similar files in them. It allows you to organize your files.

Going straight to the heading under discussion, to create a folder after logging into your account, click the My files tab and select the New command at the top of the OneDrive dashboard. The photo below shows the *New* command you are to select.

The New *command you are to select*

When that command is selected, you will see some options in the photo above. From the list, select *Folder*. As the *Folder* command is selected, a space is provided for you to type the name you want the folder to answer.

Giving a name to a folder

Type the name in that space and click *Create* button below the folder name. Once this last step is taken, the folder is created on your OneDrive. Even in that your created folder, you can create a folder in it. This will take us to the following subheading.

Getting More OneDrive Space

By default, Microsoft assigns 5GB of storage space to the user of their cloud storage platform, OneDrive. In the future, you may find out that the space is getting filled, but this depends on the volume and size of files you upload onto the platform. In this subheading, I will walk you through how you can get more storage space for your OneDrive account. This can be a minimum of one Terabyte of space.

You have to know that to be given that additional space, you will likely buy Microsoft 365 suite. That is more beneficial to you. This is because when you become part of a Microsoft 365 subscription, you will not only get storage space of 1 Terabyte, but you will be given some major apps of Microsoft which are up to date with beautiful features. These apps include Word 365, Excel 365, PowerPoint 365, Publisher 365, and Access 365. You will gain all of these.

To buy more storage space, click the *Gear icon* (Settings) positioned at the top-right corner of your Microsoft account when you log in through the web. Some options will be displayed by clicking on that icon. Click on *Upgrade*. This action will take you to a new page.

The new page will open when you click on **Upgrade**

From the above photo, you can see the features attached to any plans you may go for. They are grouped into Microsoft 365 Family and Microsoft 365 Personal.

When you decide on the subscription package you want to go for, scroll down the page and click on the Go Premium button under each package. This action will take you to a new page. On that new page, your OneDrive account email address is displayed. Click on *Send code* for a code to be sent to the email address. Verify the code by typing it in the space provided and then proceed.

Creating a Folder in an Existing Folder

To create a folder in an already created folder, the first step you need to take after signing into your OneDrive account is to click the My files tab and then click that parent folder where you want to create a new folder. As that folder opens, click the New command at the top of the interface, as shown in the photo below.

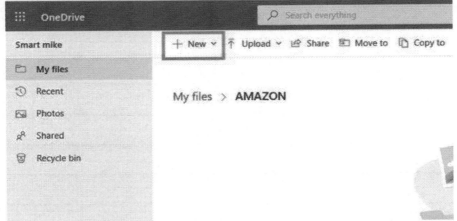

When you click the *New* command, select *Folder* from the list of options. As that command is selected, type the name you want the folder to bear, followed by the *Create* command. That is all about creating a folder in an already existing one.

Downloading Files from OneDrive

Have you been in a place where you needed a document urgently? Since you did not have your personal computer to have that document, the only option was to download that file from your OneDrive account and then print it from any cybercafé closest to you.

When you want to download any existing file in your OneDrive account, log into that your OneDrive account. Click the *My files* tab to see all the files in your account. Locate the file you want to download and get it selected. And lastly, click the *Download* button, which appears above the file.

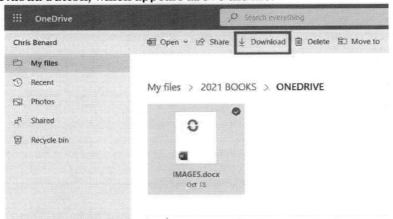

Downloading a file from OneDrive

If you are downloading on a computer, the system will ask you if you want to open the file or save it on your computer. In most cases, I choose the option to save it on my computer. Once the file is downloaded, you can find the file on your computer.

CONCLUSION

Thank you for reading this book. OneDrive is a superb cloud storage app that allows you to store your files and folders online. There are several cloud web storage systems out there that give you similar opportunities to store your files and folders on their web online storage space. Still, Microsoft has proven that the OneDrive is a real deal regarding cloud safety.

This unique OneDrive storage is good for those with a Microsoft account as it automatically comes with free 5GB storage. If you have a Microsoft account, you have a free 5GB storage space that comes automatically when you open your account.

One thing about OneDrive, besides its safety online, is that you can collaborate with your work colleagues, family, and friends and share files with them no matter where they are at any time. All you have to do is to share your email link to your document with them, and you can control whether they can edit your file or whether it is a read-only file.

Good luck.

BOOK 6:

MICROSOFT OUTLOOK

2022

Definitive Guide to Using Microsoft Outlook 2022, Staying Organized, and Adding Contacts

INTRODUCTION

Like many people, you have probably already been using Outlook for years. Because of this, you likely have countless emails in your inbox, many of which are unattended. You also may have flagged overdue emails when you decided to try using them but eventually gave up. Maybe your emails are spread across a collection of generally useful folders but still not how you would like them. This book aims to help you quickly parse these emails without losing the important items and set up your layout so that it will be most productive. Microsoft Outlook is an email management program for peak performance at all times. It's also known to save a list of people we often contact for the comfort of sending emails to each other and managing our time taking notes and appointments most effectively. And you also have the freedom to stay connected to all business and personal networks.

Microsoft Outlook has been the type of Email that users have used for quite some time, and since its acclaimed debut, it has received many positive responses from users worldwide.

Microsoft Outlook is the main deal for this decade because all forms of departments, institutions, and various offices use Outlook to send and receive emails. This is because data is stored most efficiently, simple to use, and non-complicated, making it easier for most users to use without qualms.

CHAPTER 1:
Functions of Outlook

Outlook is dedicated software for personal management; it also helps you to manage your Email effectively. So, in this section, we will be finding out the real standout features of Outlook mail. They are:

- **Efficient Email Management**: This is an outstanding feature that shouldn't be ignored. You can manage your work email and categorize them based on your needs, avoiding confusion and giving you the ease of operation you need. Besides that, you can also execute flagged commands to receive emails quickly.
- **Ability to Sync Data On/Off Your Devices**: This feature helps you to be able to work and manage mail with more flexibility. All you need is a phone or device connected to the network and then login into your Microsoft account; you can collect all related information and work with them more easily.

Questions and Problems Solved by New Outlook Features

Resetting Your Password

To reset your password, you'll have to know your old password; this is done to secure all related information. Proceed by login into the application, and on the settings page, you go to the security section. You will see an option right there to change the password.

If you've forgotten your old password, click 'I forgot my password and follow the instructions to reset your password.

Not Able to Find the Downloaded Files on Your Device

You can view all this by clicking Documents in the Oracle Content application navigation menu and proceed by clicking Offline in the filter menu. When you're done downloading the file, it is downloaded to a secure area within the Oracle Content Application. You can access it through the mobile application, even if you aren't connected to the cloud.

But for security reasons, it is impossible to be accessed outside the Oracle Content, so you won't find it in your regular download folder or any other folder on your device.

Note: If you're using an IOS device and have saved the file locally to your device, you can view it in the file application.

To delete a synchronized or downloaded file, tap and hold it, select it, and proceed by tapping the delete icon. Removing these files from your device wouldn't affect the original copy, which has been stored in the cloud.

Not Able to View the Downloaded File

You only need the right software on your device to view such a file. Now, for example, if you downloaded a PDF file, you'll need an app on your device that would be able to open the PDF file. If you don't have the correct app, you'll be unable to view the file.

Perk: One of the latest features introduced by Microsoft is the ability to enable dark mode. This is only available in office 365.

All you have to do for the dark mode is sign in to Outlook. Click 'Try new Options,' and a new function will immediately be activated.

Hidden Functions of Outlook

Outlook reminds you to attach a file and never miss a flight again. Also, add the details to the flight automatically. Outlook reminds you of a task you've never specified or an appointment you'd forgotten to write down.

If you compose an email and type the words, Outlook will remind you that you may have forgotten to attach the file. You can stop such a sending process, attach a file, and send a message. You can click Attach files or Insert Pictures in Outlook email messages for more Outlook functions.

Have you also found yourself in an email conversation that you wish to ignore? Perhaps, you work in a large company, and someone could annoyingly add you to a distribution list without your consent. Instead of deleting each message from the conversation, you can ignore or delete the entire conversation.

All messages in the conversation would be moved to the Deleted Items Folder. Future messages from that conversation would be wholly skipped from your inbox and placed directly in the Deleted Items Folder.

You can use a clean folder to wipe out extra and unnecessary messages.

Suppose you've emailed a lot of workers when you only needed a few of them. Well, here's what to do. First of all, the cause is that you used text effects like bold, underlining, or even bright font colors to make your names stand out.

Here's what you should do. Type @ followed by the name, and an operation will immediately happen.

The name would be automatically added to the recipient line of the email message. So, when the recipient does receive a letter in their inbox, they'll see the @ symbol in the message list.

Search folders; the actual case in this category could be that a user needs to do specific searches regularly. You can create a virtual folder that consists of the items that meet specific search criteria.

In this sense, Outlook does have a series of templates or custom folders that would be created. For example, we can find the unread items folder, which includes emails in various folders. It's also important to know that no mail is physically transferred to the search folder but can be displayed in that location virtually by meeting the specified criteria.

The procedure for this is simple:

- Click on the folder tab and choose 'New Search Folder.' You can select an already created template or simply customize a search folder at such a time.
- In such a case, find the last option in the list Custom, select it, and click Choose in the New Search Folder dialogue box.
- Next, select a name for the search folder you are creating and click on Criteria, which specifies the search criteria.

Perhaps you wish to set the time and date other than the time to write something down. It is possible to do it differently and is also quite simple.

Here's the procedure:

- First, you proceed as if it were a regular mailing, whether a new one or a response to one received.
- Next up, and from the message itself, you click the Options Tab and proceed to Delay Delivery in the More Options Sections.
- Then you select the box, make sure you 'Do Not Deliver Before,' and select the date and time; this is when you want the message to be sent. Choose any other option you so desire and Click Close.

Outlook is known to store scheduled email messages in your Outbox until they are further needed when transferred to your Sent Folder. In any case, it's always possible to change the date or time of the deferred Delivery or cancel it.

To do this, proceed to Outbox; this is where you'll be able to find the Email. Open and click the Options and Deferred Delivery tab, in which you can make all the changes you do feel it's appropriate.

If you use Outlook for Email, tasks, and scheduling, you may also want to open multiple Outlook windows. This permits you to view your Email, tasks, and calendar consecutively. You don't have to use the navigation buttons to keep switching views. It also gives you the freedom to use the different trays at the same time too.

With Outlook, you can search for your preferred content in specific mailboxes, subfolders, folders, and all generalized forms. But what isn't well known is this, we can also refine searches by applying particular strategies. Writing a single word (Ontek), the engine will display all elements containing that word without discriminating between the upper and lower case.

Now, if we write two words (Blog Ontek), the engine would show us those elements that contain one or two words or even both, regardless of the order.

If we use quotation marks (Blog Ontek), the elements that do contain the exact string will be displayed.

To customize a quick step, click on 'Create New' in the 'Quicksteps section.' Following this, a Quickstep would open, and you must name it. Then you choose the action we want to associate with it and click on the 'Add Action.' What you are doing here is this, you are adding as many actions as we do need for this Quickstep; for example, we can configure quick steps to mark a message as necessary or as 'Unread' and transfer it to the 'Emails to reply' folder. In such a way, all actions requiring various steps to execute can be simplified with a single combination of keys.

Suppose you'd receive a flight, hotel, or rental car reservation by email. In that case, Outlook will automatically add them to the calendar along with the related information, such as the tracking number, confirmation, and link. Unfortunately, Outlook cannot calculate travel time to the airport, so be sure to check out the traffic before you leave so that you don't arrive late.

Favorite Folders; 'Favorites' is a tab located at the top of the folder panel, and the function of this tab is simply to facilitate access to the most used folders. This is done to prevent you from scrolling or searching through numerous panels of folders, which can be pretty discouraging.

You must now drag those you need as 'Favorites,' They will be visible there as if they were direct access. By moving them within the favorites, we can have them satisfy us the most.

Perhaps you wish to remove the folders from 'Favorites,' all you need to do is right-click on it and choose 'Remove from Favorites.' And, you'll have to know it is a 'Live' folder, which is especially suitable when operating different tasks.

Major Reasons Outlook is Popular

One of the fascinating things about Outlook is the number of functions to operate your tasks efficiently. It spans from managing your contacts to creating and assigning tasks, printing attractive mailing labels, and managing your digital schedule. Outlook can do all of it.

Outlook is also known for organizing all your emails, Calendars, contacts, tasks, and to-do lists in just one space. Its organization starts with your email account; from there, you can begin working on your Email, transitioning to work or appointments, and storing information about the people you interact with the most in your contacts. All these are done, so you don't have to remember email addresses or phone numbers. Let's take a quick look at some of the essential functions.

You can use Outlook to send and receive emails to communicate with people inside and outside your organization. It can also be used to schedule all-important appointments on your calendar and manage appointments to remind you before the meeting.

You can store additional contact details such as your company name, telephone number, address, and other information.

Outlook also permits one to send high-capacity files much more easily and quickly.

It has the best features to block spam emails and mark or block special emails more safely and effectively.

It also allows the use of HTML and CSS; this is done to help you be more creative in sending mail. Perhaps, you accidentally delete your messages while using it; you can apply the 'Quick Recovery Feature.'

Best of all, Outlook is known to have high speed.

It lets users sign in with temporary passwords and can star essential messages. Suppose you wish to use that password for a certain period; you can automatically set it up in the settings. The form would be attached to

'Important Messages' so that when they are sent, they'll be notified first, which is a more convenient way to make your exchange.

You can also sort emails by time, size, ending time, and time of receiving. So, you can easily find your Email and the file you need to send.

Also known to support it with large file attachments combined with SkypeDrive or OneDrive.

You can block Emails by specific address or domain (which is highly resistant to spam).

Outlook also generates a disposable email address (used for one-time mailing operations or Email Marketing); this is done to keep you away from spam mail engines. With Outlook, you can create, change and delete these addresses more easily.

Supports recovered or deleted emails, all within the acceptable amount of time, even when deleting the trash's emails.

Unlike other apps, Outlook gives its users access to unlimited storage and permits logging in with a temporary password. It also integrates chatting through Skype.

Outlook is also known to save time; a quick step in Outlook is a small macro you do have to create. And you can use such a macro over and over again. You don't need any programming skills to make a quick step. Creating a Quickstep is much more comfortable.

All you have to do is click the necessary actions together, and all the activities become one quick step. You have the liberty to forward a specific email, ad a piece of text, and then place the Email in your archive. You can bring those three steps altogether in one Quickstep. Extra time is the result of making Quicksteps.

Perhaps you wish to create an email and want it to be sent early tomorrow morning. All you have to do is save the Email in your draft folder and send it before tomorrow. Another option is to indicate in the email options that your Email shouldn't be shipped till a certain point in the future. This is where it only has one drawback; at that specific moment, your Outlook should be working, and your computer mustn't be turned off; your Outlook must be overall active.

Using your daily task lists under your calendar, a daily task list is a handy tool that permits you to show tasks from your to-do list at the bottom of your calendar. Under the calendar, you can put a subset of your more extensive list in your to-do list.

You can also manage important mails for users to see first; all other mail parts are kept separately. You can quickly search mails by type and filter incoming grouping mail and private messages by individual's/business messages in the inbox.

There is a shortcut function for archiving, scheduling, and deleting messages. You can quickly switch between apps, Email, and calendars.

Outlook can also send large files instantly without loading them onto the device. If you have to write the same email regularly, you must use the option to create Outlook templates. You create a template in the following way, make the 'template mail,' and that's done by creating a new mail.

Type your text, the subject line for the recipients (to, cc, bcc) save the Email via File> Save As...> Outlook template.

You can also save the template file in another folder. To apply the template, go to New Items> Choose Form and then go to your 'User Template in File System.' if you've saved the template in another folder, you can proceed to use the template by double-clicking the file. It's also possible to use the template in a rule. This allows you to automatically answer emails, especially when an email lands straight in your inbox that meets all conditions.

Using an additional Calendar to write time and time tracking is one of the best ways to increase awareness of your actions. Having someone follow you all day can cost you some cash. All you have to do to resolve this is to create a different calendar. To do this, create a new folder and choose the calendar items as the folder's content.

When you are working, open your calendar or timekeeping calendar; drag the actions from your daily task list to the time in your timesheet calendar; that's when they are completed.

If you don't do an action from your list, add it manually from your calendar. You'll get an overview of what you did on a particular day. This is helpful because it gives feedback on what you did in the past week - an insight that helps you do better than next week.

CHAPTER 2:
Managing Contacts, Dates, Tasks, and More

Learn how to create and manage your Contacts list, including changing how you view your contacts, attaching photos to them, and sending them to other people, as well as how to sort your contacts and use grouped views.

Discover how to create and modify appointments, print your calendar, and work with multiple calendars using the Calendar.

In addition to keeping your entire list of names and addresses in one place, Outlook also lets you sort, view, find, and print it in many different ways, depending on the type of work you're doing. Furthermore, you can store lists of family and friends alongside your business contacts in Outlook, easily distinguishing between them when necessary.

Putting in Your Contacts' Names, Numbers, and Other Stuff

Keeping many names, numbers, and addresses is not difficult, but finding them again in the future requires magic unless you have an application like Outlook. Several programs can save names and related numbers, but Outlook is the most popular choice for working with names, addresses, and phone numbers.

If you've ever used a pocket address book, you'll be familiar with the Outlook Contacts feature. You just need to enter the name, address, phone number, and a few tidbits-and you're done!

The Quick Way to Add Contacts

A new contact can be added easily to your Contacts list:

- Click the New Contact button in the People module to create a new contact. A contact form will appear.

- Complete the form. It is not necessary to fill out all the fields; only use those that pertain to the contact in question.
- Close the document by clicking Save & Close. It's that simple. Adding more information to contact later is okay if you don't fill in all the details immediately.

The Slow, Complete Way to Add Contacts

Depending on your preferences, you can enter dozens of details about every person on your contacts list. However, if you just want to include the essentials, that's fine. Here's what you'll need to do to enter every tiny detail for every contact record.

- Select "New Contact" from the People module.
- You will see the new contact form.
- Choose your full name from the drop-down menu.
- A window titled "Check Full Name" appears.
- Take one or more of the following actions:
- To scroll down, click the triangle (called the "scroll-down button") on the right edge of the text box named "Title." You can either type a title (such as Reverend, Guru, or Swami) or select one from the drop-down menu.
- Enter the contact's first name in the first text box.
- If necessary, type the contact's middle initial (if any). Leave this field blank if there is no middle initial. The middle name can also be written here if you wish.
- Enter the contact's last name in the "Last" text box.
- Select the suffix from the drop-down menu. Select one of the options (like Jr., III, or Ph.D.), or type one in the box (such as D.D.S., B.P.O.E.).
- To proceed, click the OK button.
- Your Full Name and File Number As text boxes are now filled with the name you entered in the Check Full Name dialog box,

Complete the form by clicking on the appropriate box and entering the requested information. Please leave the box blank if the information is unavailable, for example, if a contact does not have a title. There are more options when a triangle appears after the box. If your choice isn't listed, enter it in the box.

When you enter a name in the Full Name box, you'll see that name appear in the File As box.

You can file a person under a different name by clicking File As and entering the designation you prefer. Your dentist may, for example, be filed under the term "dentist" rather than by name. In the alphabetical listing, the dentist's name appears under "dentist" rather than the actual name. You will find the full name and the file as designations in your contacts list. By doing so, you can find your dentist by name or the word "dentist."

- Enter your contact's email address in the "Email" text box. To enter a second email address, click Email 2, pick the second address from the list, and then enter it in the text box.
- Type the contact's business phone number in the text box beside "Business Phone." You will have the option to type in the contact's home phone number if you click on the Home Phone text box.
- To enter numbers other than home and business telephones, click the triangle beside the number option, choose the type of number you are entering, and then enter the number.
  There are four blocks for phone numbers in the New Contact form. The drop-down menu contains 19 types of phone numbers that you can use according to your contacts' numbers.
- Choose the type of address you want to enter in the Addresses section by clicking the triangle. Choose a business address, home address, or other address.
- Go to the Addresses section and click the button.
- An address check dialog box appears.
- Fill in the appropriate fields with the following information:
  - The street
  - The city, state,
  - The province
  - Region of zipping or postal code
  - Country
- Click OK to close the Check Address dialog box.
  - If the address you just entered will be used for mailing, select the "This Is the Mailing Address" box on the New Contact form.

o   If you want the address card to link directly to a page, click the Web Page Address text box and type the page's address.
- A contact's webpage can be viewed by opening a contact record, clicking on the More button on the Ribbon, and clicking Web Page (or pressing Ctrl+Shift+X). An internet browser will display the webpage. The URL of the page can be viewed in your web browser by entering it into the Address box. Within the Web Page Address text box, you can enter the URL for any webpage an Outlook contact has.
- Fill in the bottom right notes box with whatever information you want.
  There is no limit to what you can enter (preferably something that will help your dealings with the contact).
- Click the Save & Close button on the Ribbon after you are finished.

You're ready to start interacting when you've entered any information you need (or may need) to know about the people you deal with at work.

Viewing the Contacts

The information you enter in Outlook can be viewed in many different and useful ways, called views. By viewing your contact information and sorting the views, you can easily see the big picture of the data you've entered. Within each module, Outlook provides several predefined views. You can edit any predefined view, name it, save it, and then use it exactly as you would the predefined views.

You can change how your contacts list appears by following these steps:
- Select the Home tab from the Ribbon of the People module.
- Choose the view you want from the Current View group. That view will appear on display. Besides the card view, you can also select the phone view, the list view, or any other view you like.

View Sorting

A few views, such as the phone view of the People module, are organized as simple lists.

You can sort by a column's title once you've clicked on it if you can't find a contact in a view with columns. Suppose you want to know the names of the IBM employees in your contacts list. If you sort the company column, you can see all the names simultaneously.

Here are the steps you need to follow to sort by column name:
- Select the Phone view on the Ribbon under the Current View section of the People module. Contacts are displayed in the phone view.
- Go to the COMPANY column and click the heading.
- Contacts are listed alphabetically from A to Z (or ascending order) according to the "Company" column. Now you can find someone by scrolling to that letter. By sorting by company, all contacts appear in alphabetical order of company name.
- Upon clicking the title a second time, you will see your contacts sorted in reverse alphabetical order (i.e., descending order).

Rearranging Views

Simply drag the title of a column and drop it where you want it to appear to rearrange the appearance of a view. Below is an example of how to move
The contacts list may already be displayed in the phone view.
To the left of the FILE AS column, click on the title of the preferred column and drag it over. Red arrows appear to the left of the clicked column, pointing to the border between two columns. By releasing the mouse button, Outlook will drop the column where the red arrows indicate.
Let go of the mouse button. You have now dragged the column from right to left. The procedure is the same for moving any column in Outlook.

Using Grouped Views

Sorting doesn't always suffice. After a while, you can easily accumulate several thousand contacts; it only takes a few years. In a long list, if you're looking for something with the letter M, for instance, you'll find it about three feet below the bottom of the screen, regardless of how you sort it.

There is no need for Outlook, as anonymous groups are the solution. You already have several predefined lists that rely on grouping in Outlook.

Lists are displayed in Outlook in several different ways: Sorted lists are like playing cards laid out in numerical order, starting with twos and proceeding to threes, fours, and so on, up to picture cards. In a group view, all the hearts, spades, diamonds, and clubs are arranged together in a single row.

Here are the steps to viewing the company grouping in list view:

- Select the Home tab under the People module.
- Select the List option from the Current View group on the Home tab.
- Headings with the prefix "company represent companies." The number of items under each heading is shown under that heading.
- Expanding or collapsing the contacts under that heading is done by clicking the triangle symbol to the left of the heading.

You can group items according to just about anything you want, provided that the data you enter is accurate. Below are the steps for grouping by another field:

- Select View Settings from the View tab of the People module.
- A dialog box with advanced view settings for the list appears. You will see that Group By is set to "company."
- Group by clicking "group by."
- An appropriate dialog box opens. You will see that Group Items By is set to "Company."
- Select a different field from the company list.
- Specify the sort order by clicking "Ascending" or "Declining."
- Ascending means going from A to Z, and descending means going from Z to A.
- For the dialog box to close, click OK.
- Close the Advanced View Settings: List window by clicking OK.

Identifying Your Friends

A string tied around your finger doesn't do much to remind you to do something involving another person, and it also looks ridiculous. Fortunately, Outlook provides a better solution.

You can easily remember the name of someone you have promised to call next week by flagging their name in the Contacts list. This will trigger a reminder in your calendar. Flagging isn't limited to contacts. The same effect can be achieved by adding reminders to tasks, emails, and appointments.

The following steps will guide you through the process of adding flags to contacts:

- You can flag a contact by right-clicking on it in the People module. You'll see a shortcut menu appear.
- Select Follow Up. "
- You will see the "Follow Up" menu. Choose the day for your follow-up.
- You can choose today, tomorrow, this week, or next week. When you flag a contact for a specific day, that contact's name appears in your Outlook Calendar on that day.
- Select the contact, click "Follow Up," and add a reminder. A dialog box appears.
  If you need to avoid that person for some reason, you can choose to have the reminder open and a sound played at the specified time. Reminders are Outlook's way of telling you to do something.
  The Custom dialog box allows you to select a reminder date from the Date drop-down menu in the Reminder section.
- A calendar is displayed when the arrow next to the date is clicked. Click on the date you want.
- From the drop-down menu, select a time for a reminder.
- Set the reminder by clicking OK.

Finding a Contact from Any Outlook Module

You'd like to search for a person, but you're currently using another module. That's fine. Any Outlook module can be searched using the Search People box on the Home tab on the Ribbon.

The steps are as follows:

- Find people by clicking on the "Seek People" box.
- You will find it on the far right of the Home tab of any Outlook module.
- Enter the contact's name.

- To open that contact's record in Outlook, press Enter.

When you enter only a few letters of a name, Outlook lists names that contain those letters, so you can choose the contact you had in mind. With the word "Wash," you can search for George Washington, Sam Washburn, and any other people on your list that include "Wash."

To view a contact record, double-click its name.

Sending a Business Card

Any Outlook user (or any other application capable of displaying digital business cards) can forward an electronic business card to another Outlook user. There's no better way to share any contact record in your list with someone else.

The most obvious thing you may want to send this way is your contact information.

- Create your contact record in the People module.
- This record should contain all the information you need to send to someone.
- To send information to a contact record, click twice on the record.
- Clicking twice opens the contact record.
- From the Ribbon, click the Forward button under the Contact tab.
- Three options are provided: a business card, an internet card (vCard), or a contact in Outlook.
- Select the format that suits you best.
- If you're unsure, select "Business Card." Both Outlook and Internet cards can be sent using that program. A new message is generated containing the contact information.
- Enter the recipient's address in the "To" text box.
- You can also choose a name from your address book by clicking the "To" button.
- Press Alt+S (or click the Send button).
- A message and vCard will be sent to the recipient.

Double-clicking the icon representing the business card in the message will add the business card to your Contacts list. An additional contact record will be created. You can add the new name and all the business card information to your contacts list by clicking the Save and Close button.

Alternatively, your business card can be forwarded by clicking the contact record and selecting the Forward button in the Ribbon. The process is shorter, but you can only forward it as a business card or an Outlook contact.

CHAPTER 3:
Getting More with Microsoft Outlook

Many users prefer using Outlook as their email client and personal information manager. Over the years, as part of the Microsoft Office Suite, Outlook has proven to be a standard solution (in conjunction with the Microsoft Exchange Server) for both public and private organizations.

In this chapter, we will delve more deeply into how Outlook works, its components, and how much can be achieved without spending a lot of time trying to figure out how things work. Carefully go through the points outlined below to gain more knowledge.

Folder Pane

The folder pane shows all the folders in Outlook. If this pane is minimized, other folders will not be displayed, and you will not be able to gain access to them. There are two different ways this folder can be viewed.

The first is by clicking on the left side of the screen. This will help in expanding the folder pane and making other folders visible.

The second option is to click on view, then the folder pane, and click on normal to see things more clearly.

The folder pane in Outlook is said to be the main navigation tool between mailboxes, folders, and different modules like mail, calendar, and contacts. Note that the folder pane has a couple of other options and tips to help make the pane fit more into your style and help you work effectively and efficiently.

You can enable or disable the folder pane by Pressing the ALT + F1 buttons.

To change from one module to the other, use the icons enlisted in the lower area of the Folder pane. If you also prefer to see the names of the modules alone instead, disable the Compact Navigation through the Folder Pane Options dialog box.

Note that with the Folder Pane, you can configure the way modules are shown, and in the very order they are shown, they can also show module icons or names for easy navigation, add shortcuts to modules, and lots more. To get the best out of this folder, you should spend some time clicking on various options, including the ones explained above.

Information Viewer

The information viewer is the very place where most of the action in Outlook takes place. If we assume the folder pane is the channel sector on a TV. The information viewer will be more like the TV screen.

The information viewer is where emails are read, contacts are searched for or added, and contact names are also displayed. If you also wish to do many other fancy things like sorting contacts, tasks, and so on, the information viewer is the perfect place to get all that and more done.

Based on the fact that lots of information, more than what can be seen at a glance, can be stored in Outlook, the information viewer helps to show a preview of the information available. This way, you are up to date with all you need to know. The calendar, for example, can store dates as far back as the 16s and as far ahead as you can imagine. The smallest calendar review is displayed in a day, and the largest calendar view is a month.

The information viewer also helps to arrange what it displays into smaller units known as "views." There is an option to create your views and save them, but you can also decide to use the view with Outlook.

Move through the different previews of the information displayed by Outlook by clicking on various parts of the information viewer. Some people love to say they are browsing the information viewer when moving around; it seems more like just scanning through the pages of a notebook.

You can also browse through the calendar data in the information viewer to keep you abreast of things to come. To do that, simply follow the steps below:

- Click on the calendar in the navigation bar, use the keyboard shortcut, and press the Ctrl + 2 buttons.
- Next, click on the workweek button on the ribbon's Home tab. The workweek view of the calendar will then be displayed. Note that a workweek means five days if the regular calendar week shows seven days.

To further spice things up, you can decide to change the appearance of the information viewer in several ways. For example, there might be a need to see the schedule for a day or just the items that have been fixed for a particular category. Views can ensure you get a glance at the very preview of the information needed.

While checking out the calendar, you can also decide to check the To-Do bar on the screen's right side. The To-Do bar shows your appointments and reminds you of what you need to do. To turn on this feature,

Click on the View tab on the ribbon > click on the To-Do Bar > click the calendar button.

In Outlook, every module (mail, calendar, people, tasks, etc.) has its own version of the Ribbon, arranged specifically to meet the needs of the module. Most of all, the buttons are labeled with the actions they are used for, such as replies, business cards, new appointments, and many more.

A little button known as "properties" can be found in the lower-right corner of some groups.

Click on it if you want more information displayed than what is shown on the ribbon. Properties are also known as "dialog boxes" as they open some sort of dialog box launcher related to the group when it is clicked.

Ribbon Ties

Viewing Screen Tips

Each button on the ribbon shows a little popup called a "ScreenTip" when the mouse is placed over it. The ScreenTip informs you about the button's name and also tells you things that will happen if you click on the button.

Some buttons have a small arrow that points downwards or to the right side of the button.

Click on the arrow to have a menu or list open. A popular example pertinent to almost all the modules in Outlook on the Home tab is a button known as "Move." When you click on the Move button, it opens a menu and shows all the various places an Outlook item can be sent to.

Using the New Items Button

Each module in Outlook has a "New Items" button that enables the creation of an item in any module. For instance, if you are checking the name and address of a customer whose name was also mentioned in a fascinating article in one of the daily newspapers, you will want to remember to refer to it at any time. You can do this by creating a new item from the new contact option, selecting the particular date, and then saving it with the name of the customer or something unique that can always make you remember the incident in the daily diary.

Taking Peeks

One unique feature in Outlook is a tiny pop-up window known as a "peek," which is displayed when you place your mouse over the modules such as People, Calendar, or Tasks in the navigation bar. This little but unique feature offers great help when replying to an email about an event that needs to be scheduled. Feel free to take a quick peek at your calendar while you work on that email. If a broader view with more information is needed, there is an option to make the peek window larger by clicking the button at the top right corner of the peek screen or by double-clicking on the calendar, people, or tasks in the navigation bar.

Getting Help in Outlook

The help feature in the Office applications, which includes Outlook, goes beyond just rendering help as it tries to get things done for you. Does that sound awkward? It isn't. It is just amazing and very helpful.

When working in the help feature, a lightbulb icon and a textbox are located at the top of the screen with the inscription, "Tell me what you want to do." Once that box is clicked, type in what you might need help with, and it will display a list of things that starts with a list of things that can be done. For example, if you enter the word "delete," the help feature will link to the Delete and Delete All commands and the folder with deleted items. When one of the commands is selected, it will delete the same Outlook item chosen. When you click "Deleted Items," it will take you straight to the deleted items folder.

Note that it is vital that you request only the things that can be done in Outlook. If you type something like "what can I eat?", the choices Outlook will offer you might disappoint you. But if you are trying to do something that involves email, appointments, or tasks, Outlook should provide you with the very important links you need to get things done quickly.

Scroll beneath the list of links to view other choices that Outlook might display. Once you point at the "Get help" option, it will open a submenu of various help topics that are in some way related to what you have asked. You have to click on that yourself, as there is no option to help you do that.

The final option in the help menu is called "Smart Lookup," which helps open the Smart Lookup task pane and uses Microsoft Bing, the search engine for Microsoft, to search for the phrase that has been entered. When using smart lookup, the intelligent service may need to be activated. For example, if you type "marry a millionaire" and click on the smart lookup link, a list of marriageable millionaires will be displayed, and if not, at least At the very least, you will get the definition of the word or phrase that has been typed and probably a link to Wikipedia also.

Other Programs as an Alternative to Outlook

Postbox

This program was created by one-time Mozilla employees and was based on Thunderbird. About ten years later, the software has developed into an autonomous and extremely effective mail client. The design of its interface is like that of other solutions, and it is also easy to use. Users who want a unique look can adjust themes or design their templates.

For a more efficient operation, Postbox makes use of different shortcuts. Users can access the Quick Bar via hotkey so that messages can be moved or categorized quickly. In addition, when creating an email, a signature can be entered using the Quick Bar without the mouse.

There are lots of benefits when writing emails in the postbox. The software has various templates and text blocks that can be used to write cover letters and replies in a placeholder that can be added and created where the receiver's name is always added automatically.

Thunderbird

For both private users and those in companies, Thunderbird is one of the most preferred options as an alternative to Outlook. The open-source solution is also available for free. The program's free version is streamlined and offers only the most basic functions. One major advantage is the addition of various add-ons. This means that there is room for expansion of the email program. However, the add-ons and extensions are made to suit their respective versions. If you need to update your version of Thunderbird, the add-ons must also be updated.

Spike

Spike was released in the year 2013, and it combines certain functions of classic email programs with those used in modern messenger apps. Immediately a private mailbox is linked to the application, and elements like subjects or signatures are no longer necessary. At the same time, the basic mail client functions, which include the central inbox or contact management, will be integrated into the modern messenger environment. It is also not coincidental that the creator of Spike described it as a conversational email application. Note that audio and video calls can also be made via the software.

Spike depends on modern standards in terms of security. Communications that include attached files can be encrypted with just a single click. This way, you can be sure your messages are fully protected against unwanted access. Spike is free for private users; however, monthly fees are charged when business email accounts are added.

Mailbird

Mailbird is an Outlook alternative that is only free in the test version. This email solution combines messages and contacts from different accounts into just one box. The interface can be designed with different free themes that best suit you.

Mailbird offers different interfaces to various applications and also enhances the mailbox with helpful features for better interaction and teamwork. For instance, Twitter, Whatsapp, Calendar, and Dropbox can be integrated into the mail to change it to a multi-functional program.

CHAPTER 4:
The Essential Secrets of Email

Email is essential for all professional communication in the office. If the organization you work with uses Outlook, learning how to make judicious use of it can be vital to your professional development since the skills learned will help you arrange meetings with those you work with and send email messages easily. Furthermore, using the Outlook features, you can easily show your colleagues, boss, or team lead that you have learned well and improved over time. You can even offer to teach them what they want you to know about using these tools.

Front Ends and Back Ends

Two things are needed to send and receive an email; a program that helps create, save, and manage messages and a program that sends the messages to people and receives replies from them (exchanging messages). A few people in tech call these two parts the "front end" and "back end," as the case may be. Outlook, on the other hand, is a front end for email messages. It helps create, format, store, and manage messages, but it doesn't do much about getting the message to the intended destination. Ensuring that messages get to their intended destination is the work of the back-end service (like the Microsoft Exchange Server in your office), the Internet Service Provider you use, and an online email service like outlook.com or gmail.com.

Email messages cannot be sent or received anywhere in the world without an internet connection. The phone company you use most of the time provides internet services that can be used for this purpose. Choose the best Internet Service Provider to ensure your email messages are sent quickly and get replies as quickly as possible. Remember, though, that the easiest choices aren't always the best. There are several companies ready to offer internet services. Shop around to get the best value for money.

Creating Messages

In many ways, electronic mail (email) is much better than normal paper mail, commonly known as snail mail. Email is delivered much faster (almost instantly) than paper mail. The speedy delivery can significantly help when closing a last-minute deal, sending vital information towards the close of working hours, or for last-minute birthday greetings. Email is also very cheap to use; it is free most of the time.

The Quick Way

Creating a new email message can be very easy. Simply follow the steps below.
Open Outlook The main module will then be displayed, opening the inbox.

- Click on the New Email button
- Insert an email address in the To box.
- Insert a subject in the subject box.
- Insert a message in the message box.
- And finally, click on the send button.

Most of the time, Outlook starts in the Inbox only. This will only change if the settings have been changed. If there is a need to start up in an entirely different folder than your inbox,
Click on the File tab and choose Options.
Click on the advanced option, and in the Outlook Start and Exit part, change the Start Outlook. Click on the "browse" button to check all the folders in the Outlook data file. To begin in another module, select a folder similar to that, e.g., Calendar or Notes.

The Slow and Complete Way

You might like the more comprehensive way of creating an email message. If you love to create fancy emails, especially if you want to take advantage of every key feature Outlook has to offer, follow the steps below:

- Locate the Mail module > select the New email button or press Ctrl + N. The new message form will then open up.
- Click on the "To" text box and insert the email address of the person you are about to send a message to. If you are sending to more than one person, separate their email addresses using the comma or the semicolon. There is also an option of clicking on the To button, locating the names of the people you intend to send messages to in your address book, and double-clicking on their names to ensure they are added to the To text box.
- Click on the Cc text box and insert the email address of the person you want to have a copy of the email message you are about to send. You can also click the "cc" button to include people from your address book.
- Insert the subject of the message into the subject box. The subject should be brief and simple, as it makes someone enthusiastic about reading your message rather than a lengthy subject line. If, for any reason, you forget to insert the subject, Outlook will open a window that asks if you intend to send the message without a subject. Click the "Don't Send" button to return to the message and include a subject. If there is no need for a subject, click the Send button to send the message.
- Type the body of your message in the message box. If Microsoft Word is the word processor you use, you must be familiar with the graphics table, modes of formatting, and all the tricks in Word to ensure your email appears more attractive. These same tricks can be found in Outlook using the tools at the top of the message form on the Format Text tab.
  Be extremely careful when formatting your email. This is because not all email systems can deal with graphics or text that has been formatted like boldface or italics. This way, the text you send to your client will not look like gibberish. Furthermore, most people read their email on phones or phablets, making the text you send look odd. If you are unsure how your recipient will receive your mail, stay off of adding graphics or formatting text.
- Click on the Review tab > select the Spelling and Grammar button at the upper part of the message screen. You can also choose to press the F7 button. Outlook will then run a spell-check to ensure your message is free of spelling and grammatical errors.
- Finally, click the send button or press Ctrl + Enter or Alt + S. Outlook will move your email to the outbox. Outlook will immediately send any message in the Outbox if you are connected to the internet. If the message was composed when you were not connected to the internet, click the F9 button to send the message again when you are connected to the internet. When a message is sent, it will automatically move to the sent folder.

Another option for telling Outlook to send messages from the Outbox is to tap the little button looking like two envelopes overlapping that can be found on the Quick Access Toolbar at the top left corner of the Outlook window, which can be seen from any module in Outlook. If the mouse pointer is moved over this button, a screen tip will be displayed, notifying that it is the send/receive all folders button. Whenever messages are sent by clicking on the send button in a message or by tapping the F9 button, it is also a way of telling Outlook to receive all messages coming in.

Setting Priorities

Certain messages can be more important than others. Sending a report to your boss is not the same as sending a friendly message to a teammate or colleague. Setting the importance level of a particular message to "high" informs the recipient that the message needs urgent attention.

There are three levels of importance you can choose from:

- Low
- Normal
- High

Setting Sensitivity

Sometimes you need your message to be seen by only one person. Alternatively, you might just want to ensure no one alters your message after sending it. The sensitivity settings in Outlook help to put a restriction on what any other person might be able to do to your message after you have sent it. They also help you decide who that person can be.

In applying the sensitivity settings to a message:

- Click to open the properties drop-down menu for messages.
- Click on the list box arrow closest to the word "sensitivity" and any of the displayed levels as briefly described.

Most of the messages sent via Outlook have just the normal sensitivity, which is what Outlook uses if the settings are not changed. Settings such as Private, Personal, and Confidential only inform those receiving the message that there might be a need to treat the message differently from the way they treat other normal messages. There are even specific organizations that employ the use of strict measures in dealing with confidential messages.

Applying the sensitivity settings of a message to either private or confidential does not make it any different from other messages; all it does is inform the person receiving the message that the message has some information that might be delicate. If you use Outlook at work, double-check with your system administrators before assuming that the information you're about to send via email is secure.

Setting Other Message Options

Upon clicking the Properties dialog box, you might see that there are quite several odd-sounding options. A few of these options are Request a Read Receipt for This Message (which informs you when the receiver reads the content of the message) and the Expires After option (this marks a message as expired if the receiver does not open the message before a stipulated time). These options are pretty useful. The only glitch is that your email and the email receiver must support the setting, or it might not work. The Microsoft Exchange Server should work fine if you are on the same network. If you are both not using Outlook or an Exchange Network, it can just be a gamble.

Reading and Replying to Email Messages

Outlook has several methods to notify you when an email message has been received. The status bar towards the left of the Outlook screen will inform you of the total number of emails in your inbox and the number of messages that are still unread. The word "inbox" will change automatically in the folder pane to a boldface form when there is an unread email. The titles of unread messages will also be bold.

To click open and read an email message, follow the steps below:

- Locate the Mail Module: click on the title of the message you want to read twice. This will open up the message in its window.
- Select the close tab option (X) or press the escape key to close the message pane when you are through.

Viewing Previews of Message Text

When you begin to receive plenty of emails, some of them will be important, while others might not be significant, if not useless. Upon receiving the mail in your inbox, it can be handy to know which is important and which is not. This way, you can focus on the very important one. You cannot depend on those sending the mail to tell you how important or otherwise it is. Outlook offers help by giving a glimpse at the first few lines of the message. The message preview is always on when launched and set to 1 line. This option can be changed to 2 or 3 lines, and you can also choose to turn it off totally. The Message Preview option becomes redundant if the reading pane is turned on, but the preview can be useful if it is not.

To gain control over the previews of messages that have not been read, follow the steps below:

- Find the Mail Module>click on the View tab option in the ribbon.
- Click on the Message Preview option.
- Click on the setting you prefer (one line, two lines, three lines, or off).

If, for any reason, there is a prompt to alter the settings found in all mailboxes or just this folder, select the option that works best for you.

All the modules in Outlook have a lot of viewing options that can be used to make information much easier to use. The Message Preview option is an excellent way to scan through email if you don't want to use the reading pane. Follow the steps below to set up the Reading Pane:

- Locate the Mail Module >click on the View tab located on the Ribbon.
- Select the Reading Pane option.
- Select from the options on the right, bottom, or off.

You cannot be wrong with either of the options you decide to choose. You can also switch from one choice to another if the first choice chosen is not comfortable for you.

Sending a Reply

One of the amazing benefits of using email is that replying to a message is very easy. There is no need to know the person's address when replying; click on the reply icon, and Outlook will sort the remaining.

To reply to a message, follow the steps below:

- Locate the Mail Module>select the title of the message you want to reply to. If it is enabled, the selected message will be displayed in the reading pane.
- Select one of the options below
- Select the Reply button to reply to those in the From Field.
- To reply to those in the CC field and the From field, select the Reply All button. A reply screen will then open in the reading pane area where the initial message was. Email sent to a bunch of people can also be received at once. Ideally, it is expected that one person at the least will be named in the To field and more than one in the Cc field, which is for those you are sending just a copy of the email to. There is no need to keep replying to those in the CC field. You can also decide to respond to some of them if you wish.
- Enter your reply into the message box. Do not be dismayed if you find out that the message box already has some messages; they are part of the message you are replying to. The cursor blinking will be in the upper part of the screen. With this, anything you type will appear before the other message. When you reply, the recipient can view the initial message to help refresh their memory about the discussion.
- Select the send button, and your message will be sent with the message form disappearing and the message replying to reappearing.
- Press the escape key to close the message screen. This will make the message replied to disappear, and the inbox reappear.

Resending Messages

Asking people to do just what you want is another fantastic feature of email. Nonetheless, most people overlook things because they receive too many emails. When you discover you are making the same requests again, it is high time you took advantage of the resend feature in Outlook. With this, there will be no need to type the original request again; just find the original message and send it again with a lovely reminder about when the initial message was sent.

To send a message again, follow the steps below:

- Locate the Mail Module and click on the sent items folder in the pane.

- Search for the message with the initial request and click it twice. This will leave the original message unopened. Doing this is essential because resending a message is not done from the reading pane.
- Select the Actions Button on the Message Tab and then click on the Resend This Message option. This option will create a new copy of the former message automatically.
- Insert a reminder or make specific changes to the message if need be.
- Finally, click on the "Send" button.

Follow-Up

Very often, new mails will require specific tasks. Maybe your boss expects some contribution. One does not need to do that instantly; it only needs to be done on time. I strongly recommend getting used to instantly telling Outlook when you'd like to get a reminder - in case you haven't done that in the meantime anyway. This way, it's much easier to get sorted and cluster your tasks instead of gaining ground between pressures from all sides. Outlook is your reliable assistant and will ensure nothing will be left behind.

To get this done, click Follow-up in the open mail, in the Message tab, and for the whole choice of options, now on Custom...

The remainder will be set to the due date and the end of office hours.

You should adjust that to maybe the forenoon of that day when the first rush is done, and you're still well before the closing date.

After clicking OK, we can read in the email what settings were made.

Beware of Phishing!

Some cunning people are always looking to trick and deceive you; most of the time, it is always on the internet. Recently, a widespread scam known as "phishing" has caused people to lose their time and money, causing them grief after responding to an email from an impostor who claims to be a representative of a bank or certain financial institution.

If you receive an email claiming to be from a bank or any other business and you are asked to click on a link for verification of your data, don't do it.

Often, the link will take you to a website that seems genuine, but the data you are asked to enter can be used for theft or fraud. Reach out to the organization directly to be sure the email isn't fake. If you are unsure what to do, it is best to delete such an email.

If, on the other hand, you want to check in with the sender of the email, visit your browser and check out the organization's website if it is one you are quite familiar with. If the message looks very old, please do stay away from it.

Forwarding Emails

When you don't have the answers to an email you received, you may need to forward it to someone else who can. Follow the steps below to forward a message:

- Locate the Mail Module>select the title of the message you intend to send. The selected message will then be displayed in the reading pane.
- Click on the Forward button. The forward screen will then be opened, replacing the reading pane. The initial message will also be the subject of the new message, except for the letters FW, which means forward and is entered at the beginning.
- Select the To text box and insert the email address of the person you intend to forward the message to. If the person is already in your address book, insert the person's name into the search box, and Outlook will detect the email address.
- Select the Cc textbox and insert the email address of those you want to send a copy of the message to. A lot of people forward very trivial things to their colleagues via mail. A host of recipients are constantly added as cc addresses.

Blind Copying for Privacy

Whenever a message is sent to a large group, all those who get the message can view the email addresses in the To and Cc fields. Email addresses that some might want to keep private have just been given out. Everyone might have received too many bizarre, unsolicited messages before, and most of them will get peeved at the broadcast of their messages without their permission.

Blind copies offer the best of both worlds. If all the email addresses were inserted into the Bcc field, no one's privacy would be compromised. By using Bcc addresses, addresses that need to be kept secret can be kept secret.

Deleting Messages

It is possible to disregard an email message without having to think twice. There might be no need to read it at all. By looking at the inbox list, you already have an idea of the sender and the content of the message. Hence, there is no need to waste so much time reading some unnecessary jokes. Simply take it off.

If a message you still need is deleted accidentally, simply press the Ctrl + z button to undo the action quickly. If some other actions have been committed in error, click on the Deleted Items folder in the Folder pane; the messages that have been deleted in the past will be found there. To bring back a message that has been deleted, simply move it from the Deleted Items folder to the icon of whichever folder that it should be in.

To have a message deleted, follow the steps below:

- Locate the Mail Module > select the message title that should be deleted. It is not a must to read the message. You can delete it from the list immediately.
- Select the Delete button located on the Home tab on the Ribbon or simply click on the Delete key on the keyboard or press the Ctrl + D button.

The Delete button can be recognized easily; it is marked with a huge "X" sign, meaning "Make this message disappear."

When messages are deleted, Outlook will not remove the deleted items; it simply drags them into the Deleted Items folder. (In some other mailing accounts and mail systems, it is known as trash rather than deleted items, though they mean the same thing.) If messages have been unread in the Deleted Items folder, the folder's name will be followed by the items that have not been read. It is possible to do away with the deleted messages forever by right-clicking on the Deleted Items folder in the Folder pane and selecting an empty folder. After the Deleted Items folder empties, the messages in the folder will be gone forever.

Saving Interrupted Messages

If you get disturbed while composing an email, don't give up, as all is not lost. You can still get back to the mail. Outlook will save it automatically in the drafts folder whenever you begin composing a message and switch to other things without first sending it.

To make sure it does this,

- Press the Ctrl+S keys before it saves automatically when you are ready to continue working on the message being composed.
- Click on the message and complete it by clicking on the send button.
- You can also click the "discard" button if you decide not to continue with the message.

Saving a Message as a File

Sometimes you receive an email that is so wonderful or disheartening and wants to have the email saved. You can either print out the message or show it to someone else, save it to a disk, or simply send the message to a desktop publishing program.

To save a message as a file, go through the following steps:

- Locate the Mail Module with the message box open, choose the File tab on the Ribbon and then choose the Save As Option or F12. This will open up the dialog box.
- Use the navigation pane on the left side of the save box to select the drive and folder in which the file should be saved. Outlook will initially choose the document folder by default, but there is an option to save the message on any drive and folder as it suits you.
- Select the File Name text box and insert the specific name you intend to give the file. Insert just any name you want. If you type a name that is not compatible with Outlook, it will bring up a window that states that the filename is not valid.
- Select the triangle at the end of the save as type box and select text only as the file type. There are various file options to choose from, but the text-only file format is the one that is read the most by other applications. The various file type options are:

- o Text Only: This file format is easy to use in that it helps to remove all of the message formattings. As the name implies, only text messages are saved.
  This format saves messages that will be frequently used in Outlook. It helps to save not just message formatting but also attachments.
- o Outlook Message Format: This format ensures all message formatting and attachments are kept but can be read by Outlook only. This is the same as the former file format, but it uses the international characters that can be read by any version of Outlook that uses various languages. This is Outlook's default setting.
  This helps to save a message in a file format option that can be shown in a web browser like Edge or Firefox. Or any application that can show HTM or HTML files. File attachments are not saved, although the message formatting is permanently kept. Furthermore, in addition to saving a copy of the message with the HTM file extension, another different folder is created which has the supporting files that the HTM file needs.
  This is also known as the HTML file format; the only exception is that an additional folder is not created because all the content is saved in just one file. Applications that can show HTM and HTML files should also be able to show MHT files.
- Click on the save button, and the message will be saved to the folder specified.

CHAPTER 5:
Important Email Tools

Outlook can perform many tricks with the email messages sent out and the ones received. Messages can be flagged with reminders, customized with signatures, or have special formatting added to the messages sent as replies.

Flagging

Over the years, flags have become the most used feature in Outlook. If you are the type that receives hundreds of messages daily and needs help with remembering those you need to reply to so that they won't get lost in the mix, it is best to flag that message as soon as it is read. This way, you are sure you will get back to the sender. A flag can also be planted in a message you send to others to remind them of a particular task they have to carry out for you and the person on the other end using Microsoft Outlook.

One-Click Flagging

If flagging a message serves as a reminder of what needs to be done concerning a specific message, you should be aware of the quickest way to do so.

When you move your mouse over any message in the inbox, towards the very end on the right side, a gray outline flag will be displayed, looking more like a shadow flag. When that shadow is selected, the color will change from gray to red, which means it has been flagged. When you check through your list of messages, you can easily recognize the one that needs more attention. This way, the tracklist of flagged messages can be maintained even if they are below the bottom of the screen.

Once you have sorted the messages you flagged, click on the flag again. This will replace the flag with a checkmark indicating that the message has been taken care of.

Setting Flags for Different Days

If you select a message once to include a flag, a copy of the message will be displayed in the task list, and various tasks scheduled for that day will also be displayed. Sometimes you might not be in the mood to deal with particular messages. You might feel it is better to wait until the next day or week. All you have to do is right-click on the flag, and a list of possible dates for a flag will appear, including the next day, this week, and next week; no date and customs will be displayed. Once a due date has been picked, it can still be changed if the need arises by moving the item from one due date to another using the TO-DO bar. You can also double-click on the item to have it reopened and then choose a different due date.

If the due date comes and goes and the flag remains unchanged, the message heading in the Inbox and To-Do bar will turn red.

Changing the Default Flag Date

For those who are constantly busy or simply enjoy procrastinating, the default due date of flags can be changed by following the steps below:

- Click on the "Follow Up" button in the Ribbon Tags group. This will then have the flag shortcut displayed.
- Select the Set Quick Click, and a dialog box will be opened. The list in the box will provide different options for a due date.
- Lastly, select the date that best suits you. The date will then become the default flag due date.

If you have issues committing yourself to a certain date, choose the "No Date" option and wait until someone raises the alarm.

Adding a Flag with a Customized Reminder

Without a doubt, flags can do a whole lot more than just stand for a week or more. Flags in Outlook can pop up as a reminder, reminding you of what needs to be done. Flags can also pester someone else when a reminder is attached to a message sent to someone else. Adding a reminder to a flag cannot be completed with a single click. Follow the steps below to do that:

- Locate the Mail Module and right-click on the message that needs to be flagged. The flag shortcut menu will then be displayed.
- When this is done, the custom dialog box will open up, and if you click on the OK button at this point, the message will be flagged and ready for a reminder at 4 pm. This reminder can be adjusted, especially if the time is too close.
- Select the list box arrow at the right side of the Flag to Text box and click on one of the menu items. A handy flag means "Follow Up" and reminds you to affirm a certain arrangement or appointment, as the case may be.
- Insert the dates in the Start Date box, Due Date box, or all boxes. The date and time inserted will determine when a reminder will pop up to help jog the memory of the appointment. Ensure the dates are typed in a way Outlook will remember.
- Click on the OK button. Once the reminder date entered into the custom dialog box is up, the reminder dialog box will help offer a nudge.
- Changing the date on a reminder
- Don't get nagged with a reminder; you can always pull it off and do it much later.
- To change the date on a reminder that was sent to you by someone else, follow the following steps:
- Locate the Mail Module and select the message that has the reminder that needs to be changed. The message will be displayed as highlighted when it has been selected. To open the custom dialog box, simply right-click on the message.
- Click on the Home tab, select the Follow Up on the Ribbon option, and include a reminder. As an alternative, press the Ctrl+Shift+G buttons.
- Click on the Reminder checkbox and, if it has not yet been selected, choose a new date for the reminder flag to show up. If the checkbox has already been selected, leave it as if you click on it again, it will then leave it deselected.
- Finally, click on the OK button.

There is also an option to click on the snooze button in the reminder dialog box to turn off the reminder flag for some time when it pops up, the same way it is done with the alarm clock.

Saving Copies of Your Messages

There is nothing handier than knowing what was sent and when. All outgoing email messages in Outlook can be saved. This way, you can always go back and check the message sent. Immediately after the Outlook program is installed on a computer, it starts saving sent messages. This feature can, however, be turned off. Before attempting so, check your message folder to be sure it contains sent messages.

To save copies of the messages, simply follow the steps below.

- Choose the File tab > select the Options button. This will then open up the Outlook dialog box.
- Select the Mail button and locate the navigation window on the left side. The mail settings will then be displayed.
- Move to the Save Messages section and click on the Save copies of the messages in the Sent Items folder check box if it hasn't already been selected.
- Then finally, click on the OK button.

Setting Your Reply and Forward Options

The look of a forwarded message can be controlled as well as the replies. If you use Microsoft Outlook, your text can be made to look incredible in your messages by the addition of graphics, special effects, or some wild-looking fonts. If mail is being sent to people who use other programs and not Microsoft Outlook or those using web-based email services like Gmail, some of the effects might not be well translated.

To set your options, follow the steps below:

- Click on the File tab, locate the ribbon, and click on the Options icon. The options dialog box for Outlook will then open up.
- Select the Mail button in the left navigation window, and the mail settings window will be opened.
- Move downwards to the Replies and Forwards section and select the list box arrow at the right side of the Reply to a Message box. A menu of options will then be displayed, including the original text as the default option. The menu's diagram on the left will show how the message will be displayed when each option is chosen.
- Select the preferred style to use for replying to messages. A little diagram on the left side of the menu will change instantly to display what your choice will look like. You can try another if you don't like your earlier choice.
- Click on the list box arrow that can be seen on the right side of the When Forwarding a Message box. This menu option looks almost the same as the one above, with just one fewer choice.
- Select the style preferred to be used for forwarding messages.
- Click on the OK button. The Outlook Options dialog box will then be opened.

Using Outlook gives much room to explore and do all sorts of fancy and useful tricks with email. If the advanced options menu appears confusing, you can easily ignore them and just click on the Reply button and insert your reply.

You can also delete the original message when a forward is created or replied to, but it's best to include at least a part of the original message. This way, it will make the response easier to understand. There is also an option to choose and delete some parts of the main text that are irrelevant to your reply.

Sending Attachments

If you have created a document in another application and don't want to send it just yet, there is no need to type the same message repeatedly in Outlook; simply send the document as an attachment to an email message. Word processing documents, spreadsheets, and other presentations such as PowerPoint can all be attached. You can also choose to include pictures and music; any type of file can be sent as an attachment.

The Send From menu is the simplest way to send a file from a Microsoft Office program such as Microsoft Word.

- Open up the file in the program it has been created in.
- Choose the File tab option located on the ribbon.
- Select the "share" button.
- Choose the Word document from the share dialog box and write the message in Outlook.
- If you don't want that option, you can have a message sent directly from Outlook by following the steps below.
- Locate the Mail Module and select the New Email button that can be found on the Ribbon. You can also press the Ctrl + N button if you prefer to use a shortcut.
- Choose the Attach File button found on the New Message form's Ribbon.
- A list will then drop down to display the names of the recently worked files.

- You may be lucky enough to find the file's name and click on it. If the file name is not there, select the Browse This PC option located at the lower part of the screen. This will then open up the Insert File Dialog Box.
- Click on the name of the preferred file and tap the send button. The file's name will then be displayed in the Attached box in the message form's message header. When the email message is sent, a copy of the selected file will be sent to the recipient.
- Enter a message if you have one to send. There might be no message, and you just want to send an attachment. Note that the attachment's content will not be displayed on the recipient's screen until the attachment is opened.
- Click on the "To" button in the message form. The dialog box for choosing names will then be displayed.
- Choose a name from the contact list and click on the Select Names dialog box. This will then open up the name of the person that has been selected. This process can be repeated if you want to include more than one recipient.
- Select the OK button. The person's name can now be found in the To box of the message.
- Click on the Subject text box and insert a subject for the message. The option of a subject is not compulsory, but if you want the message to look important, a subject can be helpful.
- Finally, click on the "send" button.

Emailing Screenshots

It is often said that pictures are worth more than a thousand words. Most of those words become four-letter words when the computer begins to act up. This makes it very difficult to describe the type of problem accurately. When problems like this arise, Outlook can be of help.

A screenshot is simply a picture of the screen of a computer that is captured to show what is being done on the computer at that point in time. This ebook contains many screenshots to make certain steps and procedures more understandable. The same thing can be done with the screenshot feature in Outlook. A screenshot can be sent to help a person solve a problem with their computer. A screenshot can be sent off about anything, including pictures and documents. The possibilities of this feature are endless.

Simply follow the steps below to include a screenshot in an email message.

- When an email message or a reply is being composed, select the Insert tab on the ribbon. If you notice the screenshot button is grayed out, ensure the cursor is inside the body of the email message.
- Tap the screenshot button. This will then display a gallery of thumbnail images.
- Choose any one of the screens from the gallery. The screenshot that has been chosen will then be displayed in the body of the email message.
- Conclude with your email message and send it to the recipient.

Creating Signatures for Your Messages

Most people love to include signatures at the very end of their messages. A signature is usually just a few lines of text that show you to all who read your message and also states certain things you want them to know. Many people include their names, businesses' names, web addresses, motto, and personal information. You can automatically set Outlook to include a signature in all outgoing messages, but a signature file must be created first. To create a signature:

- Choose the File tab on the Ribbon > Click on the Options button. This will then open the Outlook Options dialog box.
- Select the Mail button in the navigation window on the left side. This will open up the Mail settings window.
- In the Compose Message section, click on the signature button. The signature and stationery dialog box will then be open.
- Click on the New Button icon.
- The dialog box for a new signature will open.
- Enter a name for the new signature. The typed name will then be displayed in the New Signature box.
- Click on the OK button to complete this process. The dialog box for the new signature will then close.

Enter the text of the type of signature you prefer in the Edit Signature box and include any formatting that suits you. Use the button in the text box to apply changes to font, color, size, or other text characteristics. You can choose to make the signature in Word and then copy and paste it into the Edit Signature box.

Shortcuts Worth Taking

The following tips will help boost your productivity, including turning a message into a meeting and resending it. You can boost your Outlook productivity with these ten accessories, including Skype, OneDrive, and an online service for backing up your data.

Also, learn why you cannot have a unified inbox in Outlook and how you cannot create a distribution list from an email.

Using the New Items Tool

In whatever module you are in, click the tool on the far-left side of the ribbon to add a new item. So you change the name and appearance of this icon when you change modules, so it becomes the New Task icon when you switch to the Task module, the New Contact icon when you switch to the People module, and so forth. Alternatively, you can click the New Items tool just to the right of it to access the menu.

New Items allows you to create a new item in a module other than the one you're in without switching modules. You might want to create a task while you're answering an email. Choose Task from the list of new items, create your task, then continue working with your email.

Sending a File to an Email Recipient

Using Outlook email, you can send a file with just a few mouse clicks, regardless of whether Outlook is running. If you're using File Explorer to view your files, you can mark any file for sending to any recipient. Here's what you need to do:

- Use File Explorer to locate the file.
- To send a file, right-click on it.
- You are presented with a menu.
- Choose the recipient.
- A new menu appears.
- Select the recipient of the mail.
- There is a form for new messages.
- An icon in the attached box represents the attached file.
- Include the subject of the file and the email address of the person you're sending it to.
- Adding a comment to your message is as simple as typing it in the message area.
- Click the "Send" button.
- The message is delivered to the receiver.

Turning a Message Into a Meeting

Occasionally, after exchanging dozens of email messages about a topic, it would be faster to talk. Creating a meeting from an email message is as easy as clicking the Meeting button on the Home tab (in the Inbox with the appropriate

You can then create a meeting based on the contents of the email by clicking on the New Meeting button.

Finding Something

You can accumulate a lot of items in Outlook in no time, which can take a while to search through when you are looking for one specific item.

Outlook can help you find items quickly if you type the item's name in the search field at the top. That launches a quick search, so you can find what you are looking for in no time.

Undoing Your Mistakes

It's time you learned about the Undo command if you didn't already. The Ctrl+Z shortcut key can be used to undo accidentally entered text, as can the Undo button in the upper left corner of the screen in the Quick Access Toolbar.

You can experiment without worrying about the consequences; the worst thing you can do is undo it!

Using the "Go to Date" Dialog Box

The "Go to Date" dialog box can access any calendar view. You'll find it under the "Go-To" group on the Home tab, under Properties. You can also use Ctrl+G as a shortcut.

Adding Items to List Views

You can add an item to a list at the top of most Outlook lists by typing something into the blank field. Simply click the "Add a New Task" button to begin.

Your new item will enter the field once you click on it.

Sending Repeat Messages

Since you might send out one or two messages repeatedly, store them as Quick Parts to save time.

The steps you should follow when finding an Outlook accessory vendor online are:

- Your email message should be addressed.
- The email address of the company appears in my browser.
- Select the Insert tab.
- Click the Quick Parts button in the message body.
- Your saved AutoText item will appear.
- Make certain changes to reflect the name of the product.
- Click on the "Send" button.

Your request can be sent in less than 30 seconds, and you can move on to the next task.

Using this feature requires you first to store text blocks in Quick Parts:

- Choose the text you want to repeat in an email message, appointment, contact record, meeting, or task.
- Select the Insert tab.
- To access Quick Parts, click the Text group button.
- Select "Save Selection to Quick Part Gallery."

You can organize Quick Part text into groups according to their purpose. You could, for instance, generate the text for introductory messages and closing messages for different types of messages and then store them.

Resending a Message

When someone forgets to do something you asked them to do, sometimes you need to remind them.

A new message could be written, telling that person how often you've reminded them already.

However, this is quicker and easier:

- Open your Sent Items folder.
- Go back to the message you sent last time and click it twice.
- Decide what action to take.
- You can resend this message by choosing this option.

Additionally, you could add the following: "Here is another copy in case you didn't receive the first."

CONCLUSION

Outlook is a dedicated software for personal management; it helps you manage your Email effectively. Outlook accounts can work with all major versions and are also known to have the best features. Yearly, Microsoft announces new features that Outlook has for all its mobile devices.

Microsoft Outlook lets you send and receive an email, manage your calendar, store your contact information, and track your tasks. Most people think of Microsoft Outlook when it comes to email, but it has many other features that may be useful to you.

With Outlook, you'll get a feature-packed email client with a higher learning curve but many more options to customize your email. Even though you may use Outlook daily, you might not know all the cool things you can do with it.

But after reading this book, I'm sure you can now use Outlook to its full potential. Thank you!

BOOK 7:

MICROSOFT TEAMS

A Practical and Effective Guide for Educators and Businesses to Use Microsoft Teams for Remote Working and Online Teaching

INTRODUCTION

Communication is undoubtedly the essential key to success in every area of life. Microsoft Teams provides toolsets designed to make communication much easier for you, family, work, and everything else. From hosting online video conferences to public conversations and private chat messages. Teams is more than a communications platform; it is a workspace that builds on and takes advantage of several other Microsoft apps. Microsoft Teams is part of a yearly subscription-based service that provides you complete control and use over Office 365 business. A well-organized collection of Microsoft tools helps you stay and become more industrious in the office. Microsoft Teams fixes a lot, but we will be looking at the major categories that have everyone's focus. Teams provides us with public group conversation threads that can only be accessible to people or contacts of your choice. The private chat section allows you to send direct messages to specified persons, which will not be visible to others. Teams provide you with public and private audio and video call services, so you can have an audio-based or face-to-face communication with people who aren't in your vicinity or anywhere around you in real-time.

Suppose you are looking for a platform intended for collaborating with coworkers or virtual meetings where you can get a group of people in one place and work on the same project or do presentations in the form of a video chat. In that case, this is the right place for you.

Microsoft Teams is unique compared to other apps like Microsoft Word, Excel, and PowerPoint because you can collaborate on those with other team members, making it a powerful tool.

It is often seen as an app for everyone because it has amazing features such as a powerful chat platform where you could go ahead and chat to reduce your emails, set up and attend live events, meetings, and webinars and perform other functions that will be useful for personal use, teachers and students, and business owners and employees.

This book is dedicated to giving you the most useful knowledge of what Microsoft Teams does, how you can get it, and exploring how it will greatly benefit you. This is broken down into the simplest details to get you started. Whether you are hearing about it for the first time or you have little knowledge about it, there is something you can do with Microsoft Teams.

At the point when you begin utilizing Microsoft Teams, you should thoroughly consider how different gatherings inside your association work together with each other. Carefully consider how to make groups with the goal that the cooperation will be as effective as possible.

CHAPTER 1:
Understanding Microsoft Teams

Microsoft Teams is a collaboration platform where you can chat, share documents, have online meetings, and other valuable features for business collaboration, online learning, teamwork, *etc.*
It has many features that you can utilize for your use. You can schedule classes, hold classes, write on a virtual board, sit in classrooms, *etc.* The only difference it'd have with the learning you are accustomed to is that it is virtual.

Students, faculty, teachers, educators, and staff can meet, interact, learn, create content, share content, and collaborate using Microsoft Teams on Office 365 Education. Distance, the pandemic, and other restrictions are no longer barriers to effective communication with this effective collaboration platform.

Microsoft is adding many new features and applications to Office 365, such as Planner, Shift, and Microsoft Teams.

Teams is a collaboration app with all your chats, conversations, meetings, and files in one location. With Teams, you can communicate and collaborate in a single and secure location. You get a messaging platform, online meeting, calling capabilities, live collaboration on files, native integration with office apps, but also integration to many non-office apps that you're currently using.

To understand what you can do with Teams and how it could allow you to collaborate more effectively, you need to be ready to practice as you go.

Installing Microsoft Teams

Direct any program to "teams.microsoft.com" and sign into your MS account. You can make a record for nothing on the off chance that you do not, as of now, have one.

When you are into your MS account, click to download and introduce the application on your Windows, iOS, macOS, Linux gadget, or Android.

The program-based web application variant does not bolster continuous assemblies or conferences, yet it is occasionally quicker to get to Teams through a program. To get to Teams through your program without downloading the application, click "Utilize the Web App Instead."

When the Teams application is first introduced on your gadget, you may need to sign in again. After, click "Pursue Teams" to start setting up your association.

Another website page will open where you can peruse a full rundown of highlights and analyze evaluating plans. Groups are free if you use them with no other Microsoft Office 365 applications.

If you are joining a current association, pick "Already Using Teams? Sign In" Once you sign in, you'll be prepared to investigate your association's current Teams framework and begin talking with your partners.

If you are beginning another association, click "Sign Up for Free."

Enter your email and afterward select "Next."

Enter your first and last name just as the name of your organization or association. At the point when there is no doubt about it, "Set Up Teams."

You and your associates would now be able to work together distantly through this association in Microsoft Teams. You can fabricate a superior correspondence stage by making new groups inside your association, incorporating Teams with Office 365, and sharing your screen, your records, or your preferred feline pictures.

Microsoft Teams as a Mobile & Desktop Application

Microsoft is quickly developing its Teams application on iOS and Android, as the cooperation instrument grasps first line and other portable specialists.

There has been something of an ocean change at Microsoft in recent years. It used to be an organization centered around gifted 'information laborers, with the trademark 'A PC on each work area and in each home.' The statement of purpose is currently 'to engage each individual and each association on the planet to accomplish more.' With the difference in accentuation from PCs to individuals, there is a move to supporting first-line laborers, who regularly work moves and are typically paid continuously.

If there is one thing that the Teams versatile application is not, it is a clone of the work area Teams understanding. While that would be simple for Microsoft to convey, it would not be the simple-to-utilize, simple-to-learn application that a first-line laborer requires. They should have the option to get it and get the opportunity to work with negligible preparation. So, the portable Teams should be intended to work like some other iPhone or Android application, with a natural look, belief, and support for versatile local highlights.

Teams include that bode well on portable, while others are there to assist you with dealing with your work/life balance more viable. That can be as straightforward as setting calm occasions to shut out calls and messages when you prefer not to be upset. Dissimilar to Windows' Focus Assist instruments, Teams offers an alternative of Quiet Days, which permit you to shut out entire days - halting warnings at the ends of the week or moving rest days.

One significant component in the portable rendition of Teams is Walkie Talkie, propelling on Android gadgets in July. Like the old press-to-talk telephones, it is a method to immediately place staff in contact with one another. Utilizing Wi-Fi or cell information gives a secure voice correspondence channel for people and gatherings. Walkie Talkie is a piece of Microsoft's organization with Samsung's cell phone gathering, with the new Galaxy XCover Pro tough telephone offering an equipment 'talk' button that enacts the element.

Walkie Talkie resembles any Teams application and should be introduced from the Teams administrator focus. When presented and conveyed to gadgets, you will have to set up committed groups and channels for Walkie-Talkie to fragment gatherings of clients and maintain a strategic distance from crosstalk and disarray. Clients will interface with a chain when they. Please move and disengage when they leave.

Firmly related is a simple method of sharing your area and guiding it into your gadget's current GPS and planning apparatuses. Tap on the '... 'In a talk, where you typically pick an emoticon or connection to video transfers, Teams will embed a guide bit and a location. It is a valuable path for field administration engineers or other versatile specialists to immediately tell others where they are according to current calls, making it more straightforward to rapidly distribute assignments to the laborer closest to a call.

Microsoft is unmistakably mindful of the contrasts between work areas and portable use. A portion of the versatile Team's highlights ensures that utilizing Teams does not take away from your gadget's look and feel. That incorporates support for a dim mode, which can be helpful in low-light conditions or prefer not to upset the individuals around you. Different choices simplify tweaking the catches and menus, so you can have the instruments and applications you use inside Teams right where you need them.

Present-day cell phones are more than versatile PCs; they are also ground-breaking cameras. Microsoft's ML-controlled Office Lens is an instrument for taking and sharing pictures of records and screens, cutting undesirable fringes, and altering points of view. It transforms a telephone into a versatile scanner, and by incorporating Office Lens into the portable Teams application, you can rapidly share paper records with partners without leaving the app.

Setting Up Microsoft Teams

First, go to your Start menu, then to "*Settings,*" and navigate to "*Accounts.*" Go to the tab that says "Access work or school account," and if you have any of these accounts linked to your device, you will see them here.

Next, double-click to open Teams. You will get a welcome screen asking you to pick an account to continue. These accounts are already linked to the device, and the number of accounts linked to your device will be displayed here. Select an account to proceed. This will link that account to Microsoft Teams, and whenever you open Teams, it will automatically log in with that account.

If you follow this step, you may not be asked to enter a password during this process because your account has already been linked to this device. This means your password has also been linked and synchronized with Microsoft 365, so it is more like a single sign-in, and you wouldn't be asked to sign in with your password.

However, whenever you change your password from office 365, then Teams would require you to enter your new password.

As technology continues to advance, life gets better with Microsoft Teams. This is because the Teams keep advancing with the inclusion of new features making connectivity possible between people in different parts of the world.

Microsoft Teams is an effective way of making the internet a learning atmosphere for students. Instructors can make use of this tool to schedule and hold meetings on the internet with students across the globe without any problem at all.

Furthermore, teachers who have urgent projects to assign to their students and do not have the opportunity to meet with them physically can use Microsoft Teams to carry on with the activities. Besides that, instructors can share the documents they need with the students. Teachers can start a meeting with the students by connecting to a web app or the Teams desktop client.

Setting Up Your Account

The first step to using the Microsoft Teams application is registering an account with Microsoft. Individuals who already have an account registered with Microsoft from Skype or any other Microsoft application do not have a problem and can move on to signing up. But if you haven't had a registration or used any of Microsoft's applications, you will have to create a unified account that can be used to access other offers from Microsoft. After registering an account with Microsoft, you must go to your Teams app or the web version to sign up with Teams.

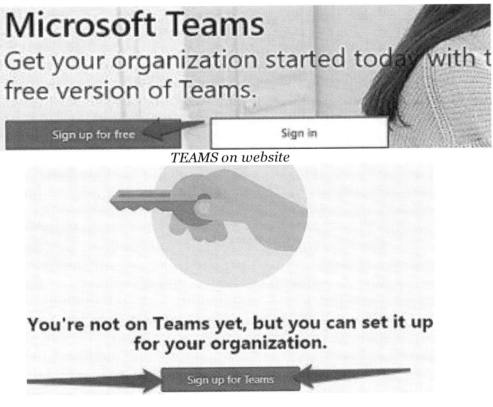

TEAMS on website

Click on the signup button, which will lead you to an opt-in page where you have to input your Microsoft user account information to continue or any other email of your choice. Type in your email and click Next.

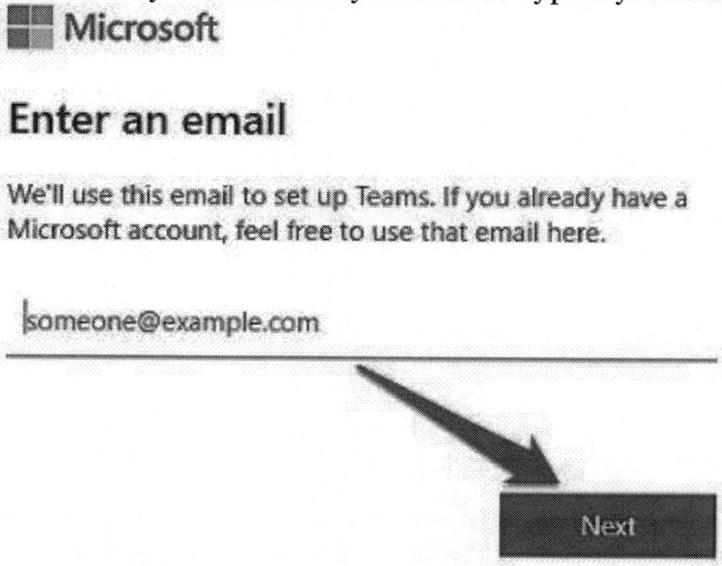

Microsoft

Enter an email

We'll use this email to set up Teams. If you already have a Microsoft account, feel free to use that email here.

someone@example.com

Next

Next up, you have to clarify what your TEAMS application is for. Be it for your office, home, or school. Choose and click next

Microsoft

How do you want to use Teams?

○ **For school**
To connect students and faculty for courses and projects, in a classroom or online

◉ **For friends and family**
For everyday life, to make audio or video calls

○ **For work**
To work with teammates wherever they are

Next

Note: Selecting Teams for Friends and family will direct you to sign up with skype because TEAMS was created for the workplace and school. So if you indeed want a video conference application just for getting together with friends and family, then Microsoft will suggest you use Skype instead.

After selecting For work or school, you will be asked to put a password for your account and then fill up information about your full name, company name, and Nationality. Fill in the information correctly and click set up teams.

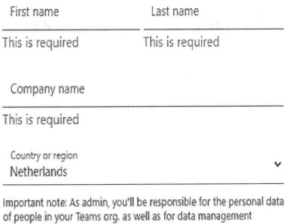

First name   Last name
_____   _____
This is required   This is required

Company name
_____
This is required

Country or region
Netherlands   ⌄
_____

Important note: As admin, you'll be responsible for the personal data
of people in your Teams org. as well as for data management
requests they submit to you. Learn more.

By clicking **Set up Teams**, you agree to our terms and conditions.

We may provision your Teams Free tenant in any facility where Microsoft stores
and processes customer data. This means that your data may be stored at rest
within any of the regions and countries where such facilities are located. We will
comply with all applicable law with respect to data transfers. Teams Free is NOT
intended for official public sector, government, or educational use.

Set up Teams

Afterward, you will be asked to download the Teams app or use the web version.

Stay better connected with the Teams desktop app

Download the Windows app   Use the web app instead

But if you already have the downloaded application on your phone or desktop, you will see a tab that pops up like this.

Open Microsoft Teams?

https://teams.microsoft.com wants to open this application.

Open Microsoft Teams   Cancel

You will then be signed in to the Microsoft Teams platform, regardless of the version you chose, web, mobile or desktop app. Click Continue.

PIPATIME

As simple as that, you would have made your way to the home page of Microsoft Teams, where you would be given a link you can share with your contacts or via emails so that they can join your organization.

Following the steps above would have enabled you to completely set up your Teams account from sign up to sign in. Let's move on.

Note: Be sure to remember the information used to sign up for Microsoft Teams, as that information will be required to fill in if you are attempting to sign in on another device, thus meaning your information can be used to sign in on any other device giving you the mobility to use TEAMS across devices.

Setting Up Video Conferencing in Microsoft Teams

Click on "Gatherings" on the left-hand side of the screen. You can either plan a gathering or start one right away. For the last mentioned, select "Meet Now." You will be given the alternative to name your audience and flip your sound and video on or off. Snap "Join now" when you are prepared. At the base, from left to right, these permit you to flip your camera on or off, switch your mic on or off, share your screen, get to more alternatives, lift your hand, see the visit, view members, or hang up. Click the three specks in the center to get extra options like entering full screen, empowering live inscriptions, or turning off video for members who join the call. When the gathering begins, you may get a spring-up window with two choices for adding individuals to the call: you can either get a connection to share or send an email welcome. If you do not get this window naturally or need to get to it later, click on the "Show members" button on the right side of the catch line. At that point, in the sidebar on the right, click on the "Offer Invitation" catch to open that equivalent window.

New members who utilize your connection to join the gathering will initially hold up in a virtual entryway and be told, "Somebody in the gathering should give you access soon." If you are facilitating the audience, when their name appears in the "Individuals" sidebar, click on the checkmark close to their name to add them to the call. If you haven't empowered the sidebar, you will get a little spring-up window over the "Show members" button at the base of the screen to caution you that they're pausing; click "Concede" to add them to the call.

To schedule a meeting for another time. Click on "Meetings" on the left-hand sidebar.

Click the "Calendar a meeting" button.

A window will spring up, letting you set the time and date for the gathering, alongside a title. Click "Timetable" when you are set.

The following box will give you the alternative to "Duplicate gathering greeting" to get a connection to join the gathering. You can likewise consequently share your welcome using Google Calendar and Microsoft Outlook, contingent upon what administrations you are at present marked into.

Also, that is it! Since your gathering is unique, you will have the option to sign onto it whenever, yet along these lines, you and different members will make some planned memories to meet.

Join Meeting on Microsoft Teams

There are several ways to access and join a meeting in Teams.

- **Joining with a Link**

Click the link given in your Teams meeting invitation. Your meeting will consequently open in Teams. Otherwise, you can click on the Join Microsoft Teams Meeting directly.

The meeting invite records a telephone number and meeting ID. At that point, you can join that meeting by Phone.

- **Joining by Phone**

The meeting may be joined by phone, and the invite will list toll and toll-free phone numbers. You can choose both numbers, depending on your requirements and preferences.

- o Dial the suitable phone number.
- o Enter the meeting ID when incited.

The meeting will also have a list of nearby numbers from which to choose. You can choose a phone number from this list if the cost and complimentary phone numbers are not close.

- **Joining your MS Teams Calendar**

To join a Teams meeting from your schedule,

- o Choose the Calendar from the menu on the left-hand side of the page.
- o Click any picture on this page to see it at full size.
- o From your schedule, click on the meeting you wish to join. A window will show up with a Join button.
- o Click Join.

Creating a Channel

- Click on the ellipse to the right of the team name.
- Click Add Channel.
- Enter the channel's name and a description of the channel's purpose.
- (Optional) Click the Privacy drop-down menu to specify whether your channel is only visible to you or public to your team.
- Click Add.

Each member of your team has access to the channels you create, but they will be hidden in the list of the channel that your team members have. If you are your team's owner, you have the additional option to Show this channel automatically on everyone's list, which adds it to the default list for each member.

Joining By Channel

Channels are MS Teams' subsets; they empower colleagues to hold discussions and offer records about discrete undertakings that do not require all colleagues' cooperation. You can also join a Teams meeting from a channel, and the gathering will incorporate the member recorded in the circuit.

Click on the Join button to join a Teams meeting through a channel.

Teams Navigation Buttons

TEAMS Navigation buttons and history

The navigation buttons in Teams are a little productivity hack that could be easily missed. This is the ability for you to navigate forward and backward as you would with the forward and back buttons in your browser, as illustrated in the Figure Below. This feature, however, is not available in the web version of Teams.

CHAPTER 2:
How to Manage Microsoft Team

As an administrator, you may need to view or update teams that your organization has configured for collaboration or make improvements, such as assigning owners for unattended teams. You can manage the teams used in your organization through the Microsoft Teams PowerShell module and Microsoft Teams headquarters. You can access the administration center at https://admin.microsoft.com.

The team administration tools are located in the Teams node at Microsoft Teams headquarters. (Select **Computers**> Manage Computers in the Administration Center.) Each team supports a Microsoft 365 Group, and this node provides a view of the Microsoft Teams-enabled groups in your organization.

Add or Remove Members and Owners

Team and group settings can be changed easily.

Make Changes to Teams

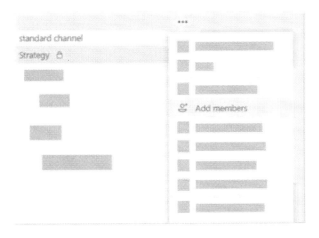

- **Channels:** You can add new channels and edit or delete existing channels. Please note that you cannot delete the default public channel.
- **Privacy:** determine if the equipment is public or private.
- **Rating:** This is compatible with Microsoft 365 group ratings. Choose secret, top-secret, or the public.
- **Conversation settings:** set whether members can edit what messages are sent.
- **Channel Settings:** Determine if members can create new channels and edit existing channels and whether they can add or remove tabs, connectors, and applications.

Any changes you make to a computer are logged. If you are changing group settings (change name, description, photo, privacy, ranking, or team members), the changes are attributed to you through the control channel. If you are taking action against specific equipment configurations, your changes will be tracked and associated with you in the General Equipment channel.

Solving Problems in the Team

- **Issue:** teams are missing from the team summary grid
- **Cause:** This problem may cause a missing property to be recognized when the computer incorrectly creates the profile (or has not yet created it).
- **Solution:** manually set property to correct value with MS Graph

Replace the "Get-Unified Group" cmdlet as the "External-Directory Object Id" attribute in Query for that actual Group Id, which you can get through Exchange Online PowerShell instead of {groupid}.

View Meetings

Select Calendar to view your appointments and meetings for the business day or week.
These appointments stay in sync with your Outlook calendar.
Choose a meeting invitation to see what the meeting is about, who will attend, and respond to the meeting.

Schedule a Meeting

- Select New Meeting
- Write the title of a meeting and enter a location
- An online meeting is created by default
- Choose a start and end time and add details if necessary
- To add people to the meeting, enter their names in the Invite box

Note: Enter email addresses to invite someone from outside your organization; even without Microsoft teams, you are invited to join as a guest.

- View everyone's eligibility in the participant list, choose a suggested time if needed, or select Schedule Wizard to see more time available in the calendar view.
- Under Select the channel you will know, select the drop-down arrow to manage the privacy settings of your meeting:
  - Select None to keep your meeting private.
  - Select a channel to open the meeting to team members.

How to Record Your Teams Meeting

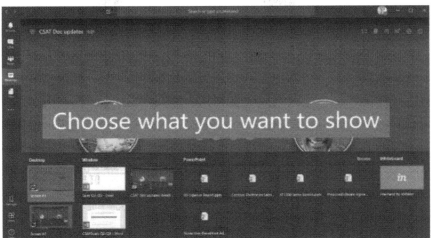

You can record a meeting, especially if you need to review the content discussed afterward.

As the meeting is about to commence, click join, to kick off.

Wait for a while for the other members to join. While this occurs, navigate down to the right side of the menu; you will see the number of people already in the meeting.

Locate the bottom of the menu bar; you will see a three-dot button; click on this button to see options for recording.

Click recording from the numerous options you'll see. You will be notified that the recording will be seen on the Microsoft Stream or in the meeting room (chat).

Note: Recordings on the Microsoft Stream can be found in the cloud. It can be accessed once the student or teacher has connected their device.

Once the recording has begun, you will notice a red dot. This implies that every conversation during the meeting is on record and everyone needs to be notified that they are being recorded so they'll be able to avoid any sound interrupting the recording.

CHAPTER 3:
Other Microsoft Teams Operations

How to Customize Microsoft Teams

Change the team name:

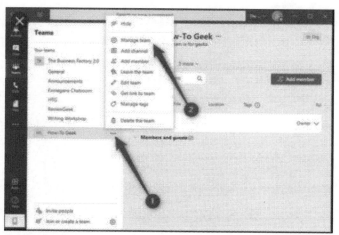

- Click the ellipse next to the team name.
- Click Edit Group in the window that opens.
- Delete the current team name and enter a new one.
- When done, click the Update button to save the change.

Edit Team Description:
- Click the ellipse next to the team name.
- Click Edit Group in the window that opens.

- Delete the text already in the Description field and enter a new description.
- When done, click the Update button to save the change.
- Change team privacy:
- Click the ellipse next to the team name.
- Click Edit Group in the window that opens.
- Click the Privacy drop-down menu.
- Itemize if you want your team to be private or public.
- When done, click the Update button to save the change.

Download a File

- Click on the downloads that are highlighted in gray when they are selected.
- The settings appear at the top. Click Download.

Create a New Folder

- Open the Files tab on your channel.
- Click New. A drop-down list appears.
- Select a folder.
- Name the folder.
- Click Create.

Download the File

- Open the Files tab on your channel.
- Click the Download button below the channel name at the top of the screen.
- Select the files on your computer that you want to download.
- Click Open.

OR

- Open the Files tab on your channel.
- Open the folder that contains the file (s) you want to send to your computer.
- Click and drag the file (s) from the current location with the mouse.
- Upload the file (s) to the Teams Files window.
- Create a new team file

Open the Files Tab on Your Channel

- Click New. A drop-down list appears.
- Select one of the file settings you want to create.
- Give the file a name.
- Click Create. The file opens automatically.
- Add text to your file. The changes are saved automatically.
- Enable the Close button above the screen to exit.
- Share the OneDrive link

Click on the Conversation Where You Want to Share Your Documents

- Select the attachment icon from the Bot Tom screen.
- Click OneDrive.
- Click on the file you want to share the link with.
- Click Share.
- Click the Submit icon to send the file in a chat.

- Share the MS Teams link
- Go to where your MS Teams website is located.
- Click on the file. The file name is highlighted in purple when it is selected.
- Click the Get Link button at the top of the screen.
- Click the Copy button.
- Click the Chat icon on the navigation key on the left side of the screen.
- Click the chat where you want to share the file.
- Click the box in the text box in the Bottom box.
- Add a link by right-clicking and pasting (or use the keyboard shortcut ctrl + v).
- Click the upload icon to share the link to your document in the chat.

How to Use Teams Features

Teams allow you and your students to collaborate and communicate effectively. You can explore many features on Teams to help you and your team and students communicate better and more easily. These features make Teams stay ahead of other collaboration apps and platforms. The features are incredibly user-friendly and can provide a smooth remote environment for all your learning purposes.

Setting Up and Managing Channel Moderation

As the Team owner, you can create channels and add moderators, those who participate in a channel. You can create a channel moderation to manage the channels. You can control those who can post or comment on the channels.

The channel moderators you add can:
- Create new posts on the channel
- Add or remove team members to and from the channels.
- Regulate who can or cannot comment on existing channel posts and messages.
- You can use channels to make announcements to other teachers or students and set up a channel for class discussions.

How to Manage Channel Moderation

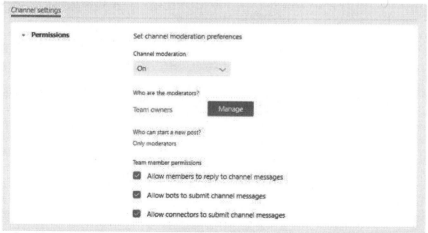

The first thing you need to do is go to channel settings. In the "more options (...), click on "manage the channel," and you can regulate your channels.

You can turn on or off channel moderation, add or remove moderators, and set members' permission.

Tabs

Teams tabs are web pages that are embedded in Microsoft Teams. They are usually HTML tags that lead to the domains in the apps, and they can be added to teams, group chats, personal apps, or users.

There are two types of tabs on Teams:

- **Channel/group tabs:** These deliver content in teams and on group chats and channels. They make the collaborative platform easier to use, primarily when they revolve around web-based content.
- **Personal tabs** are for personal users and function well with personally scoped bots and apps.

Tabs are usually pinned to the left bar of your screen so you can access them easily.

Microsoft Teams Apps

There are many apps you can integrate with Teams for practical usage. Some of the apps are:

- **Microsoft Stream**

This video app allows you to view and share a recorded video of your team's activities with your team. It is a combination of Stream and YouTube. You can use this for meetings, training, discussions, etc., and record them. So, anyone who misses the gathering can access them later.

- *Polly*

Integrating Polly with Teams allows you to insert or create polls in your Teams channels. You can use it for voting and decision makings among your teams.

- *Karma*

You can use the karma app to reward your students. This will motivate them to be on their best behavior. You can use it to applaud good presentations, proper conduction, and excellent performance of your students.

- **Project Planners**

Project planners like Trello, Wrike, Planner, and Asana will help you and your students manage your projects on Teams.

- o *Planner*: With Planner, you can keep track of the progress of the projects you have assigned to your students. This app has already been integrated with Microsoft Teams, so you don't have to worry.
- o *Trello:* This also helps you to manage your projects effectively. It notifies the team members of any member's activity on the projects. When someone does something, it updates it on your Trello cards, lists and boards.

- *Wiki*

Integrating the Wiki app with Teams is good for your Teams channels. It will serve as a knowledge repository for you and your students. You can add a lot of information to this app, and your students can go there to access it. It could be the rules of the group or channel, maybe definitions of terms, FAQs, and many more.

Other apps you can integrate with Teams are:

- **MyHub** – track and organize your Teams.
- **ScrumGenius** – to track meetings, activities, and progress concerning team goals.
- **AtBot + Power Automate** – for adding chatbots to your teams.
- **Microsoft Lists** – track and organize work for the members of your team.

This team's features help you and your students carry out your activities well. You can use any of them, especially when you think they will help aid learning better for your student. You and your students can impute these features into your Teams platforms and start learning even better and smoother.

CONCLUSION

Thank you for reading this book. Microsoft Teams has made learning via the internet a task so easy for everyone. Teachers can now sit in the comfort of their homes and help their students acquire knowledge with their parent's guidance, and it will still appear as though they are sitting in the classroom.

Microsoft Teams is one of the most helpful and powerful approaches to assembling a digital workspace in a hurry. Since the application is accessible for numerous OSs, you can interface consistently with different administrations.

Microsoft Teams is worked to see both colossal chances and massive changes in how individuals and groups complete work. MS Teams is more coordinated and authoritative in keeping correspondences and data streaming. It is an exceptionally intuitive apparatus that makes a productive and included workplace.

Another important thing this software does is that it lets teachers use it to check how well the students are progressing in their various classes. Instructors can converse with their students via video or audio calls or chats. Video calling is most preferred as it will help curb the student's actions as the meetings go on.

The importance of Microsoft teams cannot be watered down as it promises to introduce greater features that will help make learning easy for teachers, parents, and students.

Good luck.

BOOK 8:

MICROSOFT ACCESS 2022

A Complete Beginner's Guide On Microsoft Access 2022, Including Tips & Tricks On Data Management

INTRODUCTION

Many people are unfamiliar with the app, and many that have heard of it do not know what it means or how it is used. Microsoft was released in 1990 with packages, some phased out and some still in use. Microsoft Access was first distributed in 1992 and was created to sort and analyze data. It was well used and appreciated for a long time, but it faced competition with creating more software applications that perform almost the same functions. However, the successful use of this tool increased when it was made to be a part of Microsoft Office in 1995. So, it can be said that Microsoft Access has been riding on the success of Microsoft itself, which is not bad as the tool in itself performs so many functions that are needed in this modern era. Since then, the tool has become a member of the Microsoft Office evolutionary pipeline with a need to be examined thoroughly in synchronization with developing some other Office components. This has taken Access to be at the state it is now.

In simple terms, Microsoft Access is being used to bring into creation a relational database system. You enter your data, and after this, Microsoft Access sorts it out, then analyzes them in the most relational way possible. You just supply the information, and Access does the rest. Access is beneficial when you have many records to make into a database. Using Microsoft Access to sort this will remove the possibility of errors and make your work easier and much faster. This database will also be easy to work with and navigate through.

So, in all that has been said, Microsoft Access can be said to be a tool developed by Microsoft and is used as a database management system (DBMS) that combines the relational Access Database Engine (ADE) with a graphical user interface and software-development tools, allowing users to create queries, tables, reports, and forms, and connect them with macros. It was launched in November 2022, and updated versions have been released subsequently, with the newest version being Microsoft Access, 2022.

This chapter will discuss the various functions you can perform using Microsoft Access, like building big databases, creating databases with multiple tables, reaching out with SharePoint, and how to use Microsoft Access after installing the software.

Building Big Databases Using Microsoft Access

Access can carry out many activities, but a very important one is building big databases. These records run into hundreds and thousands, and management tools like Access will be important to monitor them. Typically, creating a type of database with these kinds of records will lead to a lot of errors. Still, with Microsoft Access, there is an elimination of the probability of error due to the automatic creation by the software. This database can be brought into existence within a maximum size of 2 gigabytes. Now, imagine how huge your creation can run. You can also work around the size limitation created with this software by linking to tables in other Access databases or tables in multiple database files.

Using Microsoft Access to build your big databases will also make it possible for you to sort through them easily with the sorting, searching, and other creative tools that have been made available. Imagine how hard it could be to access a particular record through hundreds of records. However, with Microsoft Access, you can quickly locate a particular record within hundreds, even thousands of records. Also, creating big databases using Microsoft Access ensures proper and insightful reporting. You can tailor the database to the activity you want to use it for, whether being left in digital form or printed out. If you are a project manager and you need the database for a presentation or to distribute amongst your team members, Access got you. Access will enable you to communicate effectively to your team members as the data created will be easy to understand.

Microsoft Access saves you from reentering your collected data and allows you to keep multiple data sources consistent. It lets you import and recycles all that you have entered into another software, for example, Microsoft Excel, when you wish to sort out using Microsoft Access.

In all that has been said, it can be deduced Microsoft Access is a very powerful software, and a proper understanding of how to explore all its capabilities will make it an inevitable tool for you if you are a data analyst or not, whether you deal with huge records. This tool will automatically record the most pleasant, easy-to-use, and navigate. And with the most recent release, Microsoft Access 2022, there sure are many upgrades that you will want to be familiar with, and this book has been written not to let you miss out on anything.

Creating Databases With Multiple Tables Using Microsoft Access

Yes, it is possible to bring into existence databases with more than one table and make different reports using Microsoft Access. Most databases you'll work with as a developer will have more than one table, and those tables will be connected in various ways to form table relationships. Hence Microsoft Access is the perfect tool for you as a developer. You can use just one table in Access, but your work might appear clumsy and have redundancy and repetition because of the large volume of records.

Access is a tool that allows you to hold your information in a very neat and easy-to-use way, and using a single table can deny you this opportunity. Hence, the ability of Access to create multiple tables for a database is a powerful software tool.

Imagine you have a reason to create a database that contains different information. For example, if you work for a company that supplies different products to different customers, creating a single table for this database will make your work look messy and complicated to navigate through and understand. Instead, you can create a database with multiple tables, with a table serving a particular purpose. Below is a prototype that can be used for this kind of information:

- The first table contains each customer's name, location, email address, and phone number.
- The second table contains the products to be supplied to each customer, including the name of the customer who placed the order, shipping information, the salesperson who handled the sale, and the order date.
- The third table contains information about each product, including the product name, batch number, expiry date, number of items in a package, and so on.
- The fourth table contains information about the suppliers, i.e., information about the employees in the company. This includes the employees' names, numbers, and names of products handled by each employee.

This can continue, and creating multiple tables like this will produce a database that virtually anyone can easily understand.

Steps to follow to create a single table or multiple tables will be thoroughly discussed in subsequent chapters of this book.

Using Microsoft Access in Creating Databases with User Forms

User forms in Microsoft Access are objects through which you or other users can edit, add, or display the data stored in the Access desktop database. You can create a database that can be used by multiple users using your Microsoft Access. There are many ways you can create forms in Microsoft Access, including- from an existing table or query in Access, creating a blank form, creating a navigation form, creating a split form, creating a form that covers another form (a subform), creating a form that displays multiple records.

A form in Access is a database object you can use to create a user interface for a database application. A user form simply creates a form that users have access to and can create and edit as much as the creator.

CHAPTER 1:
Getting Started with Microsoft Access

The primary purpose of using Access is to help you to store large arrays of data, arrange the data and retrieve the data when it is needed. Some users thought Access and Excel have the same purpose, be it? Storing data in Excel is limited to the number of rows in an Excel worksheet. It can only help you sort and filter a minor list of data, but Access deals with compound and bulky data arrays beyond what Excel can do or try to do.

Introducing You to Access Database

A database can also be called a database file. It is an organized collection of an item that relates to specific information. The item can be a product, employee name, etc. For instance, Amazon is a database with organized items you can purchase. The items contain attached information such as name, price, author, title, and many more. Another example of a database is a library catalog with an organized collection of information about books.

Basic Terminology to Become Proficient in Access Database

Understanding the basic term of accessing databases in and out of the database is expedient. The table below explains ten database terminology you must recognize if you run the access database conveniently.

Basic Database Terminology You Need to Know	
Database	This is an orderly method of organizing information for easy retrieval when it is needed for any purpose.
Database table	It is referred to the orderly arrangement of data information into fields (columns) and records (rows).

Fields	It can be likened to a column in a conventional table, the categories of information inside the database table.
Records	It can be likened to a row in a conventional table. It shows all the recorded data about each category, whether of a person or anything.
Cells	Like a conventional table, a cell is the intersection of field and record inside a database. It is the point where you can enter a piece of data
Foreign key or field	It links information in database tables, i.e., it shows the relationship between two database tables by relating it with the primary key. The unique column compared with another column during comparison is known as a primary key.
Primary key field	This is a field in each database table whose values uniquely identify other fields across the table.
Relational database	This is the type of database where data is stored in more than one database table. It helps to organize data into a table that can be related together because data must be common to each other, for instance, a company that recorded the first database table with customer details and another database describing individual customer transactions. The database used to have more than one database table, but a situation may warrant that it will have only one database in such a situation. It is called a flat-file database.
Dynaset	It is the process of taking data or a set of data in one or more database tables, i.e., the outcome of your search within the database.
Object	The object comprises various components in constructing a database, such as database tables, queries, forms, reports, macros, and modules. They will be discussed at length later in this section.

Launching into Microsoft Access Application

Launching means starting an application. The best and easiest means to start Access is via the start menu. Observe the following instruction to start Access:

1. Tap on the **Window Start** menu located at the bottom left or middle of the desktop window, depending on the position of the Start button.

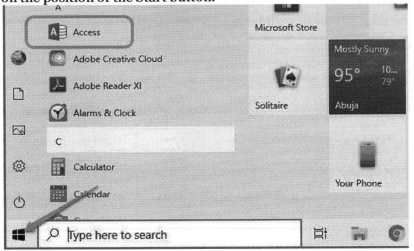

2. Scroll up/down to search for the Access application and click on the **Access** icon to open the Access application.
3. The above steps (1-2) will lead you to the Access opening screen.

Working with Access Opening Screen

Access opening screen is the starting point of getting started with Access. Use the privilege of the opening screen to do the following activities.
1. **Blank Database:** this is used in creating a new database or database file.
2. **Template:** this is the available template you can get on the system without going to the internet.
3. **Online Template**: you can click on this to search for more templates over the internet if you are not satisfied with the available template offline.
4. **Recent Documents**: it helps you to access the recent database document you have recently worked upon.
5. **Open All Documents:** this is the folder for accessing all the database documents.

Creating a Database File

The database file is the document where your database work is being stored. Access permits you to create a Database file in two ways, either from scratch, also known as a blank database file or from the preformatted template. Both ways will be made from the opening screen after launching the Microsoft Access start screen.

Creating a Blank Database File

To create a blank database file from the opening screen, kindly:
1. Tap on the **Blank database** command on the right side of the opening screen.

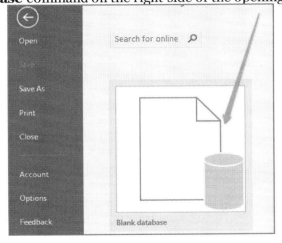

2. Move to the **file name** and change the name Access guess for you to the name you want, then click on the **Folder icon** to change the file location to another folder location, provided you desire that.

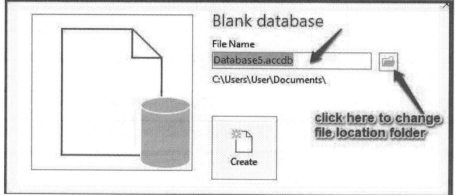

3. (Optional) Select another location and click on Ok to confirm the selected folder for the file location storage.

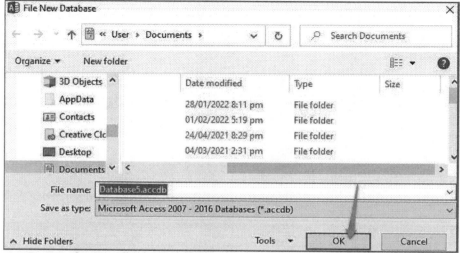

4. Then click on **Create** button below the file name box to create an Access blank database with a blank table by default.

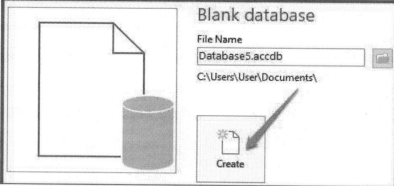

5. Take a look at the Access blank database file.

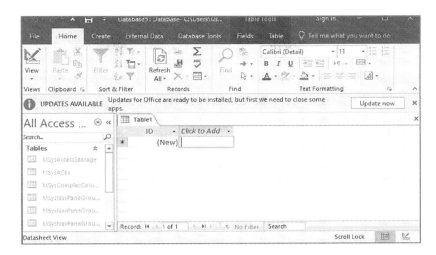

Creating a Database File from the Preformatted Template

Preformatted templates are easier to start with, provided you understand all the database elements and know how to edit them to your information. Templates are for those who know how to work well with the database. To create a database file from the template, follow these listed steps:

1. Choose **"New"** from the opening screen of Microsoft Access, then look at the template. You may scroll down to see all the templates available on Access or use the search box to search for more templates. Click on a template immediately to find the one that relates to your information.

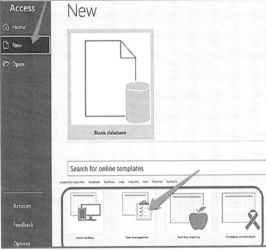

2. You will be provided a preview panel where you can change the **template's name, select a folder, and view the selected template.**
3. Click on **Create** button once you are satisfied with the preview template and click on enable editing to permit you to work on the database.

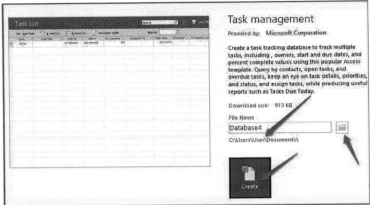

4. Behold a template database file with an inbuilt design table comprising fields and records that you can easily edit on your own.

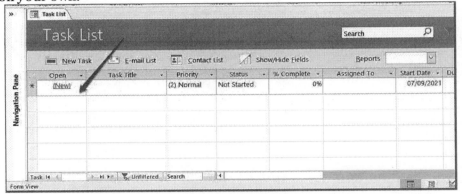

CHAPTER 2:
Navigating the Workspace in Access

Starting with the Workspace in Access

The workspace in Access 2022 is very similar to the previous version, although, as expected in every upgrade, there are some changes. Going through this section will introduce you to these changes. If you are familiar with Access, you will find the workspace very familiar.

Starting with the File tab, you would see a vertical list of commands that creates context-sensitive changes to the main workspace, and this main workspace essentially represents everything to the right of that left-hand menu panel. Follow these procedures to carry out any of the activities mentioned in each bullet.

- If you want to start a new database, click "New" in the File tab's menu of options found on the vertical pane. Starter templates show up and the Blank Desktop Database button. In most cases, you'll be clicking on the Blank Desktop Database button so you can begin a new database.
- If you've opened an existing database, right-click on the database and select "Info" to get relevant statistics similar to the open database. Two big buttons and a link will show up, from which you can click on any of these commands - "Compact & Repair" to compact and repair the database files, "Encrypt" to create a password for the open database to deny access to others apart from you or click on "View and Edit" to see the properties of the database.
- There are also "Save," "Save As," "Print," and "Options" command. Each of these commands operates directly or leads to a dialogue box. For example, the "Save" command will automatically save your work, whereas the "Save as" command will open a dialogue box from which you can select what you want to save in the database and maybe create a new name.

Working with the Onscreen Tools in Access

Opening an existing database or a blank space in Microsoft Access changes the workspace, offering the Ribbon and its tabs (Home, Create, External Data, and Database Tools). These tabs, however, are not to be confused with the context-sensitive tabs that appear when various database objects (the tables, forms, queries, or reports that make up your database) are created or edited.

The ribbon tag at the top of the screen contains the tools you can use while working with your database. Although the tools here are dimmed if you have not used any of these tools, making use of even one of these tools will make all the other tools available for use, and the buttons that are relevant to what you have opened and active in your database are available when you need them.

Working with the Buttons

The Onscreen buttons in Microsoft Access are either action buttons - this means they perform an action when clicked, or they are buttons that represent lists or menus of choices. Each view in an Access app displays the specific predefined action buttons in the Action Bar that can be performed from that view. These buttons are found on the Action Bar, and although predefined, they can be customized, and you can add or remove them. The buttons that represent lists or menus can be represented in two ways: drop-down list buttons that, like a small triangle, appear when clicked, a list of options appears, or the menu button that displays a list of menus.

The File Tab in Microsoft Access

At the top of the screen in Microsoft Access is a red ribbon, and on this ribbon is the File tab. It gives you access to the file functions when you open a particular file. These functions include - Open, Save, Properties, and Close. Opening a database and clicking on the File tab opens information about the file you have opened.

The Quick Access Tools in Microsoft Access

Quick Access Tools in Microsoft Access is a toolbar that can be customized and consists of commands that are not dependent on the tab at the ribbon on top of the screen. This tool can be customized in the sense that you can shift the location, and you can also add and remove tools that perform specific functions. Quick Access Toolbar is in the uppermost left of the workspace. Clicking the small triangular shape at the right corner of this tool will allow you to edit the tool by adding or removing specific commands to suit your style.

Using the Panels, Panes, and Context-Sensitive Tools in Microsoft Access

A very nice thing about Microsoft Access 2022 is being offered tools based on what you are creating. Microsoft Access provides the tools you need for the file you are working on or the feature you are using. A relevant onscreen panel will be shown at the top of the screen, and you can choose whatever option you want to complete your task.

Customizing the Workspace in Access

Like much other software, you can customize the workspace using Microsoft Access. There are three main components in the Access workspace - the ribbon, the backstage view, and the navigation pane. The ribbon contains the Quick Access Toolbar, and you can customize this tool to suit your style. You can customize your workspace by working on any of these three elements. The following section will discuss how you can customize the Quick Access Tools.

Changing the Location of the Quick Access Toolbar

The Toolbar of Quick Access is in the uppermost left corner of the file explorer window, but if you wish to change this position because you don't like it, you can do so. Follow these steps to carry out this action.

1. Select the arrow located at the bottom left corner of the home screen.
2. Select the "File Explorer" under the windows section to access the file explorer.

3. After you have opened the file explorer, open a folder, and select any of the files you want.

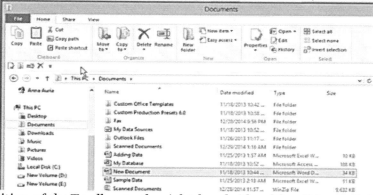

4. To change the position of the Toolbar to the right-hand side of the ribbon, click on the down arrow to the right of the Toolbar and then click on "Show below the ribbon."

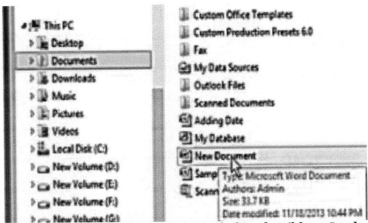

5. Now, you will see that the Quick Access Toolbar is just below the ribbon. Look at the position of the ribbon in the image represented below.

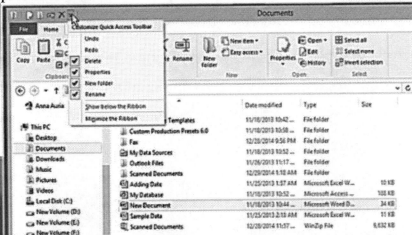

6. You can take it back to on top of the ribbon by clicking on that down arrow to the right of the Toolbar and then clicking on "Show above the ribbon."

Adding Tools to the Quick Access Toolbar

There are default tools that come with the Quick Access Toolbar, but the good thing is you can add to these tools, although the tools you want to add must perform specific functions. Now, follow these steps to add a command to the Quick Access Toolbar.

1. Click on the drop-down button by the right of the Quick Access Tool.
2. Clicking on any of the commands will make a checkmark appear on the command, which means this particular command has been added to the Quick Access Toolbar.

Removing Tools from the Quick Access Toolbar

It is very easy to remove commands from the Quick Access Toolbar, and just like how these commands have been added, they can be removed. To remove a command, simply follow these steps.

1. Click on the drop-down button by the right of the Quick Access Tool.
2. Uncheck any of the commands you want to remove by clicking on them.

Minimizing and Maximizing the Ribbon in Access

The Ribbon at the uppermost part of your window contains the commands required to carry out everyday tasks while using Access. It has multiple tabs, each with several groups of commands. The red ribbon that appears at the uppermost part of your screen in Microsoft Access can be minimized. If you feel the ribbon is taking too much space on your screen and wish to minimize it, simply click the arrow in the lower right corner of the screen. To make the ribbon reappear, click a tab, and when it is not in use, it will disappear again. To maximize the ribbon, click on a tab. After this, click the pin icon in the lower-right corner. The Ribbon will appear at all times.

Working with ScreenTips

ScreenTips in Access 2022 are the brief descriptions and little names of onscreen tools that appear when you place your mouse pointer over buttons, menus, commands, and many other pieces of the Access workspace. You can show or hide the screen tips when working with your Microsoft Access.

To show or hide screen tips, follow these steps.

1. Click on the File tab.
2. Select "Options"
3. Click on "General."
4. Under the options that display the User Interface, click the option you want based on these self-descriptive options.

    - **Show feature descriptions in ScreenTips**: This option turns on ScreenTips and Enhanced ScreenTips, and this will allow you to be able to view more information about a command, and this includes the name of the command and keyboard shortcuts on your desktop, art, and links to Help articles. This is the default setting.
    - **Don't show feature descriptions in ScreenTips**: This option turns off Enhanced ScreenTips; you can see only the command name and maybe a keyboard shortcut.
    - **Don't show ScreenTips:** This option turns off ScreenTips and Enhanced ScreenTips; this way, you will only be able to see the command name.

Navigating Access with Shortcuts on Your Keyboard

For some people, navigating Access with their keyboard makes them work more efficiently. The most frequently used shortcuts include:

- Alt or F10: Select the active tab and activate the Key Tips.
- Alt + H: To use the home tab.
- Alt + Q: To view the "Tell me" Box.
- Shift + F10: View the shortcut menu for an item you have selected.
- F6: If you wish to move the focus to another part of the window.
- F11: Use this to make the navigation pane visible or not.
- F2: To change Edit mode to Navigation mode.
- F4: If you want to hide or show a property window.
- F5: If you are in the Design view and wish to switch to the Form view.
- Ctrl + O or F12: If you want to open an existing database.
- Alt + F5: to go to a specific record.
- Alt + F4: To exit Access.
- Ctrl + P: If you want to print, and you want to open the print dialogue.
- Ctrl + F: To open the Find tab in the Find and Replace dialogue box when you want to look for a specific record.
- S: To open the page, set up a dialogue box.
- Z: To zoom in or zoom out of a page.
- Ctrl + H: To open the Replace tab in the Find and Replace dialogue box.
- Ctrl + plus sign: Add a new record in the Datasheet or Form view.
- F1: To view the Help window.

CHAPTER 3:
Composition of Database Object

Database objects consist of all the elements that allow you to enter, store, analyze, compile and extract your data the way you want. There are many numbers of an object, but we will focus on the main objects, which are Tables, queries, forms, reports, macros, and modules, as I have mentioned in the database terminology. Without these components, you can't effectively operate the database. I will quickly discuss them one after the other below.

Using Tables to Store Database Data

A database table is the database component where related information is stored in **fields (columns)** and **records (rows).** A table can store all information in a field such as a Supplier ID, employee Name, Contact Address, Position, etc. Still, each table must contain related information. The record must contain the information that relates to the field.

ID	First Name	Last Name	Phone Cont	Faculties	Email Address	Level
1	Jos	David	(555)415-671	Educations	josclaire.st@yahoo.com	Associate
2	Thomas	Faith	(555)171-253	Arts	thomasfaith.st@yahoo.com	Associate
3	Christopher	David	(555)791-452	Sciences	christophergraace.st@yahoo.com	Master
4	Claire	Daniel	(555)103-694	Arts	clairedaniel.st@yahoo.com	Bachelor
5	Jacob	Faith	(555)127-326	Engineerings	jacobfaith.st@yahoo.com	Associate
6	Brandom	David	(555)223-410	Economics	brandomjos.st@yahoo.com	Master
7	Jordan	Leah	(555)312-654	Arts	jordanleah.st@yahoo.com	Master
8	Anthony	Noa	(555)642-124	Educations	anthonynoa.st@yahoo.com	Associate
9	Emma	Olivia	(555)122-341	Arts	emmaolivia.st@yahoo.com	Bachelor
10	Charles	Sophia	(555)189-543	Arts	charlessophia.st@yahoo.com	Bachelor
11	Olivia	Jos	(555)433-127	Educations	oliviathomas.st@yahoo.com	Bachelor
12	Noa	Paul	(555)354-921	Engineerings	Noapaul.st@yahoo.com	Master

On most occasions, a database used to have more than one database table; nevertheless, when the information is not large, you may use only one database table.

Generate Forms to Enter and Maintain Database Data

The next action after creating the table is to enter data into respective fields and records. The Forms help you to enter, edit, view, and delete data. In short, form is used to create data and to carry all forms of data manipulation such as editing, viewing, modifying, and many more. However, you have the choice to enter and modify data straightway without form, but it won't be as easier compared to when you use form.

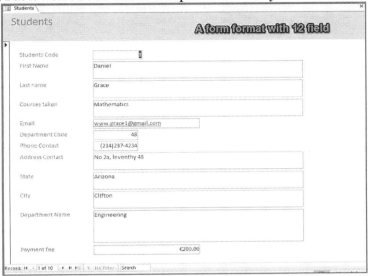

Selecting Queries to Extract Database Data

A query is designed to extract specified information that you want to work with from the table. The query is used to sort and filter the data based on the search criteria. Query means passing a question to your database by defining specific search criteria based on the needed information. For instance, you may ask who the customer cares for. In this case, you are asking your database to find your customer care under the job title category.

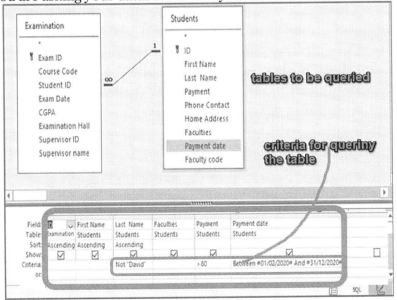

Result of the above query

Using Reports for Data Presentation and Inspection

Reports are usually an output result from selected queries or tables. Reports are always on paper in printed format, which is meant to be presented to higher or recognized authorities for proper inspection and scrutinization.

Macro

Macro is simply a programming language invented by Microsoft for creating instructions and commands in the form. Using Macro extends what you can do with Microsoft Access. For instance, you can add a button to the form for opening another related form or report, which will introduce a wizard to guide you with the command, but you can only do it once. Nevertheless, Macro can repeatedly help you achieve such a command with a drop-down list. Macro can help you to open an executive query, view, and print reports. The limiting factor of Macro is that you can't make any choice outside the command within the drop-down list.

Module

The module is designed to help you store VBA code. Either you wrote the code, or that is available on Microsoft Wizard Access. The module works as a macro, but the Module permits you to write your code without any limitations depending on your skill and language. Macro is limited depending on the command writer by Microsoft Access available on the drop-down list.

Working with the Navigation Pane

A navigation pane is the center area where all database works are executed in Microsoft Access. The navigation pane is on the left side of the database and displays database objects such as tables, queries, forms, and other objects. Navigation Pane permits you to carry out diverse operations on the database. I will explain those operations one after the other.

Open/Close and Resize the Navigation Pane

You may decide to open or close the navigation pane based on the space you need in the working area. To do that, kindly:

1. Click on the **Shuttle Bar to open/close** the navigation pane at the top right corner of the pane or press **F11** on the keyboard.

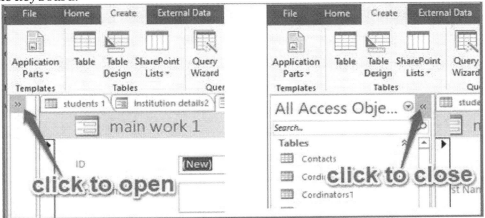

2. Depending on the extent of the space you need in the working area, it may not necessarily be needed at times to close the pane but rather resizing. To resize the navigation pane, place the cursor on the **upper right side of the pane** till you notice a change from the cursor to a **two-headed arrow,** then drag it to the desired size.

Selecting a Predefined Category

Immediately you create a new database file, the category by default will be the table and Related views with All tables as the group. You may, however, change to other categories by:

1. Clicking on the **"All Access Object"** to display All objects.
2. Then move to **Navigate to Category** and select another **category**.

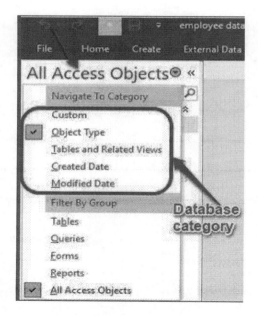

Finding an Object with the Pane

To search for any of the database objects you have created, simply:

1. Tap on **All Access Object** and Enter the name of the needed object you are finding in the **search box**.
2. Perhaps, you want to search for another object again, simply clear the previous object name with a **Clear** button and insert the new object you want to find.

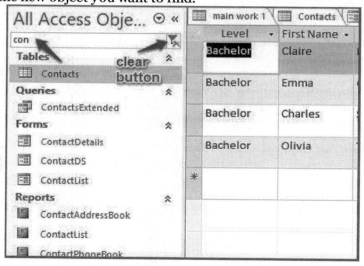

Selecting Database Object

To select any of the database objects, kindly:

- Tap on All Access Object, then click on the object type under navigate to category.
- Then move to the filter group and click the Object you want to select.

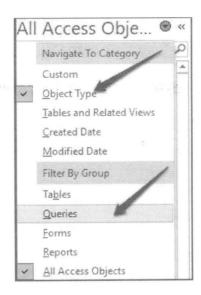

Sort Objects

You can dictate how you want to arrange your object with Sort. The object, by default, is sorted by type. A sorting arrangement can be changed with the listed process:

- Right-click the **title bar** of the navigation pane.
- Then tap on the **Sort by** menu and select the sort order you prefer.

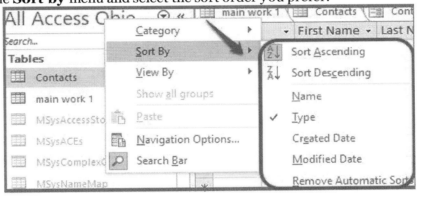

CHAPTER 4:
Constructing a Database

Any database that misses the designing aspect will not be appreciated. Still, a well-prepared database commands respect and regard from its User; therefore, it is of great importance to design the database properly to serve the purpose for which it is created. Developing a database comprises diverse activities. Kindly pay maximum attention to this section regarding designing a fascinating database.

Ascertaining Kind of Information that is Needed for Your Database

The basis on which your database will be built depends on the type of information you want to store in the database. It is this information that determines the type of database you will prepare. For instance, the information may be stock taken, customer details, or revenue information depending on the organization's need. To ascertain the information needed on the database, look at the form the organization will give you in preparing and recording the database information. This form clearly shows the kind of information that is needed on the database.

Distributing Information into the Different Database Tables

The next action immediately after you have gotten the information to be recorded into the database is to distribute such information into different database tables for relational purposes among the tables involved, which will make a query across many tables convenient because access is more concerned with the relationship that exists among the tables. Using one database table for very large information is not ideal as such will obstruct relationships across tables. Check the diagram below to understand how the information is distributed across many tables.

Distributing information into different database tables may be worrisome if you are unfamiliar with distributing information. Check the below guides on principles to follow to distribute information across many tables:

1. **Assign one subject only to one table:** each table should contain one subject only to make dealing with data of one table independently from the other table. Putting two subjects on a single database table will obstruct the relationship and cause data to depend on one another.
2. **Do away with duplicate information:** do not repeat the same information or put duplicate information into the same database table. This principle will help you deal with each piece of information conveniently when information is entered once in each table. Nevertheless, you may use a single database table to store data, provided the data is simple and short.

Note: when preparing a database with the student application form, you should be able to distribute information into different tables as explained below:

1. **Students table:** this is the table to store information about student Identity, name, sex, and so on.
2. **Lecturers table:** this is the table to store information about the Lecturer names, State, Code, and so on
3. **Departments table:** this is the table to store information about Department names, codes, mottos, etc.

Assigning Fields to the Database Tables

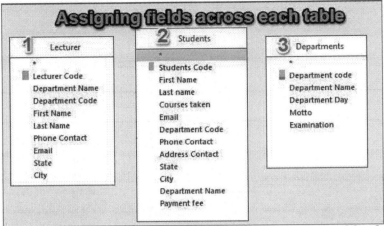

Each database table needs one or more fields depending on the subject of each table, do not forget that fields are equivalent to categories. In short, each database table must deal with one subject, and the subject must have different fields (categories), such as the Employee database as the subject with employee addresses, salaries, and ranks as the fields. The database will be useless until you split the subject into different fields (categories).

Assigning categories to database tables on a specific subject is as easy as ABC if you can obey the following basic guiding principle:

1. Break the information of each table down into components. For instance, rather than having only a contact address, you may split it into residential and company addresses or names; it should be broken down into first and last names. Breaking down information into different components and formulating a field for each piece of information requires deep thought.
2. Give each field a descriptive name to make its identity clearer. For instance, rather than having staff I.D, it is more prudent to put staff Identity numbers.
3. Exclude every information that will involve any formulation from the calculation. The field has no concern with the calculation. Every computation will be initiated and sorted in the query.

How to Select a Primary Key Field for Every Database Table

A primary key field is a special field where unique data is stored. A primary key field is structured uniquely so that it must uniquely identify each record in the table. It can be called one unique key; consequently, it will never allow you to enter similar data into its field; whenever users try to enter similar data, it will issue a warning message via a dialog box.

The primary key makes finding data more fitting for Queries because it won't allow the same data entering into its field and therefore lessens the effort of Query when searching for data. After all, all data are not alike.

Among the table fields, Primary Key is the special field that can be selected as a primary key field. For instance, the student identification number may be the primary key, but the student name can't be selected as a primary key field because two or more students may have the same name, it may be the first or last name, it may even be both names at times. An employee's staff identification number can also be selected as the primary key field because the company can't assign the same identification number to the two staff.

Establishing Relationships Among the Database Tables

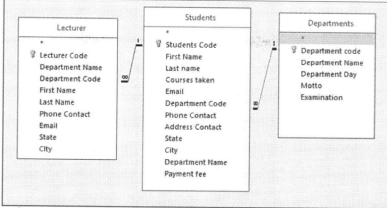

This simply means liking the relationship between tables with the primary and foreign key fields. Foreign key fields are the fields that have the equivalent field like a primary field. You can say the primary key is one unique key that will be compared with many other keys, known as a foreign key field. Establishing a relationship between these common fields makes gathering information with reports or queries easier. Failure to relate these fields together will make query and report very difficult.

CHAPTER 5:
Constructing Database Tables

A database table is the source and starting point of every database assignment. After the creation of the table, the construction continues with entering the field that will be used to establish a relationship among the table for database queries, allowing you to generate a report from the concern tables.

A fantastic database is defined by how you construct its table and enter the data. Do not worry about how to construct database tables. Every apparatus needed for constructing has been fully explained in this section, including sorting, searching, querying database tables with primary keys and indexed, and creating links among tables. Kindly do yourself good by paying more attention to this section.

Creating a Database Table

As I have said earlier, the most crucial part of constructing a database start with table creation and how to enter data into the table. Kudos to Microsoft Access, as it permits its user to create a database table with three different approaches, as I listed below:
- Creating a database table from scratch.
- Creating database table with the In-built template.
- Importing table from another database table.

Creating a Database Table from the Scratch

This simply means you are creating a blank database table in which you must enter its fields one after the other. Kindly open a database file and observe the itemized methods to create a database from scratch:
1. Tap the **Create tab** and click on the **Table Design** command to access the blank table.

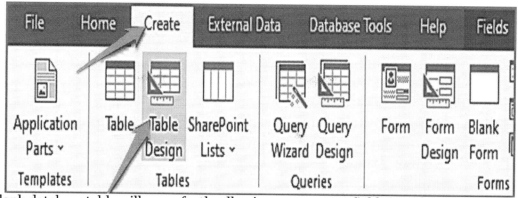

2. The blank database table will come forth, allowing you to enter fields into the table. We will be discussing how to enter fields later in this chapter.

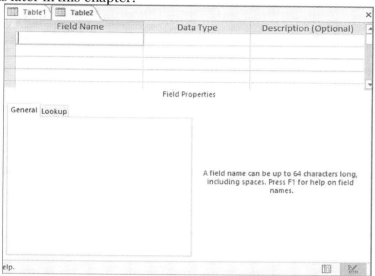

Create a Database Table Using an In-Built Template

A template makes database table creation easier. It involves minor modification; nevertheless, any user who wants to use a template to create a database table must be proficient in Microsoft Access and know how to manipulate access gadgets. You have to pick one of the parts of the template in creating a database table, as you can see below:

1. **Contacts:** This is ideal for creating a database table related to contact addresses and phone numbers.
2. **Users:** it is the database that deals with email address storage.
3. **Tasks:** monitoring the project, such as the status and condition of the project.
4. **Issues:** it is concerned with a database table structured to deal with issues based on their importance.

When you create tables with templates, you will also be provided with preformatted forms, queries, and reports that can be attached to the tables. Observe the following steps in creating a database table using a template together with the preformatted forms, queries, and reports:

1. Kindly close all the **Open Objects** if any object is opened in the database working area by right-clicking any **open object title** and selecting **close All** from the drop-down list.
2. Once you close all the objects from the working area, tap on **Create** tab and click on the **Application Parts** menu.

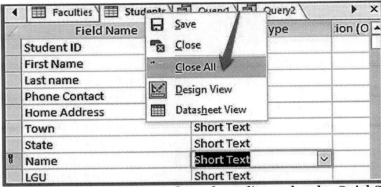

3. Select template parts from the Application drop-down list under the QuickStart heading **(Contacts, Issues, Tasks, or Users).**

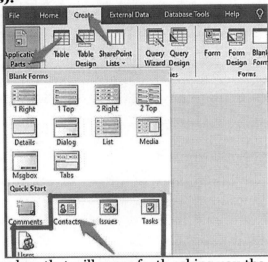

4. Create a relationship dialog box that will come forth asking you the pattern of relation you want. This warning will come if you have any other table in the database. Immediately you see the warning, kindly click **"There is no relationship"** and tap on **Create** Button.

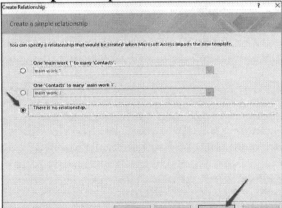

5. The new table has been created with an in-built form, query, and report. You may have to click on design view at the status bar to view the table, field, and data type for any modification. Modifying the template field name is another topic in this section.

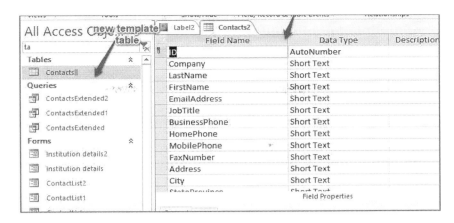

Importing a Database Table from Other Database Table

The easiest way to create a database table is when you import it from another database table. It gives you work-free effort in creating a database table, just like copying and pasting. To import a database table, ensure compliance with the following guidelines:

1. Tap on the **External tab** and click on the **New Data Source** menu, then pick **From Database** menu on the drop-down list and select **Access** from the fly-out list.

2. Get External Data-Access Database dialog box will come forth, then Click the **Browse** button to access File Open dialog box.

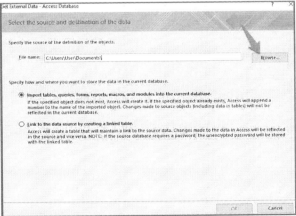

3. Select the **file** with your desired database table and tap on the Open button to access the Get External Data-Access Database dialog box.

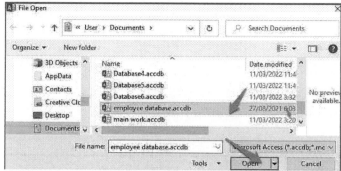

4. Pick the first option with inscription (**Import Tables, Queries, Forms, Reports, Macros, and Modules into the Current Database**) and tap **Ok** to access the Import Objects dialog box.

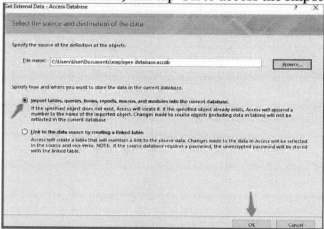

Select the **database table(s)** you need with **Ctrl + click** for multiple selections under the Table tab (you have the option to "import table fields, format, and data" or "table fields and format only" by clicking on the Options button and select either Definition and Data or Definition only respectively on the Import Table section.

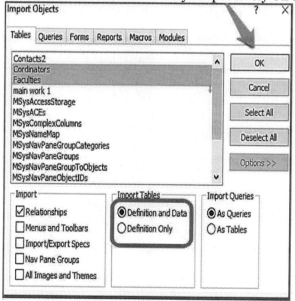

5. Then click Ok for authentication.

Note: you will be provided with a save import dialog box; simply click on the close button. If the table you import includes lookup fields, the imported table will include lookup fields. You will learn more about lookup fields as we proceed in this section.

Two Ways of Opening a Database Table

Access provides only two ways for opening its table, but the two ways are structured for different purposes. You can either open the database table in the datasheet or design view. Why do I have to open the table in two different ways? Because they serve different purposes, which are explained below:

1. **Design View**: when you open a database table in design view, this view permits you to carry out two different tasks: **entering fields** into the table and **suggesting restrictions** for each field you are entering.

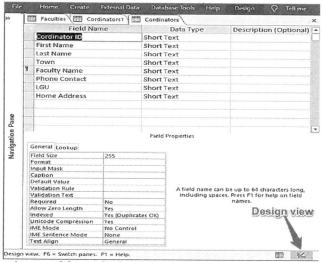

2. **Datasheet view**: opening a table with this view allows you to **enter data** into the table and **perfect examining** of the table.

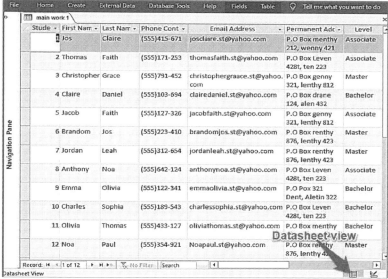

To open a table either in Datasheet view or Design view, kindly move to the navigation pane and click on the "All Access object" then:

- Double-click the **Table** to open in the datasheet view or select the table you want to open and **right-click over it**, then select **Open** to open in the Datasheet view.

301

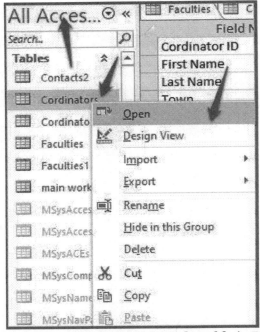

- Right-click the **Table** and select **Design view** to open the table in Design view.

After you open the table in either of the views, you may want to change the view. To **change the view of the current table** that is opened, you will have to **switch the current view** with any of the three options listed below:

1. **Using the status bar:** move to the **bottom right** of the application window to switch between the **datasheet and design view.**
2. **Using the table's title tab**: right-click the **table's title** tab that its view needs to change and select either **datasheet view or design view**.

3. **Using the view menu:** tap on the **Home tab** and click on the **View menu**, then choose Design view or Datasheet view.

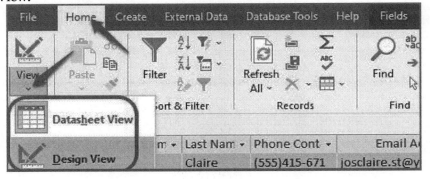

Determining Data Type

You are advised to study data type very well before jumping to the ocean of entering fields because data types are the basic parameter in deciding if the field data is entered accurately. Data types are the guiding principle for entering data into each database table field. For instance, if you select short text for a field name, you must also type a short name into such a field. If you try to enter a webpage address, there will be an instant warning that your entry is invalid because the webpage ought to be a hyperlink. This warning allows you to correct your error immediately after it occurs speedily.

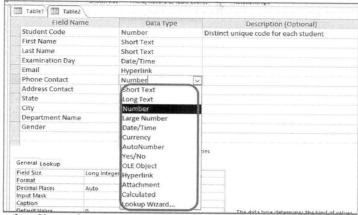

Data type selection completely affects the size and performance of the database. It is also a yardstick measure for the perfect running of the query. Classifying currency as short text under data type will obstruct the running of the query, which is why effort should be made to understand how data type works. Study the table below to get how to deal with data type very well, as it deals directly with the kind of data you will enter into each field without making an error.

Data Type for Entering Fields

Data Type	Description	Size
Short Text	It can be used to store all forms of text that can't be used for calculation, such as addresses, telephone numbers, names, and so on	Ability to hold 255 characters.
Long Text	It is designed to store large forms of text. Only a few users use this type of data type	Ability to hold 63,999 characters.
Number	It is used for storing numerical data that can be used for calculation and currency computation.	Up to 16bytes
Large Number	It is used for storing a very hefty data of numerical numbers for calculations and computations	Big integer of about 450 bytes
Date/Time	It is used for storing dates and times. This can as well be used to determine the range of calculation	8bytes
Currency	It is used in storing monetary data for calculation	8bytes

Auto Number	It stores numbers in a particular sequence depending on how you set Auto Number. You can assign it as the primary key, provided there is no unique data in the database tables	4 bytes to 16 bytes
Yes/No	It stores logical values, such as yes/no, true/ false, etc.	At most 8bytes
Attachment	It is used to store files, charts, and images. You can use it to attach files to the database table just the same way as attaching files on the email.	About 1GB
OLE object	It is used to insert database file links into another application file such as a Word document	About 2GB
Hyperlink	It is used to store data that has webpage format.	Maximum of 2048 characters
Calculated	It is used to store mathematical values from one field to the other.	Not much dependent on the data to be calculated
Lookup wizards	This is mainly used to create a drop-down list from which the worker can use to enter data in a way to eliminate the error of data entering	About 200 bytes

How to Enter and Modify Fields of a Database Table

The next activity immediately after you are done creating the database table is to enter the field, provided it is a blank table created from scratch, or modify the field table, if necessary, for the table you created from the template and the table imported from another database. This section is prepared to enlighten you on all the required assignments you have to know concerning fields.

How to Enter a Field into a Blank Database File

Entering a field is visible after you must have created a blank database table, then switch to the design view and critically follow these guiding principles:

1. Click on the **first field** and enter **its name,** then click on the **Data type** menu to select **data restriction** because Access sets restriction limits to the type of field data you can enter to ensure that field data are correctly entered; quickly check back the previous lesson about (Data type for entering fields)

2. Do the same to the next field until you are done inserting all the fields you have to enter.

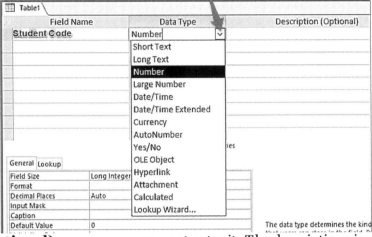

3. **Description (Optional),** you may or may not enter it. The description gives more explanation about your field name and makes those who see the description understand what the field name entails.

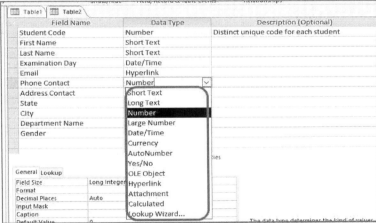

4. Then save your database table before carrying out any other activities by pressing **Ctrl + S or right-clicking the default table name (table 1) and selecting Save** from the drop-down list.

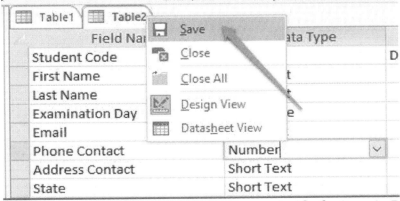

5. Insert a **brief and explanatory name** into the field name inside the Save As Dialog box and press **OK.**

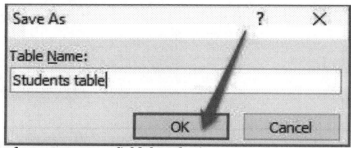

Note: Sometimes, you might forget to enter a field, but that's not a problem. You can easily insert a new row by:

- Selecting the field that will come after the new field, move to the ribbon, and tap on **Insert Rows** under the **Design tab**.

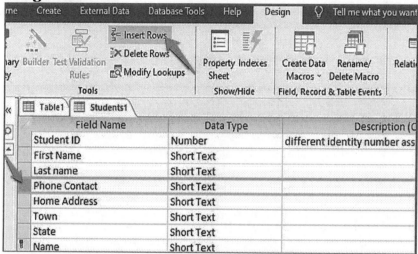

- Insert the missing field and move on with the database construction.

Field Name	Data Type	D
Student ID	Number	different identity
First Name	Short Text	
Last name	Short Text	
email address	Short Text	
Phone Contact	Short Text	
Home Address	Short Text	
Town	Short Text	
State	Short Text	

CHAPTER 6:
Entering Data into the Database Table

This is the most crucial section of constructing a database table. It is the main reason for creating a database; without data (the records), there is no excess of creating a relationship between the table and the printing of the report.

This section is the toughest section for many users when building a database. Nevertheless, it is the easiest section provided you have done justice to the previous chapter, such as entering of field, selecting the necessary data type, setting field properties for entering data, and linking relations between database tables.

All these are the sources for constructing a meaningful database table. If you miss it at those levels mentioned, entering data into the table will be so horrible. As a result, you are advised to go through those sections very well before moving to this section to exempt yourself from unnecessary stress.

Data Entering Approaches

There are two approaches to follow when entering data into the database table. Both approaches are good depending on the one users know how to use best. The two approaches are the following:
1. Data entering by switching to Datasheet view
2. Data entering with the help of a Form.

Data Entering By Switching to Datasheet View

Most users like this approach because it is almost the same as entering data on an ordinary table with grid cells where rows and columns intersect, which many users have previously used. Aside from that, many like using the datasheet view to enter data based on the following benefits:

- Numerous data can be viewed on the screen for proper record comparison.
- Scrolling here and there, up and down between the record, is easier.
- It makes sorting and filtering of each column possible.

Let us start entering data into the table via datasheet view. To do that, study this guiding principle:

1. Open the concerned **Table** in the datasheet view or switch its view if it has already been open in the design view.
2. Enter the **data** into all the empty row cells with **asterisks** marked according to the categories of each field. As you are done entering data into the first row, create a new row by pressing the **down arrow** or clicking the **new (blank) record** in the datasheet navigation button or click on the **New** button in the ribbon under the Home tab or press **Ctrl with plus** key **(Ctrl++).**

3. Repeat step (2) to enter all the available data into the database table.

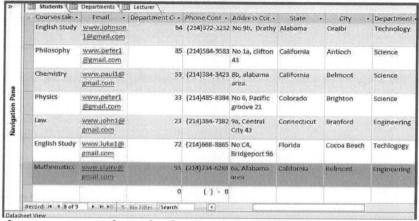

Note: an indication of the current row where the data is currently being entered in the presence of a pencil icon on the current row selector. You can remove any record by selecting the row via its row selector and clicking on the delete button in the ribbon under the Home tab.

Tips and Tricks for Entering Data in a Datasheet

Navigating and manipulating some tools makes entering data with a datasheet view the most interesting. This section deals with three particular tips you need to know when entering data into the datasheet such as:

- Keyboard shortcuts for easy navigation here and there within the datasheet.
- Freezing and Hiding a field

Keyboard Shortcuts

Keyboard shortcuts help you move here and there in the datasheet within the shortest period, which speeds up the data entry rate; check the table below for the necessary moving shortcut within a datasheet.

Keyboard Shortcuts	Destination
↓	Moving to the next record of the same field
↑	Moving to the previous record of the same field
Enter or Tab	Moving to the next field in the same record.
Shift + tab	Moving to the previous field in the same record.
Home	Moving to the first field of the current record.
End	Moving to the last field of the current record.

Ctrl + Home	Moving to the first field in the first record.
Ctrl + End	Moving to the last field in the last record.
Page up	Moving up one screen.
Page down	Moving down one screen.

Freezing and Hiding Field (Column) in the Datasheet

Understandably, Access deals with bulky data, which makes it an exceptional database application compared to other spreadsheet applications. Consequently, you may need to lock those field (s) by freezing them so that you will always see them locked to the screen because they serve as a clue for entering other records or data. They will be locked onto the screen irrespective of how far you navigate to the right side of the screen. Hiding on the other side is ideal when a user notices field congestion on the screen, and such obstructs data entering. A user may decide to hide some fields in such a way to free some space for easy entering of data.

To freeze and hide fields (columns), kindly:

- Click a field or drag the "down arrow" over multiple fields to select more than a field. You can hold down the shift key and click on each row you want to select to select multiple rows.
- Then right-click and pick either **Freeze Fields** or **Hide Fields** from the drop-down list, depending on the one you need.

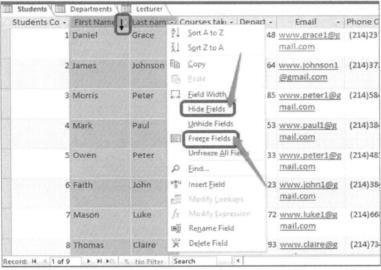

- If you pick **Freeze Fields,** this is the result you will have, irrespective of how far you move to the right side, and those frozen fields will be locked to the screen at the left. You can unfreeze the fields by right-clicking any **field name** and selecting **unfreeze All fields** from the drop-down list.

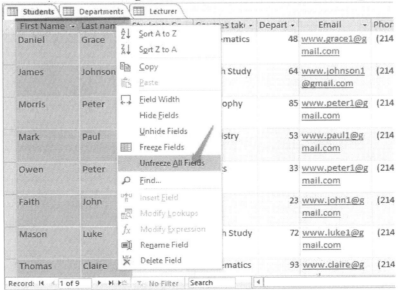

- If you pick **Hide Fields,** this is the result you will have, and those fields will not be visible on the screen. You can unhide the fields by clicking on any other **field name** and selecting **Unhide** from the drop-down list to access unhide columns dialog box.

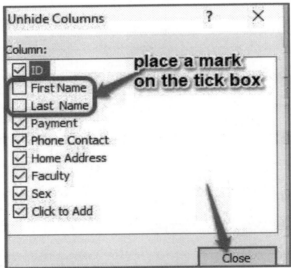

- Unhide Columns dialog box will come forth. Place a **mark beside** the columns you want to unhide and **Close** the dialog box.

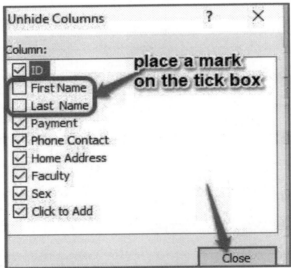

Note: you can quickly hide a column by dragging its border to the left side until such a column vanishes.

Amending the Look of the Datasheet

Access permits you to adjust the look of your datasheet until it is acceptable to your taste and preference. The following are one or two activities you can carry out within the confine of the datasheet to make it look incredible as you may want it:

- **Columns/Rows adjustment**: you can adjust the size of the columns and rows by placing the mouse over one row and column selector boundary till you notice a change of mouse into a two-headed arrow, then drag right, left, up, or down depending on the side of the column/row at the moment and size you want. When you adjust one row or column, other rows and columns will be adjusted automatically.

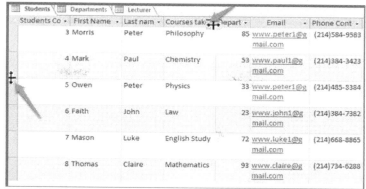

- **Switching the fonts:** to switch default font text and size, move to the Text formatting section under the Home tab, then select different font aside from Calibri and font size aside from 11 points.

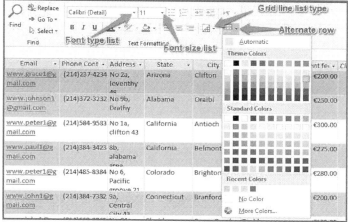

- **Alternate row colors:** the default alternate row color is white, and you change it by clicking on the Alternate color menu and picking different colors from the drop-down list.
- **Amending the gridlines look:** you can select another format for the gridlines by clicking on the gridline menu and selecting different gridlines formats from the drop-down list.
- **Repositioning columns:** you can shift any column's location to another by selecting the column and clicking, then dragging it to another location.

Email	Phone Cont	Address	State	City ↓	Department
www.grace1@g mail.com	(214)237-4234	No 2a, leventhy 48	Arizona	Clifton	Engineering
www.johnson1 @gmail.com	(214)372-3232	No 9b, Drathy	Alabama	Oraibi	Technology
www.peter1@g mail.com	(214)584-9583	No 1a, clifton 43	California	Antioch	Science
www.paul1@g mail.com	(214)384-3423	8b, alabama area	California	Belmont	Science
www.peter1@g mail.com	(214)485-8384	No 6, Pacific groove 21	Colorado	Brighton	Science
www.john1@g mail.com	(214)384-7382	9a, Central City 43	Connecticut	Branford	Engineering

Entering Data Using a Form

Some users prefer and prioritize using a form to enter data rather than a datasheet. They claim forms have many benefits, which may be so. That is what people call individual differences. However, there are truly certain benefits to entering data with a form; some of them are the following:

- Each field has a clear name inscription for easy recognition for entering the data.
- There is no chance of skipping any unfilled field because you can simultaneously see the whole field for each record on the screen.

- Moving from field to field is very convenient.

Entering data into the form you created:
Entering data into a form starts with the form itself, and thus there is a need to create such a form before you can fill it with data. To create a form, do well to follow this guiding principle:

- Tap the **Create** tab and click the **Form wizard** to access the Form Wizard dialog box.

- Select the **Table** that needs the data you want to enter from the Tables/Queries drop-down list and click the **Next** button.

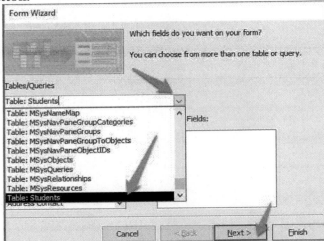

- Press this button (**>>**) to enter all the available fields in the selected table into the Selected Fields box and click the **Next** button.

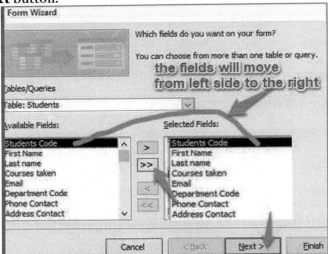

- Pick the **Columnar** from the layout option, which is the best option that is good for entering data into the table, and click the **Next** button.

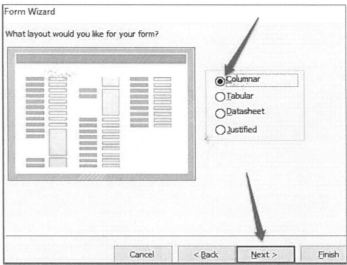

- Give the form the same name as the table you link it with for proper recognition in the navigation pane, then click the **Finish** button.

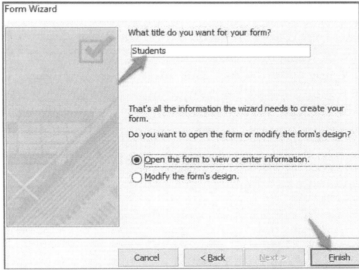

Note: you can remove a Form from the database by right-clicking its name in the navigation pane and selecting delete from the drop-down list.

Now that you are done creating the Form, you can move further by opening the form and entering the data into the form by:

- Double-clicking the form name in the navigation pane under the Form section to open it.

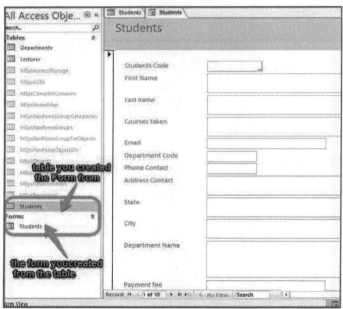

- Enter the data into the form, and **use the tab, shift + tab, and arrow** keys to move here and there within the record. When you fill out the current record, click the **new blank record** button in the navigation button below the screen to move to the next record until you enter all the data into the form.

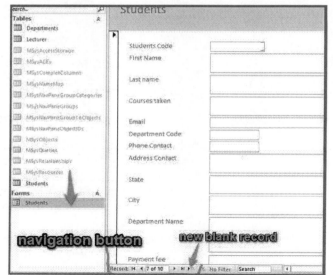

CHAPTER 7:
Finding, Filtering, and Sorting Your Data

Filtering in Microsoft Access allows you to view only the data you are interested in. When you filter, you can view only the information you are interested in, and the rest is hidden. Filters are necessary as they allow you to focus on the information you need and remove unnecessary baggage.

This chapter will discuss how to create filters and sort out and find information using them. Creating filters helps you to create a neat workspace, which can be easily used not only by yourself but by others too. It also allows you to control the information you see around your workspace.

Creating a Simple Filter

To create a simple filter, go through the following steps.
1. Next to the field you want to filter, click the drop-down arrow that you will see.

ID	First Name	Last Name	Street Address	City	State
102	Theodore	Achi	120 Baker St.	Raleigh	NC
195	Kris	Ackerman	1311 Coretta Scott Way	Raleigh	NC
78	Michiko	Akiwana	901 Glenwood Ave.	Raleigh	NC
188	Nathan	Albee	76-C Meadowview Ln.	Raleigh	NC
13	Mariah	Allen	12 Jupe	Raleigh	NC
37	Carol	Allenson	3201 Glenwood Ave. Unit A	Raleigh	NC
38	Zoey	Altman	817 Hillsborough St. Apt E1(	Raleigh	NC
163	Franz	Angelou	291 Hinton St.	Raleigh	NC

2. After clicking on the drop-down arrow, you will see a drop-down list. This list contains all the information in this field, and checking the box beside each data will create a filter that allows you to see only the data you have checked. Clicking on "Select all" will select or deselect everything.

3. Click on the "OK" when you are done, and your changes will be saved. You have successfully filtered the information you want to see in your database.

At the top of your window, on the red ribbon, is a command, "Toggle filter." This command allows you to turn on and off your filter. Selecting this command will allow you not to use a filter, and deselecting it will enable you to use the filter you have created.

This is further illustrated in the image below, with the arrow key on the "Toggle filter" command.

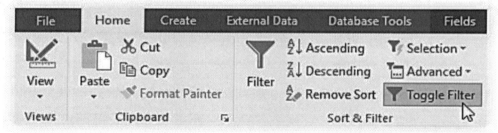

Creating a Filter from a Selection

In Microsoft Access, you can also create a filter from a selection, which is different from a simple one. Creating a filter by the selection means you select a particular data from the table you have created, and you find data that is like it or not. Let's make an instance, imagine you are working for a hospital, and you want to search for all patients who have been admitted for malaria; you simply select the word in one of the patient's data and create a filter with that selection.

To create a filter from a selection, you can choose from the following options.

- **Contains:** This contains only records that have cells that have the data that has been selected.
- **Does Not Contain:** This includes all other records apart from those with cells that contain the data that you have selected.
- **Ends With:** This includes only records whose data for the field you have selected ends with the search term.

- **Does Not End With:** This includes all records except those whose data for the selected field ends with the search term.

Now you know what it means to create a filter from a selection, but how do you do this? How do you create a filter from a selection? It is a straightforward process if you follow these steps.

1. Open a table. Choose the cell you want to create a filter with. This cell will include the word or data you want to use to create a filter.
2. Go to the Home tab on the Ribbon, click on it, locate the "Sort & Filter group," and click on it. There will appear a "Selection" drop-down arrow; click on it.

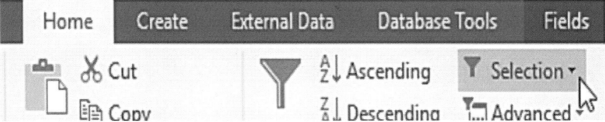

3. Select the type of filter you want to create from the list of options from the drop-down list.
4. The filter would have been applied. Your table now displays only products containing the selected word as a filter.

Creating a Filter from a Search Item

You can also make a filter from a Search Item, which will be discovered in this section. You can do this by typing a search term and deciding the way your Microsoft Access should match data to that term.

Like the options listed when filtering by selection- Contains, Does Not Contain, Ends With, and Does Not End With, you can choose from these and some more which include- Equals, does not Equal, Begins With, and Does not Begin With. You can apply any of these based on self-explanatory individual options.

Now that you know what it means to create a filter from a Search Item, how do you carry out this process? Simply follow these steps.

1. Open a table, select the field you want to filter by, and select the drop-down arrow next to this field.
2. In the drop-down menu, place your mouse on "Text Filters." From the list that pops up, select the way you want the filter to match the term you enter based on the options explained above.
3. The Custom Filter dialog box will show up. Type the word you wish to use for your filter.
4. When you are done, click "OK," and the filter will be applied.

Using the Find Command

The use of filters has been extensively discussed, and if studied adequately, you would have understood how to apply different filters to your database. In this section, it will be discussed how to use the find command. The find command is critical when working with Microsoft Access. Imagine you have thousands of records and are trying to locate a particular record; how best do you think you can find the one you are looking for? Carousing through the files? This will be so tedious! Going through thousands of records just to locate one record. However, you can quickly locate a record by using the find command.

The Find feature in Microsoft Access allows you to quickly search tables, queries, and forms for specified database tasks. A practical choice for finding a specific record when the record you want to locate satisfies specific criteria is using the Find tab in the Find and Replace dialog box. To use the find command, follow these steps.

1. Click on the table or form you want to search a record in to open it, then click on the field this record is likely to be located.
2. Go to the Home tab, and in the Find group, click "Find," or you can do this step on your keyboard by pressing CTRL+F.
3. This makes the Find and Replace dialog box appear, and the Find tab is already selected.
4. In the "Find what" box will appear, type the value for which you want to search.
5. If you wish to change the field you want to search or the entire underlying table, click the right option in the "Look In" list.
6. In the Search list, click "All" and then select "Find Next."

7. The item for which you are searching would have been highlighted, then select "Cancel" in the "Find and Replace" dialog box to close the dialog box. All the records that have met your search conditions are highlighted by now.

Sorting Your Records in Microsoft Access

Sorting records in Microsoft Access means logically arranging your records with similar data grouped, making the database easier to read and understand. You can sort records alphabetically or numerically by assigning numbers or other ways. This even makes it easy to search for data.

To sort your records in Microsoft Access, go through the following steps.

1. Open a table and select the field you want to sort by.
2. Go to the Home tab on the Ribbon and locate the "Sort & Filter" group.
3. Sort the field by selecting the Ascending or the Descending command, and the selected field will sort the table.
4. Click on "Save" to save your changes.

CONCLUSION

This book is about the newly released Microsoft Access 2022. You can do many things with this software application that will be easy to miss. However, this can be averted if you go through this well-written piece. Throughout this book, the importance and uses of Microsoft Access are discussed, starting with the description of a particular function and a step-by-step explanation of how to carry out each function.

The book starts by explaining what Access is about and what makes a database. Subsequent sections discuss the creation and use of tables, queries, forms, and other things associated with Microsoft Access 2022. It also discussed the uncommon tips that will be useful for you when working with this newly developed software.

The complete book is a success. I am sure it will be helpful for anyone who wants to use it as a guide manual for the newly released Microsoft Access 2022, whether a novice, an average user, or a professional user. Read it thoroughly, follow the outlined steps to carry out a procedure, and operate Access like a wizard.

Thank you for reading this book!

Made in the USA
Las Vegas, NV
21 August 2022

53709273R00175